John Williams is a journalist specializing in crime fiction and music. He contributes regularly to the *Independent*, the *Guardian*, *The Face* and *Arena*. He lives in London.

JOHN WILLIAMS

Into the Badlands

PALADIN
GRAFTON BOOKS
A Division of the Collins Publishing Group

LONDON GLASGOW
TORONTO SYDNEY AUCKLAND

Paladin
Grafton Books
A Division of the Collins Publishing Group
8 Grafton Street, London W1X 3LA

Published simultaneously in hardcover
and paperback in Paladin Books 1991

A CIP catalogue record for this book
is available from the British Library

ISBN 0-586-09075-4
ISBN 0-586-09018-5 (paper covers)

Printed and bound in Great Britain by
HarperCollins Manufacturing, Glasgow

Set in Baskerville

For Charlotte

Contents

Acknowledgements

I would like to thank: Sandhya Ellis for her friendship and support throughout; Mike Hart, without whose knowledge and help this book would never have got started; Nick Kimberley, Chris Render, Kevin Allerton, Pete Webb, Paul Hammond and Liz Young for sharing their knowledge and insight; my various editors, including Sheryl Garratt, Dylan Jones, Kimberley Leston, Nick Logan and Sean O'Hagan for helping me make a living out of writing; everyone whose hospitality I enjoyed while travelling around the States, particularly Marcia Pilliciotti in Detroit, Lee Esbenshade in Los Angeles and Sarah Edkins in New York; my agent Anne McDermid, my editor Ian Paten and copy editor Chris Parker for the work they've put into this; the writers themselves for giving me their time; my parents for their belief and support; and my wife Charlotte Greig for everything.

Note

Some parts of a few of the interviews here have previously appeared in considerably different form in *The Face*, *Arena*, the *Independent* and the *New Musical Express*.

Introduction

I wrote this book because I wanted to go to America. I wrote about crime writers because it is largely down to them that I wanted to go to America. It seems to me that crime writers are the most astute chroniclers of America today, and yet they are routinely ignored or patronized by the arbiters of taste in literature – not just in patrician England but in the US too. Europeans propagate the myth that America has no culture, and Americans tend to believe them. Those Americans who can afford to are forever coming to Europe in search of culture: suggest to the average New Yorker that there might be culture to be had in Texas and he or she will laugh. So onward they'll proceed to visit the great museums of Europe, paying tribute to a culture in its death throes, leaving it up to crazy people from Europe and Japan to identify *le film noir*, worship Charlie Parker, reprint the novels of Jim Thompson, and make the pilgrimages to the Sun Records studios in Memphis or the cajun dancehalls of Louisiana. American culture is seen as not measuring up to the great tradition of European culture; its newness is seen as déclassé rather than vital; it is constantly undervalued for the reason, ultimately, that it is not dead.

The one area of cultural activity in which American innovation is grudgingly recognized – with the very debatable exception of cinema – is popular music. And it's through music that I came to crime fiction. In the early 1980s, in the aftermath of punk, I was working in a record shop and, like a lot of other people, I started listening to the rootsier forms of American popular music: soul, country, gospel, doo wop, cajun. All of which seemed to have in common a directness of approach and a depth of feeling absent from the vast majority of new wave rock music, which I began to see as shallow, merely clever, emotionally withheld.

Meanwhile I fancied myself something of a reader; this meant that I would consume, at a rate of approximately one every three months, a book by the vogue serious novelist of the moment, Salman Rushdie, Milan Kundera . . . global Booker Prize types. These books I would read about, faithfully buy and faithfully get about halfway through, admiring the wit and elegance and being too embarrassed to admit boredom.

Then came Elmore. For once, when I went into the bookshop across the road from where I worked, I asked for some advice and the man placed an imported Elmore Leonard paperback in front of me. And there it was: the America of Stax and Motown, George Jones and Grover Washington Jr, present in fiction as it simply never is in the work of the major American moderns – Updike or Tyler or Bellow – all of whom seem possessed by the idea that it is the duty of an American writer to render the American experience into English literature.

Even when American literary figures are concerned with the working population they tend either to dwell on the past – Doctorow, Kennedy, Alice Walker, even – or to write about 'ordinary people' as if they were zoological specimens under a microscope – Raymond Carver, Richard Ford etc. Where the best crime writers are different is in their involvement: they are not simply writing about the people; they have a necessarily closer relationship, born, if nothing else, out of the demands of writing for a mass audience, not a literary one. Out of which comes the fact that they are, by and large, more political than the mainstream; crime, after all, demands a political response.

Which also may contribute to its neglect: political and popular culture – from Mayakovsky to Billie Holiday – tends to be appreciated only in retrospect. Once again this is particularly clear in the instance of popular music. Old soul or country artists, Otis Redding or Patsy Cline, are deemed to be 'legends' while new artists are ignored. Likewise Hammett and Chandler are greats while the contemporary likes of James Crumley or James Ellroy are ignored. And this seems symptomatic of a wider ill. There is something particularly depressing in the spectacle of the US beginning to fetishize its recent past. It's a sign that this is no longer a culture at least united in one dream of advancement. The have-nots are still making something new: the hiphop culture of the streets. The haves are looking back fondly at the 1950s, the time, not coincidentally, before civil rights, before Vietnam, a mythical Ronald Reagan time of white picket fences, Jimmy Stewart and 'The Dick Van Dyke Show'. Out of the tensions these discrepancies provoke comes crime on a new scale and, as a corollary, the necessity for any writing about America today to deal with such crime.

One thing led to another. I read Elmore Leonard's *Stick* faster than I'd read a book in years. I read whatever else of Leonard's I could find, and discovered or was introduced to other contemporary writers: George V. Higgins, James Crumley, Ross Thomas, Charles Willeford; discovered also – and once again in common with a lot of other people – the forgotten *noir* writers of the 1930s, 1940s, 1950s, even 1960s: Jim Thompson, David Goodis, Horace McCoy, Charles Williams; discovered originals like Chester Himes or Patricia Highsmith. I started writing about these books, and got published because too few other people were paying attention.

And, back to where I started, I wrote this book because reading Elmore Leonard made me want to go to Miami Beach, reading James Crumley made me want to go to Montana, reading Sara Paretsky made me want to go to Chicago. And so on. Not that they portrayed these places as necessarily lovely, but because they portrayed them always as alive. And I wanted to write a book that would convey something of why I liked these writers. I knew what I didn't want such a book to be: a work of apologist literary criticism ('actually some of these crime-writer types are nearly as good as real writers . . .'), an absurdly patronizing tack, as if novelists are not all engaged in the identical business of making fictions. As far as casting literary bouquets goes, it'll do for me to say that a good writer is one you want to read.

What follows is not literary criticism. I may point out bad books that a writer has produced, but in general it'll have to be taken as read that these are writers I admire. Instead, what I have attempted to do is give some idea of their America. It has become the cliché in reviewing these books to commend them for their sense of place. I figured that if James Ellroy gives you a good sense of Los Angeles, and Tony Hillerman of Navajo country, then maybe if you put a selection of writers together, they'll give you a sense of America . . . So I decided to find out.

What follows is the result of that finding out: two months spent circling America with the aid of a flight pass and a series of rental cars, radios tuned into soul and country stations, staying in what seemed like one endless motel room, equipped always with the same TV set showing the same out-of-focus cable channels, fuelled on the best breakfasts and the worst beers I've encountered, talking to crime writers along the way.

1

Miami: the City that Coke Built

The cab driver didn't want to go to South Miami Beach. 'This car don't speak Spanish,' is how he put it. That's the way the day was shaping up. The hotel I'd booked had never heard of me or my reservation when I called up from Miami/Fort Lauderdale Airport. Having no idea where else to go, I persuaded the guy that, seeing as we were already in his cab, and halfway there, he might as well keep on and take me to whatever street had the most hotels – at least test his theory that South Beach was not where I wanted to be. So at this point talkative, six-foot, sandy-haired Burt stops telling me about the time he spent in London when he was in the forces and confines himself to grimly pointing out salubrious North Beach hotels that would provoke any decent tourist to exchange a couple of hundred dollars for a room. 'I hope y'all like Spanish people,' he says darkly, and slumps into resignation, barely cheered by the meter's upward progress.

Miami Beach is a long thin island reclaimed from the sea and running north–south in parallel to the city itself, like a densely populated offshore reef protecting the city from the ocean. It's connected to the city proper by a series of causeways. The main drag is called Collins Avenue, the one link between toney North Beach with its country clubs and private housing estates and the sleazy South Beach, sometime Crime Capital of the USA.

North Beach, round about Bal Harbour, is mostly boring, the kind of place where Frank and Dean and Liza may show for a winter engagement at the Fontainebleu Hilton; not so much a family resort as a place for rich people to keep warm in winter. The hotels, with the exception of the spectacularly swanky Fontainebleu, are mostly bland modern as are the North Beach's latest developments, the endless condos, well-guarded apartment blocks thrown up by Miami's building boom.

South Beach really starts when you get down to Collins Park at Collins and 22nd Street. We stop at a hotel a couple of blocks further down. I go in, leaving the door open, and ask for a room, talk to a bearded guy in shorts who says he's full but try another hotel a block back. I go back to the car and tell Burt. Who gets immediately, and bizarrely, mad. Jumps out of the car and accosts the guy. 'How come you're full! This guy's come all the way from England! What do you mean you're full, asshole!' . . . About to explode, he gets back in the car. I attempt to explain that I want to try a hotel one block behind us. Burt refuses to grasp this and shoots off in the wrong direction. I tell him to turn around, my voice rising to a kind of nervous near-shriek. Reluctantly he hangs a right and circles back a couple of blocks, belatedly delivering us at hotel number two. This time I jump out and, my mistake, shut the door behind me. It takes less than a minute to run in and secure a room, which is fortunate as, when I come back out on the street, the cab is starting to edge along the kerb with my worldly goods securely inside. I run up to the car and pull the door open, gabbling, 'Yeah, great, I've got a room, how much do I owe you, thanks, 'bye.' Burt refuses to be rushed, opens the trunk, pulls out the bags and looks disgustedly at the Latinate cast of the guy running the hotel; then he gets back in the car and burns rubber. Welcome to Miami Beach.

This of course is too good to be true. Arrive in Florida and the first person you meet is the prototype Florida psychopath. Sitting down in the hotel room I'm laughing at the absurdity of it; Burt fits just too perfectly the blueprint for a bland, blond killer that Elmore Leonard came up with in his first Florida thriller, *Gold Coast*, developed in *Stick/La Brava*, which Charles Willeford picked up and ran with in his Miami cop novels.

Back at the hotel, I've had time to shower, admire the deco chest of drawers and shudder at the discomfort of the bed. I've switched to my 'hey, I've seen "Miami Vice"' outfit – shorts, loafers, no socks – and it's time to take a stroll round the neighbourhood. From ground level and in daylight what Miami Beach does not look like is anywhere's crime capital. Simply,

South Beach is beautiful. I was expecting to see a few art-deco hotels, but here are twenty blocks of Jazz Age deco dream hotels. A few are refurbished in 'Miami Vice' pastels, but most are faded, immaculate in windblown ice-cream colours: peach, pistachio and strawberry. Mine has been recently repainted, awaiting the beach's return as a yuppie tourist centre, following the Deco District's newfound status as a Heritage Zone. It even has the fountain out front working again. The hotel is on 21st Street, half a block west of Collins Avenue. On the corner of Collins there's Wolfies, one of the last of the great American Jewish delis (*x* million muffins sold since 1935); on the other corner, and every bit as much the fading monument, is the Gaiety Burlesque Theater, now a forlorn husk showing porno movies to crowds ever dwindling since the arrival of the VCR. Keep going a little further over Collins on 21st and I pass the Beirut Cafe, local surf-punk hangout, before arriving on the beach at the same split second as a police jeep tears down 21st behind me, mounts the pavement and heads, tyres screaming and dust billowing, on to the beach.

The jeep pulls up 400 yards down the beach, next to a small cluster of people. Words are exchanged and the jeep tears off again, heading further down the beach. Wondering what next, I walk on to the beach only to discover that it isn't really a beach at all; what it resembles is concrete covered in a kind of rock dust. Certainly you don't want to walk on it in bare feet, unless you want them cut to ribbons. It's strange: I'm standing in the midst of twenty miles of what looks like prime beach, next to a major city and, on a hot sunny day, it's virtually deserted with scarcely anyone at all in the water. On the basis that the locals probably know something I don't, I decide to forgo swimming for the moment and head back to Collins to find something to eat.

Walking down Collins is as surreal a stroll as I've made. First off, there's the abundance of deco hotels, all with rows of chairs laid out on the front verandah for the retirees to sit and watch the world ebb away from them. These represent the toughest strain of old folks, the ones who survived having the Marielitos boarded alongside them in the hotels when the city couldn't think of anything else to do with them – a decision akin to

billeting a group of hungry wolves in a sheep-pen. These old
people have seen Miami Beach descend from being a retirement-
age reward for blue-collar northern Jews to a crime capital, and
are now seeing it move tentatively towards a kind of regeneration
that may, like as not, reward them for their steadfastness by
evicting them in the name of escalating property values.

Now, mid-afternoon in May, things are quiet. Collins Avenue
has an amiable mix of population: Latin, Jewish, Anglo, a few
blacks. The shops and restaurants are mostly low-income, Woolworths and Burger King, drab haberdashers and fifty-cent
novelty shops. There's a bunch of Cuban *cantinas* offering subsist-
ence-level eating, *arroz con pollo*, black-eyed beans and plantains,
and while there aren't many bars, there are a lot of liquor stores
where you can stand and have a drink before you take the six-
pack home. Strangely, there's an almost complete absence of any
of the normal seaside stores: nowhere selling Miami souvenirs,
hot dogs or rubber rings. Parallel to Collins, a block east, is
Ocean Drive, running along the beach. Here I pick up a Cuban
tuna sandwich before settling down at a beachfront bar with a
windswept, end-of-season feeling. There's a Cuban guy cooking
chicken on a barbecue, trying to conjure up the spirit of summer,
and another guy with a beard, a halfway biker type, hammering
out 1970s rock classics on an electric guitar. After a couple of
Eagles numbers he tries to placate his predominantly Latin
audience by playing 'La Bamba' at some length, quite unboth-
ered by the discrepancy between the song's Mexican origins and
his audience's Cuban roots. The barmaid claps anyway and I
get offered some free chicken barbecue. By now the wind is
starting to chill, so I head back to the hotel in time to see the
street people start to emerge from their daytime resting places.
The corner by the burlesque theatre and the liquor store is
getting seedy as thin, wired folk congregate, each starting to
figure out where they're going to get the money that'll get them
what they need for another night. As mean streets go, though,
it's more pathetic, even absurd (given the setting and the number
of oblivious retirees strolling by doing their shopping), than
threatening.

Sitting in the hotel again I turn on the TV just in time to catch

a show called 'America's Most Wanted'. This features drama-
tized reconstructions of a selection of crimes whose perpetrators
are currently at large. First up are a couple straight out of the
movie *Badlands*, a blonde teen called May and her lowlife
boyfriend Jason leaving a trail of havoc across South Carolina.
After the ads it's the 'Prime Time Burglar'. This is a guy,
described as 'black' and little else, who likes to burgle people's
houses in the middle of the evening while they watch TV or eat
dinner. To illustrate this there's a piece of footage lifted from a
French farce of a generic black guy walking around the background of a dinner party stealing things until someone notices,
at which point he runs away. A rent-a-shrink is then dragged on
screen to opine that the 'Prime Time Burglar' is 'attracted to
danger'.

Reeling with amazement at this disclosure, I pick up the *Miami
Herald*. The local news section shows that Miami still has its fair
share of urban mayhem. Among the stories currently running
are the contract killing of a black guy in West Perrine, a man
named Lee Lawrence who ran a corner grocery store and had
the nerve to speak out against local drug dealers. A Melvin
Garcia shot his prospective son-in-law, essentially for being an
asshole, and tried to claim he thought he was a burglar. Another
guy, Frank Stramaglia, part-owner of Vito's Trucking and
Excavating Co., a firm involved in building expressways in
Florida, was found in a hot tub in a Detroit motel, his body
pumped with twenty times the lethal dosage of cocaine. More
prosaically, a ton of marijuana was found on an Air Jamaica jet
at Miami Airport, and a fifty-two-year-old high-school athletic
director was arrested for supplying half a kilo of coke. And senior
citizens in Royal Country Mobile Home Park are organizing a
crime patrol following the theft of two pink flamingoes from Jerry
Rivero and a statue of the Virgin Mary from Rolando Scott.

All of which is the kind of thing you'd expect if you've been
reading Florida crime fiction over the past ten years or so.
Leaving aside the vast body of writing by John D. Macdonald,
author of the Travis McGee novels, the modern Florida crime
novel started in 1977 with Douglas Fairbairn's *Street 8* and began
to gain greater currency when Elmore Leonard broke through to
mass popularity with his series of novels set in Florida. Leonard

was the man who brought Miami crime to a wider audience. His first Florida novel, *Gold Coast*, dealt with the people who don't call themselves the Mafia, the kind of people who the Frank Stramaglia that my *Miami Herald* told me was found dead in the hot tub doubtless had no connection to. It was with his third Florida novel, *Stick*, however, that Leonard assembled the combination that caught the public imagination: Miami, Marielitos, movies and drugs.

At one point in *Stick* one of the bad guys, a Vietnam vet turned big-time coke dealer, is thinking of making a semi-legit investment in the movie business; a B-movie producer is in town hustling investors for a script about two slick Miami cops, two undercover guys caught up in the glamour and danger of the drug trade, he wants to call it *Shuck and Jive*. In the book no one goes for it. In real life a man called Michael Mann must have read the same script because, within a year of *Stick* coming out, 'Miami Vice' was on screen, and a city started to remake itself in the image of a TV show. Suddenly the Coconut Grove boutiques started selling unstructured Gianni Versace suits to drug dealers whose idea of style six months previously had been Al Pacino in *Scarface*: white suits and black shirts with big collars.

Going out at night in Miami Beach, 'Miami Vice' is literally inescapable. Walking down Collins in the evening I have to start sidestepping seriously thin people with nothing in their eyes heading up towards 21st Street and temporary salvation. Down on 14th Street I see a regular-looking neighbourhood bar called the Deuce. Inside the Deuce it is such a regular bar as to approach self-parody, like looking for an average pub and finding the Queen Vic or the Rovers Return. The Deuce has a pool table, a TV showing the basketball game, 1950s neon bar signs and a big figure-eight bar crowded around with cheery regulars exchanging wisecracks with the two tough, sassy women bartenders. It's as if the whole place has conspired to construct a *tableau vivant* of what makes America great (or at least what made 'Cheers' great). The feeling of being in an advert for American beer is so strong that it comes as something of a surprise to be asked to pay for the drinks and more of a surprise to discover that this is the kind of real bar that charges around double what most real bars charge, which in turn prompts you to notice that most of your fellow drinkers are perhaps a little less blue-collar than they seem: the baseball caps are a little too new, the T-shirts too freshly laundered; in fact the place seems to be full of junior execs who think they're Burt Reynolds on weekends. Leaving, I catch sight of a newspaper clipping on the wall, extolling the Deuce's virtues and going on to mention that it's regularly used as a set for 'Miami Vice', whose production team installed the neat neon signs in order to give it more of that 'real bar' feeling.

Having absorbed this, I walk back along Collins. The next cross street is cordoned off and drenched in spotlights. I edge towards it, wondering if this is the scene of a police shootout. Turns out they're shooting 'Miami Vice'. This will be the last series and the locals are about to be deprived of useful income. Sitting at a bar a little while later, Karen, the waitress in the Wet Paint Cafe, tells me that virtually everyone on the beach has worked as an extra or had their shop or bar or hotel used as a location. The Wet Paint Cafe is no exception: it's a kind of upmarket bohemian hangout in the distinctly unreal Lincoln Road Mall, a failed 1950s shopping centre deserted for years and now attempting a regeneration as an artists' community, the shopfronts being converted into studio spaces. Lincoln Road Mall has some way to go though: at ten o'clock it's closed down – apart from the Wet Paint – and the only people in there are myself, Karen and a guy named Ed. Ed is a thin Latin-looking guy sitting slumped over the bar wearing dark glasses. I'm the only other person sitting at the bar but he hardly seems to register me. Hey! Time for some field research: 'Well sir, what's it like being a Miami Beach cokehead?' – that kind of stuff. Karen introduces us; Ed turns out to be a nice guy who DJs around the local clubs. Twenty minutes later he lets slip the reason for his apparent terminal hipsterdom: he's blind from diabetes, has moved to Miami from New York because the climate's easier on him and DJs because he can't paint any more. Feeling like a fool, I promise I'll come and hear him play records the next night. He tells me to head to Ocean Drive below 14th if I want a little more nightlife.

So I do, and find a strip of refurbished deco on one side, palm trees and beach on the other; perfect territory for cruising in your convertible. Latin jazz drifts out of the hotel bars, urban dance from car stereos, reggae and punk from the clubs, but beneath the noise it's a quiet night.

Next morning I go to see about renting a car. Apparently there won't be one available till this evening, so I'm going to have to take the bus to visit Carl Hiaasen. Carl Hiaasen, aside from writing novels, has a day job as star columnist on the *Miami Herald*, so it's to the *Herald* offices in downtown Miami that I'm headed next day. The bus from Miami Beach takes us over a causeway across Biscayne Bay into Miami itself. Sitting on the bus I read a Miami weekly magazine that promises to expose 'the brotherhood of crack'. In best 'I've been there and I want a Pulitzer' factional style this attempts to paint a picture of life as it is lived on Miami Beach's worst crack-dealing street. This is apparently 21st Street at Collins, i.e. the one on which I'm staying. What emerges from comparing this attempted dramatization of the situation with the comparatively low-key experience of actually walking down what I am now tempted to call crack street is an underlining of the sheer boredom of the drug world at this level: guys nodded out on park benches, guys standing on the corner doing ten-dollar deals all day long. Crack's a fast-food drug and the society it engenders is similarly minimal; there's none of the endless chatter about what great shit this is that goes with a dope deal; you just hand five bucks per rock out of your car window, the guy gives you the rocks and you drive off. Later you come back. And again, and so on, until you don't have a car any more and then you buy your rock in the crack house, an abandoned hotel down the street. Calling this a brotherhood is about as appropriate as calling people who eat in McDonalds a brotherhood. As drugs go, its demonstrable effects are about as community-oriented as a neutron bomb.

The bus is a great equalizer in the States. You can understand why the back of the bus was such a pillar of Jim Crow as this Miami bus careers across the causeway: a whole rainbow coalition of folks are thrown into each other and it can easily damage people's stereotypes to watch the homeboys giving up their seats to the little old white ladies. Ken Kesey said you're either on the bus or you're off the bus – in Miami if you're on the bus you know it's because words like growth and regeneration were never meant to have to do with the likes of you. Public transport is strictly for the have-nots.

Downtown Miami is completely alienating, the centre of a place that doesn't have a centre, just a financial zone. The bus drops me off in an urban jungle of endless discount hifi stores and shoe shops. After thirty minutes of trying to locate some basic amenities – a phone, a post office, a record store – but finding nothing except more shoes and hifi, I give up and try to find a bar. There are no bars to be seen. I don't know what time it is so I go to Woolworths and buy a four-dollar watch. The strap breaks as I leave the store. I'm getting near hysterical as I ask a newspaper seller where I can find a bar. Simple, he says, and directs me between a couple of stores into what looks like an office block, 'just follow the signs to the bar'. The bar, La Cucuracha or somesuch, is in the basement and has a miniature lake and an aquarium and a *nuit americaine* atmosphere. It also has a phone, so I call Carl Hiaasen and he tells me to come on over.

Sitting in the *Herald's* lobby I pick up a copy of the paper and there on the front of the local news section is Carl Hiaasen's column. Today it's a disgusted assault on the practice of lawyers touting for business. Carl Hiaasen hit the bestseller lists a couple of years back with a book called *Tourist Season*, a furious assault on virtually every aspect of the Florida establishment in the shape of a black comedy. It starts with the head of the chamber of commerce being washed up on Miami Beach in a trunk, wearing a Hawaiian shirt, minus his legs beneath the knee and with a rubber alligator blocking his windpipe. This is merely the first salvo in a campaign of surreal terrorism being waged against the Florida tourist industry. The terrorists include a Cuban bomber called Jesus Bernal, a man who has been thrown out of every far-right anti-communist group for incompetence; a Seminole Indian bingo millionaire named Tommy Tigertail; a black ex-football player turned anarchist in Carrera frames called Viceroy Wilson; a demented newspaper columnist called Skip Wiley and a saltwater crocodile. Further stunts include dive-bombing a cruise liner with designer carrier bags which turn out to be filled with live snakes. Tracking down the terrorists is a newspaper man turned private investigator called Brian Keyes, in his thirties but irredeemably boyish. Not unlike the tousle-haired photo that adorns Carl Hiaasen's book jackets.

The Carl Hiaasen who greets me as I come out of the lift on the fourth floor of the *Miami Herald*, however, looks as if he is in process of transmuting from nice boyish Brian Keyes into drawn, demented Skip Wiley, the gonzo journalist gone too far. He's dressed soberly enough in a corduroy jacket and a tie, but, compared with his photographs, he looks drawn and there is a distinct touch of wildness around his eyes. We cross the news offices of the *Herald* (which are irresistibly reminiscent of the amiable chaos familiar from 'Lou Grant', right down to the proliferation of characters in bow ties) and enter an office overlooking Biscayne Bay that Hiaasen has commandeered for us to talk in. Hiaasen needs no encouragement to talk. He is angry, going on furious, at the state of Miami and Florida. 'Some mornings I sit in the traffic and I think the best thing that could happen would be for a force 5 hurricane to blow through here and make us start all over again – nothing would better remind people of where we came from . . . God didn't want condos on the beaches and someday he's going to tear the shit out of this place. That would be fine with me, separate out the people who really love this place,' he says, starting out in Skip Wiley, by-any-means-necessary fashion.

Then he reverts to the mild-mannered Brian Keyes persona to talk about the human impact of Florida's growth over the last twenty or thirty years. 'My grandfather was a lawyer, my other grandfather was a doctor and I grew up in West Broward County at a time when it was very rural, very undeveloped, when I could get on my bike and in a couple of blocks there'd be animals, you'd catch snakes and birds. There wasn't anything else to do, there was no city to go to to see a play or a movie. My dad had an acre of land; that doesn't sound like much, but, in South Florida now, that's like an estate because instead of one house they put eight houses on it. So all the dumb things you do when you're a kid, camping, fishing . . . I have hardly been able to show my son. I live about three doors down from where I grew up and all those places are gone. There are five shopping malls on a strip of highway where all there was before was pastureland

and canals and lakes. As a result, to give my son any sense of the outdoors I have to go farther and farther west, or actually go out west to Colorado or Montana. I used to fish in little canals and creeks for bass; he has to go to a golf course and sneak on and cast into the man-made lakes. That's what hits home.'

Hiaasen is a newspaperman through and through. There's clearly nowhere, with the possible exception of fishing on Biscayne Bay, that he'd rather be than in a newsroom. His novels make him more than enough to live on but he's committed to writing the column: 'You know, when I wrote *Tourist Season* I wasn't writing a column. Halfway through, my editor called me up and asked me to write one. What's scary is the feeling that I'm turning into one of my characters!' Writing the column gives him the sense of having some kind of say in the way things are done. 'Little victories, I've done a couple of things . . . my job is to hold the corruption up to the light and, if the people decide that's how they want their state run, then that's their decision, but at least they should know what's going on.'

The newspaper business also gives him the raw material for his novels. 'I have a kind of mental rolodex. I file away characters I meet and episodes I read about. In real life my job's here as a journalist, then I go home at night and instead of using this one quote in a column I can invent a character based on someone I met in the street or someone who called me up and I can spin off a whole line of a novel that way. It's fun, you get to work a whole lot out of your system, and the best part is I can get to write a happy ending. I don't get to do that much as a journalist. When I write a novel the bad guys get what they deserve and the good guy gets the girl, or the good girl gets the guy.'

Before writing *Tourist Season* Hiaasen co-authored three novels with another *Herald* journalist, William Montalbano. These are more conventional thrillers set among the Miami drug trade, a subject that occupied much of his time as an investigative reporter in the early 1980s (Elmore Leonard told me that it was investigative pieces by Hiaasen in the *Herald*'s *Tropics* magazine that provided much of his own background for tackling the subject). As for the drug trade in Miami now, Hiaasen is fairly fatalistic.

'Is this the drug capital of America? Of course it is, because it's the entry point for most of the drugs. It's not that it's an evil city, it's just geographic, it's the big American city nearest the places where they manufacture the drugs. Also the huge Latin population makes it possible for bad guys from Colombia and Bolivia and other places to converse and do their business in their native language. They're not going to be in Helsinki trying to do a cocaine deal, they wouldn't connect, but in Miami you can be on the street an hour and you can sell your cocaine. Crack has added a whole new dimension. Cocaine has gone through several phases in this country: back in the 1930s it was a society toot, then in the 1970s everyone was snorting the stuff, and then you got freebasing among the rich and famous, people started blowing up and a lot of middle-class people started going off cocaine. Now you've got crack, which goes right into the ghetto and is in my view a more dangerous drug than heroin. It's cheaper, more accessible, you can blow it or smoke it and it's created an enormous new cycle of crime. Cocaine users, being largely middle-class, were not typically thieves and killers, just people who got high; they may have had a psychological addiction and it may have wrecked their lives, but they were not out on the streets killing over it. It's scary as hell but it's not unique to Miami. Some of what's written about Miami is a little fanciful, a rub off from "Miami Vice", but every day in the paper there's something that makes you go "Holy Shit! I can't believe I still live down here." '

What infuriates him, though, is the craven attitude of the administration, who are interested only in maintaining Miami's public image. This reached a high point when riots broke out in the black ghetto of Overtown in February 1989, just as the city was preparing to host the Superbowl. 'You literally heard people saying, "What a terrible time for a race riot." Like when is a good time? In the dead of summer? Screw the Superbowl, we're talking about human lives!'

The hypocrisy of Miami's 'see no evil, hear no evil, speak no evil' policy was summed up for Hiaasen by a typical little Miami news item: 'Our Chamber of Commerce is continually telling people what a safe place it is. Well, the former chief of the Chamber of Commerce, his house is burgled and an Uzi machine gun is stolen out of a bedroom where he kept it for "personal protection". Like, "It's perfectly safe, here, but yeah, I do own an Uzi." These are the people who are lecturing us about overstating crime! I don't own a gun!'

Ultimately too, all these problems go hand in hand. The growth that is destroying the Florida Hiaasen loves is fuelled by the vast sums of money generated by the drug trade: 'A lot of real estate is bought and sold with drug money, not just lately but since 1974/5. You look at that skyline.' He waves out of the window at downtown Miami's futuristic skyline rising out of Biscayne Bay. 'Very impressive, lot of empty office space up there but the banks are full up with money, so they've got to loan it out which creates this cycle as they loan it out for construction. Even if there's no demand the developer is going to make his money anyway and leave and what have you got? Another shopping mall, another cheesy condo development you don't need, all because you've got to lay off the money someplace. To me, that's the most unsavoury aspect of it because it feeds the growth and all the other problems. I couldn't tell you precisely how much coke money is sitting in Miami now. I'm sure there's a ton of it in New York and in LA too. But I did a piece on where the Medellin cartel invests; we detailed apartments, shopping centres . . . look out the window – you see the condo with the blue awnings? The building's owned by them and was seized by US marshals after we wrote about it. It's a hell of an investment, right on the water in Miami. People I know who lived there said the service was great – you had a plumbing problem, boy they'd fix it! – but these are drug dealers, they're spreading misery. But the County Commission does not want to pass a law requiring people who come before the zoning board to reveal their names – the County Commission think it will *deter investment*. You're goddamn right it will! No one is going to come up here and say, "Yeah, I'm a cocaine dealer from Medellin and I'd like to invest in that tomato ranch out west, do you mind?" It's just greed and the price you pay is you have drug dealers who love it here, this is their playground, the place where they buy their cars – you can't buy the kind of Mercedes you want in Bogota. That's what happens when you hang out the welcome mat, and in the ghettoes of Washington, Chicago and LA they're paying the price for this greed – the greed which Florida has always been about.'

Since *Tourist Season*, Hiaasen has written two more novels. The first was *Double Whammy*, another black comedy, set this time in the world of pro bass fishing. More out and out funny than *Tourist Season*, particularly in a hilariously gruesome sequence involving the irrevocable attachment of a pit bull terrier to a bad guy's arm, it uses similar characters – newspapermen and berserk conservationists – and again arises out of Hiaasen's Florida background. 'Where I came to that was from growing up down here fishing when it was a bucolic, friendly sport. Now it's big money. It's very much a corrupted pleasure for me. In the book this crooked developer/TV evangelist builds this development which is totally phony, he digs a bunch of lakes so he can put that name in the title, and of course it's built on a landfill and the fish that are put in there all start dying. Well, if you picked up the *Miami Herald* a couple of weeks ago, you would have read that the largemouth bass, which is, believe it or not, our state fish, the most popular game fish in Florida – well, from northern Florida to the tip of the Everglades – all the tests that are being done on these fish are finding dangerously high levels of mercury. So the state is now warning people not to eat any largemouth bass caught in the Everglades. They don't know the source; it's probably agriculture, pesticides. You're in a bad state when the state government has to announce – come look at our state fish, but don't catch it, don't eat it.'

Corruption is also at the root of *Skin Tight*, an ultra-black comedy involving a lethal plastic surgeon and the death by liposuction of a talk-show host. Hiaasen comments, 'It doesn't stress the environmental themes so much, it's more about corruption, the corruption of everything, a black comedy of Florida as a refuge for scoundrels. In this book the main scoundrel is an inept plastic surgeon who has failed at every other specialty. The great thing about the States is once you get a medical degree you can practise in any damn thing you want, you don't have to be good at it, you don't have to know the first thing about brain surgery and you'll still find a place to practise. He hires a hitman to kill one of his enemies; everyone is corrupt including the hitman. The hero, the victim of all this, lives out in

Stiltsville in Biscayne Bay, an extraordinary place – these houses rising on pilings out of Biscayne Bay, there's not even a dozen of them left. Storms have taken most of them down. It's a very romantic place and at the same time incongruous because you've got this tropical setting and then you turn around and there's the Miami skyline. And here I am writing about a guy living out there and having a killer come out to the stilt house, and I pick up the paper and sure enough there's a story about some couple out fishing in Stiltsville with their kid, minding their own business, when two guys come up in a boat, both armed, they hop out of the boat, put a 9mm to the husband's head, rob them in broad daylight and roar off. Then, typically stupid criminals, they go drinking in the marina bar. So then, when the couple limps in after their day of terror, a fight has broken out between one of the robbers and a patron at the bar. They immediately recognize the bad guy and everyone gets arrested. But it's just such an obscenity – you're out for a day on the water and some geek with a 9mm hops in your boat.'

By now Hiaasen is looking edgy, clearly wanting to get back to writing tomorrow's column, trying for another small satiric victory against the bland, the pompous, the corrupt and the vicious. As I'm leaving he tells me that if he were choosing a state symbol he'd go for a 'gator. 'That's a really primordial beast that has somehow survived, and to me it's a symbol of nature, a reminder that, given half a chance, it'll fight back and bite your ass off.' So ends an audience with Carl Hiaasen, an eminently courteous, all-American (he's at great pains to tell you that his views 'don't make me a communist') madman – Brian Keyes and Skip Wiley still just about managing to cohabit in the one body.

It's late in the afternoon. Hiaasen has suggested I take a look at Bayside Market, one of Miami's latest developments, says it's a pleasant place to go, get something to eat or drink. It's no more than half a mile from the *Herald* so I decide to walk. Walking is clearly an ultra-low-rent activity; there are virtually no pedestrians on the roads apart from a couple of black guys waiting for cars to stop at the traffic lights so they can manically clean windscreens and demand ready cash in exchange. The sidewalks that connect these high-tone downtown developments are derelict and overgrown with weeds.

Bayside Market is a typical waterside/dockland development, a dead ringer for countless other such places from London's Hays Galleria to San Francisco's Fisherman's Wharf, designed to look 'traditional', thus a mock-industrial setting for a collection of boutiques, bars and restaurants, dominated by brightly lit stores selling ersatz Americana, ready-made kitsch at inflated prices. I stopped for a coffee and a sandwich at a Cuban-style cafe. I eat a *media noche*, a Cuban sandwich apparently constructed by taking two thick slices of Cuban bread, and about a dozen slices each of cheese and ham, then compressing them savagely. However, what is remarkable about Bayside Market is how much it appeals to an Anglo idea of good taste. Its clientele are as lily-white as you'll find in Miami. I find myself wondering what Hiaasen meant when he said he thought I might find this place 'fun'. Still, sitting on what could probably be described as the dock of the bay and listening to a Latin band strive to sound pop it's a pleasant enough place to take a breather and wait for evening to come down.

Then it's a bus ride back to Miami Beach to pick up the rental car, and get ready to take a ride round Little Havana. Driving through Miami is great: wide roads, not much traffic, I've got the radio tuned to the loudest, nastiest hiphop (or urban dance as they're calling it these days) station I can find, they're playing De La Soul, hiphop surrealism which sounds oddly out of place here, too clever by half. Listeners phone in, say 'That's wack' – in Miami music has got to be upbeat, American flash and brash, like the next record, Ton Loc's sassy and suspect 'Wild Thing'. Soon enough, having figured out the one-way system, I'm driving down South West 8th St, Calle Ocho, window down, radio up, looking for Little Havana and . . . there's nothing there. Not quite true, there's a bunch of other people driving along with their radios on and there's a couple of drive-thru McDonalds, and some flash funeral parlours and a whole heap of car showrooms and even a couple of *cantinas*, but an all-singing, all-dancing Latin version of Chinatown it is not. Partly this is for topographical reasons. Four-lane highways tend not to be too atmospheric. Partly it's a result of the economic success of the

Miami Cubans; what was a ghetto is now just a place you come back to from the suburbs to go for a meal or buy a new car. Finally, though, it's simply a reflection of the fact that Miami is now a predominantly Latin city and to isolate one area and call it Little Havana has little resonance any more; you'd perhaps do better to call the whole city Great Havana.

I park by the side of a funeral parlour and take a walk along the street looking for somewhere to eat and, at close quarters, I'm able to admire the window displays of the shops selling religious artefacts with no sense that the holy and the gaudy should be divisible. Eventually I pick on a basic *cantina*, a working men's place where everything is written in Spanish only. The waitress is a voluptuous teen with an extravagantly punk coiffure. She doesn't speak English nor me Spanish and more by luck than judgement I end up with a Mexican beer and a plate of shrimps, black-eyed beans and rice with a side order of fried plantain. As I'm struggling to finish this lot I realize that I have no cash, just travellers' cheques, on me. This kills off what's left of my appetite, so I get the bill and present a cheque to a reaction of considerable incomprehension. Oh shit! Time to start washing up, chopping the chillis and so forth ... but no, with great courtesy the cheque is passed round the staff until it reaches a white-haired guy in a suit who pockets it and leaves. Five minutes later he's back, presumably having visited one of the more tourist-oriented establishments up the street. The cheque is cashed and all is smiles.

By now there's a few more young bloods cruising the street but still a little less than action, so time to head back to Miami Beach and catch Ed playing records, Latin night at the Wet Paint. It's a cool breezy evening so I find a Quiet Storm station on the radio, soft soul music from Anita Baker, Luther Vandross, maybe a little laid-back jazz from the likes of Grover Washington; it's the smooth, sophisticated sound of middle-class Black America relaxing just a little, soulful but refined. Arrive at the Wet Paint only to find a small gathering outside and hear some bad news: Ed's had a bad diabetes attack, so no show tonight. Back to the hotel to sleep before tomorrow's meeting with James Hall, the hottest new property on the Florida writing scene.

Next morning James Hall shows up at the hotel around eleven.

He's somewhere around the bottom end of medium height, wearing docksiders, shorts and a polo shirt, plus a baseball cap over a hairline in retreat and a light beard. He's very upfront friendly and quickly launches into an apology for not being entirely himself as he's only half recovered from a vicious bout of flu. James Hall is a 'Hey! I'm a nice guy' kind of chap.

He's also an English Professor at Florida International University, a poet who has published four volumes of modernist verse and the author of an elegantly mean first novel, *Under Cover of Daylight*, that moves from the pastoral to the vicious with disquieting ease. *Under Cover of Daylight* is the story of a man named Thorn who is trying to live a completely natural life, outside of society, in the remotest part of Key Largo. The reason for his remoteness is a self-inflicted penance for a terrible act of vengeance he wreaked as a teenager upon the person who had killed his parents in a traffic accident. Twenty years later Thorn is finally forced to face the consequences of his actions as he returns to the world to help a conservation battle on the Keys and finds himself mixed up with ruthless developers, a pair of psychopathic but semi-competent hitmen and a woman who almost loves him but has good reason to hate him.

Under Cover of Daylight achieved the rare feat of reviewing well and selling well. It was the right book at the right time. Its mixture of thriller plot and lowlife characterization, combined with an elegantly crafted style that evokes Thomas McGuane at least as much as Charles Willeford, has struck a chord at a time when readers are finding serious fiction unbearably parochial, but are unwilling to put up with the formula writing that characterizes too much crime fiction. Hollywood has bought the film rights and, if Hall had a day job that required him to work more than two evenings a week, then he would no doubt have given it up. As it is, he's just finished a second novel called *Tropical Freeze* in the States and *Squall Line* in Britain (the publishers thought *Tropical Freeze* sounded like a brand of ice-cream), again featuring Thorn, and is now starting work on a third, this time with a new cast of characters.

James Hall drives a distinctly flash red convertible. We're driving across town to his house to pick up his boat and get out on the water where much of the action in his novels occurs.

Coming to an intersection there's some frantic blowing of horns and a couple of guys yelling abuse at each other out their windows. 'Jesus,' says James Hall, 'you see that? Miami's like a wild west town; all the time there are these encounters in traffic where everyone is packing a weapon. I just had one recently – a guy cut me off two feet in front of my front bumper going sixty miles an hour, so I shot him a sign of disgust! He was in a red BMW. He immediately got behind me and followed me for twenty miles to where I was going. I couldn't remember where a police station was in that part of town so I pulled into the parking lot of a bank thinking there'd at least be someone there with a pistol. Then the BMW drew up next to me. The guy was a Latin with a pained regretful look that kind of said "I hate to have to discipline you dumb fucks" and he told me I shouldn't shoot birds at people in traffic. I said, "Why?" – I live in Miami and I ask why! – and he said, "Because you could get shot." That was it. When I got home I realized that I'm driving this kind of cocaine dealer type car and the guy must have figured that I was armed, so when he said what he did, he must have had his gun ready. Jesus!'

By now we've crossed over the causeway into Miami and we're driving up Biscayne Boulevard, round about the neighbourhood they call Little Haiti, basically a standard piece of run-down, genteel gone sleazy, inner-city real estate, with enough traces of economic activity to raise it a notch above the next-door Afro-American neighbourhood of Overtown in the good ghetto stakes. The Haitians in fact are being trumpeted as the latest immigrant group to make good in Miami, this latterday El Dorado for downtrodden Caribbean and Latin American populations.

James Hall tells a joke that neatly captures the fragility of Miami's self-publicity: 'A tourist comes to Miami to see if it is a suitable place to bring his family on vacation, he stops a guy on the street and asks him, the guy says, "Yeah, it's a wonderful city." The tourist says, "What about the riots, the blacks burning down part of town?" The guy says, "Ah no, that's just a very small number of people, a localized problem." The tourist says, "What about the Cubans, the Marielitos?" The guy says, "No problem, the Cubans are very hard-working industrious people who've added an incredible energy to the community." The tourist says, "What about the Haitians, all the pictures I see of the Haitians coming in on their little boats?" The guy says, "Ah no, they're an artistic, colourful, interesting people who bring a cultural vigour to the community." So the tourist says, "Well, that sounds good, I certainly am sold on Miami. By the way, what do you do for a living?" The guy says, "I'm a tail gunner on a bakery truck." That's a typical Miami story.'

James Hall lives in Miami Shores, a couple of miles from Little Haiti. It's in a different world, the world familiar from family sitcoms, where the Cosby-Huxtables and the Van Dykes live in perpetual harmony: barbecues, picket fences, bungalows with neat front lawns. Just to complete the picture of Pleasant Valley Sunday-style suburbia, when James Hall opens the door, a big, cute dog leaps up and starts licking our faces. Past the doggy embraces and I'm introduced to Evelyn, the high-school teacher with whom Hall lives and to whom he has passed on his virulent flu. Inside, the house is light and roomy: an open-plan living area, with a heavyweight Hemingway biography left strategically on a coffee table, gives on to the garden, which in turn gives on to a canal. Moored in the canal we find James Hall's boat. This is his pride and joy, the treat he bought himself with the profits from *Under Cover*. Knowing doodley squat about boats, all I can report is that it's between twenty and thirty feet long, motorized and seems to go very well.

Hall navigates us deftly along the canal past ever more upmarket suburban gardens and even flashier boats. We come out into Biscayne Bay to be faced by some severe choppiness but, Hemingwayesque to the last, we decide to brave it and are rewarded by a rapid decline in turbulence. Over the bay Hall points out Indian Creek, where the likes of Julio Iglesias live in a community protected from the outside world by armed guards. We turn north – idly following Hall's route to work, as FIU is conveniently located on the waterfront of Biscayne Bay – and Hall directs my attention to some of the more apparently green and charming parts of the shore. He explains that the trees are growing to camouflage a toxic landfill. Inevitably the conversation turns to the ecology and the writing of *Under Cover*.

Like Hiaasen, Hall is appalled by the crassness with which Florida is despoiling its natural beauty, and he explained that his time spent living on the Florida Keys, a couple of hours' drive south of Miami, provided the background for the novel: 'That was the sociological ingredient, my new awareness of the fragile and extraordinary beauty of the Keys, coupled to a growing awareness of how endangered it was. I started going to conservationist meetings and it came out of that.'

The other strand that fed into the writing of *Under Cover*, however, and which gives the novel its edge of bitter violence, is taken from Hall's emotional rather than political life: 'My eighteen-year marriage was breaking up and I had this sort of love/hate betrayal thing with that woman and I brought that to the story – do you love this person or do you want to murder this person? That was the psychological ingredient of *Under Cover*.'

Thorn, however, is far from being a simple projection of Hall and he is not used as any kind of fictional vindication of his creator's private life. In fact he is viewed with a distinctly critical eye. This is one of Hall's strengths – too many crime writers will create lone-wolf heroes whom no woman can tie down, and slip all too easily into an apparently unquestioned misogyny. Hall, while imbuing Thorn with some of his own emotional ambivalence, has resisted the temptation to make him a kind of superhero alter ego, working out his relationships for him by proxy: 'Thorn is somewhat based on a neighbour of mine who was a sports fisherman there, but he is also Henry David Thoreau living in Walden Pond – trying to discover what's it like to live absolutely naturally, close to the rhythms of nature. I don't think that is possible, so he's really a fantasy character. I don't take him too seriously, I see him in some ways as slightly comic. He's an ageing hippie, who doesn't realize it; he's going to be, by God, true and natural, almost a parody of Hemingway. He's going to do things exactly by the code. I admire that but I also see it as somewhat unreal. Though I must say I felt it myself, when I lived there. In Key Largo my life was much more adapted to a natural pace than it is here.'

Hemingway is clearly the literary lion that looms largest for Hall, himself a fisherman and possessed of a considerable ambivalence as to whether he wants to be seen as an intellectual or a man's man, suspecting them to be mutually exclusive. In *Squall Line* Thorn spends a lot of time in a bar called Poppa Joe's, presided over by Poppa Joe himself, a man who fished with Hemingway and has the morality of a conger eel. Hall comments, 'Poppa Joe's is based on a number of bars. Poppa Joe, himself, is based to some extent on Tony Terrassino of Captain Tony's in Key West which is really the bar that Hemingway used to drink in. There's another bar, Sloppy Joe's, that claims to be where Hemingway drank and everybody goes there. Actually he drank everywhere! But Captain Tony is an old conch renegade sort of guy. I found him fascinating and thought I'd like to have a character whose values are pirate values, who believes that anything you can get away with goes. There's a good deal of America that believes that still, as you can see from Wall Street. Then there's this other set of people who are puritanical and are relentlessly trying to punish these other guys, and the rest of us are somewhere in the middle trying to figure out who's right – the Captain Tonys or the FBI? Is his maverick sensibility noble? I'm interested in that moral ambiguity.'

Hemingway's desire to be a 'great writer' is a pull too for Hall. He dreads being seen as simply a genre writer: 'I have a longstanding interest in thrillers, and as a fan I wanted to participate in the genre, but my training is more in literature. I come to this more from the Hemingway tradition via Hammett and Chandler. What interests me in crime fiction is to deal with the issue of a human being's existential struggle, a human being thrust into a situation where his life and values are in extreme danger. Writing would be a lot easier if I just said, "I'm going to write a genre book using a formula I know exists" or if I said, "Screw it. I'm going to write *Farewell to Arms*. I'm not going to bother with this melodramatic bullshit." But I'm interested in both things. I'm interested in the romantic tradition which is the detective story and the realist tradition which is the novel.'

By now Hall has turned the boat round and we're heading directly towards the downtown Miami skyline. The bay is getting busier, tugs and customs boats pottering about their business. Suddenly to our left a boat appears, going like a bat out of hell. Behind it comes a coastguard boat. Both are travelling at a speed that would be dangerous on land and looks lethal on water. In little more than a minute they're out of sight behind one of the little islands dotting the bay. 'Miami Vice', phew! Hall points out the opening of the Miami River to me: 'I took a trip down there the other day; it's where the ships come from the Caribbean. I was looking at these ships that are ready to go back and they're stacked with the strangest stuff . . . stolen bicycles, plastic buckets . . . All these things you can't believe another culture places a value on, that they'll all be saying in Haiti, "Oh, great, a ten-gallon bucket."'

Next morning the *Miami Herald* does an exposé on this river traffic. Ships flying the flags of Honduras and Haiti are coming in to Miami, bringing in Colombian cocaine, and then returning to Haiti loaded up with items as diverse as school buses, rice, beans and, as Hall observed, stolen bicycles, all hidden under tarpaulins stolen from pest-control firms. None of this strange cargo is listed on any manifest, and all disappears on arrival in Haiti. The sinister part is the identity of the people running this Miami River traffic: none other than Baby Doc's infamous Tonton Macoutes. Now minus their trademark sunglasses, they are currently upping the craziness stakes in Miami drug wars. A guy from the Sheriff's Office, quoted in the *Herald* says, 'The Macoutes don't think they can die. They think they're immune to bullets. They do drug deals based on info from voodoo priests.' The man from the DEA then chips in with some less than reassuring words: 'We know there are some Tonton Macoute-type individuals controlling drug trafficking. But we don't know if they're out and out running the port or not.'

Echoes here of *Squall Line*, in which the main villain is an FBI renegade who specializes in smuggling Latin American bad guys into Florida and giving them legit new identities. As the book opens he is processing a former drug enforcer from Haiti, a green-eyed albino called Claude who is scary even to people used to dealing with severely anti-social types. *Squall Line* keeps the same central character, Thorn, as *Under Cover*, but this is far less his story. Here there are a whole range of protagonists looking for the limelight, all morally compromised to some degree. There's no easy identification with good guys or simple condemnation of bad. In this world we all do bad things, and the most we can hope is that some decency is left in our hearts. Typical is Ossie, a Florida country boy obsessed with making it as a Florida country singer (allowing James Hall to indulge himself by writing a neat parody of one of Key West country singer Jimmy Buffet's epic Florida ballads) and smitten from afar with a TV weather girl who is in turn smitten with Thorn. Ossie is in the employ of the dangerously amoral Poppa Joe. Ossie buys Poppa Joe's romantic outlaw *schtick* wholesale and he's ready to kill, but underneath all he wants is to use his songs to get out from where he's been, and to that degree he has something in common with James Hall.

'I grew up in Kentucky with guys like Ossie who talk lahk thi-i-is, where every one-syllable word is actually three. It was a kind of backwoods moonshine environment so until I was seventeen years old I was this hick from Kentucky. Then I went to Europe and I saw the cathedrals and I developed this other part of me that thought I was cultured. Then I went to college and got a civilized education, so part of me is at war over who am I? Am I this redneck Ossie, or am I this other person who is talking now, who talks to my students? I can go home and talk to my friends in Kentucky and I slip back into the old twang. But there's still a lot of Ossies in Florida because Florida's got a real rural side to it. If you go about twenty or thirty miles inland people listen to country music, bluegrass, they ride around in pick-up trucks with the shotgun up on the rack behind the window – we call them Florida crackers. They could be from anywhere rural – Nebraska, Indiana . . . but here they are, twenty miles from the ocean.'

We're heading back to James Hall's house. We moor the boat and go inside, where he makes enormous sandwiches for us and Evelyn. We go outside to eat and drink some Californian white wine, talk about how much Hall enjoyed his trip to England; as evidence of this last he shows me his Wimbledon tennis baseball cap, blandly tacky as only British souvenirs can be. James Hall is a major tennis fan. Kentucky redneck days are long gone. Tennis is Florida's sunshine sport; up at Fort Lauderdale is Nick Bolletieri's production line tennis academy where baseliners from Chris Evert to Monica Seles are launched to the top.

Later in the afternoon we take a drive south through Miami. The interstate takes us safely over the Overtown ghetto. Major roads through ghettoes always seem to come with Berlin Wall-type security to prevent the natives from dumping rocks on passing Mercedes. Underneath the interstate, Hall tells me, live a fair percentage of Miami's too numerous homeless. Then we pass through downtown. It's hard not to be impressed here by the sheer modernity, the sense of being in a place which has not given up on the idea of progress, which believes you can still build high and build new. Best evidence of this are the two Arquitectonica skyscrapers. These are a completely contemporary mix-up of the aesthetics of the shanty town with those of post-modernism. One of them leans too far to the tired post-modern convention of painting your piping in bright colours, and ends up looking like 'something from a Mexican suburb where they had a lot of specials on different colour paints', as James Hall puts it. The other skyscraper works triumphantly: rounded, tall and primary-coloured, its masterstroke is the conceit of incorporating a huge hole two-thirds of the way up. This hole houses a large atrium with a spiral staircase and a potted palm tree. T. D. Allman puts it on the cover of his excellent book, *Miami: City of the Future*, and well he might: it's brash, funny and beautiful, designed by an Anglo/Latin team, and it makes you think for once that the future might not be too bad a place.

Driving down towards Coconut Grove, the conversation roams over a mêlée of subjects: Oral Roberts, the TV evangelist – 'he's the guy who puts his hands on people's heads and says, "Heal, heal" and they throw away their crutches and stuff. On Sunday I saw him on TV and he was healing people's wallets!' – or Charles Willeford.

Maybe the quintessential Miami crime novelist, Willeford died last year. Willeford was a spectacularly crusty twenty-year army veteran turned novelist who finally hit the big time in his sixties with his first Florida-set crime novel, *Miami Blues*, which appeared in 1984 (his publishers choosing the title in the hope of getting a free ride on the coat-tails of 'Miami Vice'). His speciality was bad guys. If Elmore Leonard produced a blueprint for the bland, blond Florida psychopath with the moral sense of a horsefly, then Willeford refined the characterization and added an appalling sense of humour. First off, in *Miami Blues*, Willeford created an amiable psychopath called Freddy 'Junior' Frenger, a nice guy till he's crossed. Junior, however, is easily crossed. As he arrives at Miami Airport, at the book's opening, he is confronted by a disguised Hare Krishna pinning a stick of candy on his lapel and asking for money. Junior reacts by grabbing the guy's middle finger and bending it back, then further back till it breaks. Unfortunately the guy goes into shock and dies five minutes later. This sets the tone for one of Willeford's distinctive ultra-black comedies. Junior just wants to settle down to a quiet respectable life of petty crime, but fate keeps conspiring to provoke him.

Three more novels featuring Miami cop Hoke Moseley, the least style-conscious man in Miami, followed before Willeford's death in 1987, at a hard-lived sixty-seven years old. The third of them, *Sideswipe*, features a character called Troy Louden who is pretty much a *reductio ad absurdum* of the Florida psychopath: blond, thick sideburns, cowboy clothes, six foot one or two with a broken nose and an easy charm. He also has a neat line in self-analysis: 'I'm a professional criminal, what the shrinks call a criminal psychopath. What it means is, I know the difference between right and wrong and all that, but I don't give a shit.'

So it was with some curiosity that I ask Hall if he'd known Willeford. 'His wife was in a class of mine,' he tells me, 'and I had him come to some of my classes in mystery fiction, so I got to know them socially. He was a funny guy; he was such a cantankerous personality, he made people think by being aggressively provocative. He could come in and be extraordinarily insulting, like a radio talk-show host, just trying to stir people up. He wasn't that way privately, he was a very sweet man with his friends, but in a group, when he was performing, he would put on this hostile baiting attitude that would make a lot of people angry. I never related to his work as much as I felt I should. When he tried to use ideas, he wasn't very good; his strength was this withheld Hemingwayesque thing, and the tone. He found a lot of absurd things very amusing.'

Coconut Grove is where Willeford's cop, Hoke Moseley, moves when he's forced out of the South Beach hotel he's been living in by the sudden arrival of his daughters, pissed off by their mother's remarriage. Coconut Grove used to be the bohemian area of Miami, its Greenwich Village, but that was years ago when James Hall, like Hoke Moseley, lived in a garage apartment. Now, like Greenwich Village or Hampstead, but without the literary self-regard, the Grove is a place for trendy rich people. The architecture and the look of the residential parts is similar to the Keys: Spanish-style houses and clapboard cottages shrouded in a forest of greenery. The streets have coral walls and all around is dense overbearing nature. The foci of the area are the shopping malls with the boutiques and discos which attract the Latin playboy crowd and their female associates, places to be seen to spend money – cold cash not credit cards – nightclubs full of guys who think Al Pacino in *Scarface* – one man with a machine gun taking on an army before diving suicidally into a huge mound of pure cocaine – was a tragic hero.

I ask James Hall how he sees the morality of crime writing, why he didn't write about a cop but an outsider, a lone wolf: 'Maybe I would have written about a cop if I had a greater sense that I knew what a cop was like – I don't know any cops. People in America have this strong contempt for the judicial process, so the individual is given a licence to do these Dirty Harry/Bernard Goetz kind of things, but I don't really believe in that vigilante ideal, I think it's anarchic and scary and dangerous when you have a lot of people packing guns. The problem I have with these books is that they play on that kind of cynicism. I'm trying to figure out a way of having my character be heroic and find some form of justice in an individual situation, and at the same time be humane. I'm trying to figure out what is appropriate moral behaviour in a world where people are eating lobster thermidor on the top of a slagheap.'

Hall is careful to avoid the cosy morality that too many crime writers slip into, with idealized cop or PI heroes (they may be flawed but you can be damn sure they are lovably flawed) and plots in which the really good guys never die, always win through at the last. The strength of these conventions is made brutally clear in both *Under Cover* and *Squall Line* when in each case the most lovable character available – in both instances an elderly and doughty woman – has to fight for her life, and in both cases loses. I ask Hall whether this reflected a desire to break the conventions or simply homicidal feelings towards old ladies: 'Oh God!' he says, 'I feel guilty about that. I guess I want to give the reader a feeling that no one is safe, that anything can happen. When I first started writing I was under the influence of some of the 1960s avant-garde writers – John Barth, Robert Coover, Donald Barthelme, even Richard Brautigan – people who by today's categories would be magical realists. The problem with that legacy is that I have to resist a strong temptation to write something surreal, which would come out silly in this kind of book, but the good part of that is that it does make me break the conventions – killing the old ladies and stuff!'

Whether killing lovable grannies will feature in the Hollywood version of Hall's novels is a moot point, as of course is whether there will *be* a Hollywood version. Hall is going through the classic drama of almost every novelist with a first hit book: the saga of the film rights. It starts every time with a whirlwind courtship and peaks with the excitement of the purchase before precipitately hurtling downhill into despair (it doesn't get made) or disillusion (it does get made) and ending with a moral dilemma: to scriptwrite or not to scriptwrite. Here's James Hall's account.

'My agent put *Under Cover* up for auction, a bunch of people bid on it including Bruce Willis. It came down finally to two similar deals, one from a guy called Paul Monash, who produced *Carrie* and a bunch of big movies, and the other from a Canadian company who had made *Atlantic City*, one of my favourite movies. So I went to Hollywood, which was a mythic journey for me, something I've always dreamed of. I even rode first-class. I got out there and stayed at the Beverly Wilshire. I went out jogging in the morning, through Beverly Hills, looking at the houses and wondering which one I was going to own. I got back from the jog and was sitting in my hotel when a 6.8 earthquake hit Los Angeles. The hotel rocked, windows broke, down the street people were screaming. I didn't know what was going on, I thought I was having a heart attack. I thought, "Holy shit, would you know, on the brink of all this success I'm dying in this hotel room." Then I realized what was happening and ran downstairs, wondering what do you do in an earthquake? It was a real existential moment and it made me think I was getting carried away with this. What always mattered was that writing this stuff was fun, not the success. So I went and had that day with a whole different attitude, it didn't matter any more, which was a good thing because those guys are every bit of what all the myths suggest.

'The first words out of Monash's mouth were: "Are you ready to be rich?" I said, "Well, I don't know." That was the wrong answer – I should have said, "Yes, yes, pleeease make me rich!" Almost the next words were: "You're not planning to write any more novels, are you?" I said, "Yes, what else would I write?" They can't understand it: a wildly successful novel might make 150,000 or 200,000 dollars, but write a screenplay which may never see the light of day and you make 100,000 dollars minimum and it only takes a couple of months. So they bought the film and they had me write the script, paid me 25,000 dollars to write it and then shitcanned it right away and stuck an expensive screenplay writer on it. They told me the reason they didn't like my script was that it was too much like the book. Which had me confused. "Sorry, you paid me all this money, I thought you liked the book, but you want a different story. OK, sorry, my mistake." Then I started reading all these books about Hollywood and realized I'd had the classic Hollywood experience for the *schmuck* with the Underwood. They steal his little precious thing, his novel – they pay 40/50,000 dollars for it, then turn around and sell it to a studio for 500,000 dollars. They make 450,000 for just turning round and selling it to their buddy and meanwhile you think you're the luckiest person on earth.' As for *Under Cover*'s chances of actually making it on to film Hall is phlegmatic: 'They've just bought up the option for another year, but it's unlikely it'll ever see the light of day. Nine out of ten books that are bought don't.'

On this rather sombre note we arrive back on Miami Beach. As we drive down 21st Street he says, 'You know, this is really a bad neighbourhood.' Apparently a police-reporter friend took him down here to investigate the crack trade. Then, remembering that this is where I'm staying, he diplomatically adds, 'Of course the worst part is down the street a little.' We pull up to the hotel and he says, 'Uh, can I just see inside your hotel room?' So in we go, James Hall to research interior life in a crack-street hotel room and say goodbye ('tell them I'm a nice person') and me to rest up and watch some TV (a teenage soap pussyfooting around the abortion debate).

*   *   *

That night the heavens open and I go briefly down to Ocean Drive where I eat a pizza in the Cardozo Hotel, the first of the South Beach deco hotels to be refurbished. It's tastefully done, but tonight the place is empty and I have to deal with a theatrical waiter who has just discovered what he called 'English music'. He is determined to share this fondness with me by playing a tape of an old Art of Noise LP unreasonably loudly. Combined with the weather, this seems like God's way of hinting that an early night is in order.

Next morning it is up early for breakfast in Wolfies, the great American meal served with a spectacular assortment of home-baked rolls but delivered by a waitress who won't see seventy-five again yet still clings to baby-doll make-up and matching manner. On hearing that I'm bound for New Orleans next she coos, 'Oh, but it's so dangerous there.' This is said in a diner from which you only needed to look out of the window to see crack deals made.

After breakfast the Everglades beckon. The quickest route turns out to be back over the causeway into downtown Miami then on to Calle Ocho (symptomatically reAnglicizing to SouweSayda now Spanglish replaces Spanish in the new generation) and keep going. As Calle Ocho leaves Miami it becomes the Tamiami Trail, the Seminole route to the Everglades. Miami disappears in a welter of superstores and gas stations and the swamplands take over. First Everglades attraction you hit is Frog City, real old-time folksy tack, rustic surreal on the outside, credit-card machines on the inside, frogs and dilapidated boats out the back. A while further on down the road you encounter your first Indian tribe, the Miccosukee: Seminole Indians who were once farmers in northern Florida and are now reduced to making a living off tourists by wrestling alligators and manufacturing knick-knacks. It's to one of their villages that, near the beginning of *Squall Line*, Haitian psychopath Claude takes the car salesman whose Porsche he's test driving and stakes him out as alligator meat.

Maybe it's at the same place that I stop to eat some very bad truck-stop food and drink some diabolical coffee. It's an unhappy place. The woman on the cash register not only doesn't speak

English, which is common enough in Florida, but doesn't understand money, which is rare and makes you wonder why she should have to. There's precious little dignity in being sat behind a tourist cash register but there's little option once you and your people have been consigned to a swamp. Actually there is one option: enterprising Indian leaders have discovered that the peculiar sets of laws governing their reservations have loopholes which allow them to have legal bingo (unlike the vast bulk of the States) and to sell tax-free cigarettes. In *Tourist Season* one of the terrorists is a Seminole leader called Tommy Tigertail who has made a fortune out of this legalized bingo. I had asked Hiaasen about this character and the role of the Seminoles in Florida.

'I have only passing contact with the Seminoles,' he told me. 'They don't have many dealings with white culture. By and large they distrust white people, and who wouldn't after all they've been through. I get a perverse satisfaction that we're all upset because they're selling cigarettes and bingo. They've taken advantage of every loophole the law has given them – you go by one of the Indian reservations round five o'clock, there's a line of cars waiting to buy tax-free cigarettes. Seminoles don't have to pay tax on the cigarettes they buy – so what do they do with them? Sell them to white people, cancer sticks! Great idea! You go into a bingo parlour in Hollywood Florida, huge aircraft hangar of a place, and there's all these blue-haired old white ladies playing bingo . . . I just can't imagine the shock when it was explained to them. You have this silly little board game, put it in a giant arena and all these white people will come to win four or five bucks a pop. They've got to be thinking these people are nuts. I find great poetic justice when you drive by a Seminole village and you see all these Cadillacs with their free licence tags. That's one of their little perks – the state, after literally raping them and driving them out of any piece of property that's worth anything, gave them free licence tags. Which I think is pretty generous! But now you see them on Cadillacs. Great! People say they're cheating the state out of taxes, but they were here first; we should be paying them taxes. God knows they have enough problems with alcoholism and severe depression. Let them have the loopholes, whatever's left.

'I know a writer who spent a year with them to research a

book and he said they never opened up, he was lucky to get a hello, which is very strange for an American. We're used to being gregarious: "Be my buddy, tell me what it's like to be an Indian." I'd love to know more about them but they want to be left alone and I can respect that. Their history is a metaphor for how Florida has screwed people from day one. They never wanted to be in the Everglades; they were in cattle country in the north part of the state, they were great ranchers and they've been driven south and south into the hottest, swampiest, most dangerous part of Florida, the Everglades. They're left with nothing – spearing fish – when these were tremendously industrious people.'

Declining the chance to watch the dubiously traditional Indian entertainment on offer, I head to the National Park. Here you pay and park and set off on a nature trail. Now, call me naïve, but I was not expecting to walk along a path and then see, a couple of yards to my right, lying by a little stream, a basking alligator. This is a situation where etiquette failed me, and I wished I'd been more interested in natural history. Was the right reaction a) to run screaming back whence I came or b) pat the critter on the head and have my photo taken with it? I went for the middle course, hoping that, if it was too hot for me to run, the same would apply to the 'gator. Fortunately this seemed to be the case, and throughout the trail the only 'gators who were prepared to do more than roll an eyeball were the ridiculously cute, foot-long baby 'gators frolicking in the stream. Savouring an unaccustomed and entirely ridiculous Hemingway-style, big-game hunter 'I saw the 'gators and lived' buzz, I got back in the car and drove to the airport, pausing only to buy a green enamel lapel 'gator from Frog City.

2

Southern Louisiana: Tell It Like It Is

Within three hours of arriving at New Orleans Airport I'm walking down Bourbon Street. Bourbon Street is a kind of Dixieland Carnaby Street, offering a titillating whiff of debauchery for tourists from the Mid-West. For five or six blocks the three main businesses are bars, novelty T-shirt shops and strip clubs. Tourists are expected to file an itinerary along the lines of get drunk, buy a stupid T-shirt, get even more drunk and go to a strip show.

I do my best. Drinking can be done either indoors at inflated prices or alfresco from paper 'go-cups' filled with either beer or a sickly local concoction called a Hurricane which is alleged to be a N'Awlins (as tourists are ordered to refer to New Orleans, to make us feel in the swing of things or something) Tradition and appears to be made from dark rum and sugar, both in lethal proportions. On spotting an Oirish-style pub, however, I experience a sudden yen for a glass of Guinness, so in I go to enjoy an overpriced and indifferently kept sip of stout while listening to a band dressed in Nashville cowboy outfits declare that they'll play the wild rover no more, and generally express their longing to return to Erin's green shore.

A little of this goes a long way at this remove from Tipperary and soon I'm back on the street savouring the strains of 'When the Saints Go Marching in' piping out from the novelty shops. I can't work up much enthusiasm for the souvenirs, which are tacky in a disappointingly half-hearted kind of way. Stroll further along Bourbon and I'm enticed into another bar by its relatively downbeat appearance and the sounds of R&B percolating on to the street. Inside, though, it's much like the rest of Bourbon: the waitress hits you up for your two-drink minimum within seconds and the R&B group prove to be a bunch of young black guys

trying not to yawn as they wade through a selection of the kind
of 1960s soul numbers likely to appeal to white college kids who
think the Blues Brothers invented funk. Clearly they know their
audience; they have only to hit the intro to 'Sitting on the Dock
of the Bay' for all the collegiate couples to start smooching
ferociously. The one black girl in the audience then goes up to
the bass player to make a request, he grins and briefly the band
comes alive as they careen through the big black pop hit of the
moment, Bobby Brown's 'My Prerogative'.

Considerably fortified by the rapid ingestion of my two-drink
minimum I head back on to Bourbon Street and look for a rats'
nest of vice. Soon enough I'm standing outside a place offering
'Live! Male and female! Topless and bottomless!' So in I go to a
dark room with a bar at one end and a small raised stage
surrounded by rows of seating. The seating is mostly taken up by
whooping student types equally divided between the sexes.
Towards the back are seated a number of middle-aged couples
who look to be on a Kiwani Club outing from Des Moines. The
waiter relays my drinks order to the biker-clad barman and
suddenly it's showtime. First up is a shortish muscular guy in a
jockstrap who proceeds to cavort about, swing round the pole set
into the centre of the stage, clench his buttocks and grind his
crotch into the faces of the women sat adjacent to the stage, in
the apparent hope of provoking lust-crazed females to stuff
dollars into his jockstrap. These basic manoeuvres are then
repeated for some considerable time to the accompaniment of
much giggling and cat-calling from the women in the audience,
encouraging the performer to remove his remaining clothing.

This, however, he declines to do and his place is taken by a
skinny woman with a California wavy perm wearing a pair of
rather worn white knickers and a baggy T-shirt. When she
performs the first of the many handstands which are the mainstay
of her performance – and which add a saddening little-girl-
showing-off quality to the act – the T-shirt falls off to reveal a
boyish torso. Essentially her act is the same as her predecessor's,
except that it's the men in the audience who get her crotch
rotated in their faces. She seems in a worse temper, though: when
marks like me refuse to stuff her knickers with loot her hard
mouth gets harder. And who could blame her? As the act finishes

I head out back to the toilet, where I am confronted with a wall dispenser offering a product called Brisk that promises 'to increase alertness and aid highway driving', while assuring me that it is 'no more dangerous than caffeine'. No *more* dangerous, huh, I muse while inserting the appropriate coinage and waiting for the ersatz speed to fall into my hand. The machine calmly takes the money and gives nothing away. When a poorly aimed karate kick fails to set matters right I head, chastened, back into the club. As I pass the stage a man approaches to offer me the chance to see 'a real show' somewhere out back. At which point I make my excuses and leave.

Next morning, following what passes in the States for a Continental breakfast, I decide to take a stroll along Magazine Street, which stretches from the Central Business District, just west of the French Quarter, for several miles alongside the elegant Garden District to end up at Audubon Park, home of the Zoo in which Nastassja Kinski transforms herself into a panther in the course of Paul Schrader's *Cat People*.

Magazine Street, in the morning sunshine, where it runs through the Lower Garden District, is just about perfect. It has old wooden houses with wrought-iron decorative work, it has porches with people sitting on rocking chairs and yet it is not gentrified or prettied up for the tourists. It is clearly a somewhat down-at-heel neighbourhood, but it is also beautiful and, on seeing a couple of 'To Let' signs, I think that I could very happily live here. What is amazing is that, as with the Deco District of Miami, there is just so much beauty and that it is just *there*, has not yet been reconstructed as a theme park.

Keep walking and I come to a clump of shops. There's a sign saying 'records' which lures me into a record store that looks as if it has been kept in a time capsule since 1963. It's a huge and chaotic shrine to the music that came out of the South in the 1950s and 1960s: country, soul and blues from all over; cajun and zydeco from the Louisiana swamplands and, above all, the music from the New Orleans melting pot; from Fats Domino to the Neville Brothers, via Smiley Lewis, Ernie K-Doe, Irma Thomas, the Dixie Cups, Lee Dorsey, Allen Toussaint and the Meters. The stock of albums is remarkable, but the selection of singles phenomenal; original pressings of virtually every great

New Orleans record are piled up all over. Unfortunately the pricing policy, unlike the decor, has kept firmly up with the times. The place is run by a wiry white guy in his fifties who succinctly sums up the difference between retailing and collecting when he tells a regular customer, a black guy who's come in for the new Neville Brothers album: 'Your trouble is you have a passion for this stuff, I don't. I don't take all this home with me!'

And so the morning wears on; 1960s records and 1950s paperbacks are acquired, antique shops are gawped at, the neighbourhood turns entirely black for a while and I pay a disappointing visit to Soul Train Fashions, which is just a rather poorly stocked version of any white high-street discount-clothing store. Eventually, exhausted, I wind up in a bar half full of ageing rednecks where the jukebox alternates Hank Williams with Aaron Neville's aching New Orleans classic 'Tell It Like It is' and I eat a Po' Boy Sandwich, something like a regular French-bread sandwich only much, much bigger.

After lunch I decide to catch a bus back to the French Quarter, see what it has to offer outside of Bourbon Street. Which turns out to be a lot, almost too much. There is something overheated about the French Quarter. It is startlingly elegant, with long narrow streets of houses boasting overhanging wrought-iron balconies, and it is so much of a piece, so distinctly atmospheric as to approach the overblown. It is no accident that the most popular writer working in New Orleans at the moment should be Anne Rice, whose modern vampire novels represent Louisiana generally, and the French Quarter particularly, as less a place than a narcotic, an essence of sickly sensuality.

Certainly the French Quarter is an appropriate enough place to set an occult novel. After the obligatory and wonderful coffee and *beignets* (fritters) at the Cafe du Monde on Jackson Square I head up Dumaine Street to the Voodoo Museum, where a startlingly Gothic young woman with an alabaster face and a black dress that, severe from the front, proves to be backless to the waist, ushers me through to the rooms where they keep the altar and the snake.

The history of voodoo is the hidden history of New Orleans. Its existence stems from New Orleans' unique historical role as the landing point for the slave traders. Much of the trade's terrible effectiveness came from the systematic way in which the slaves were stripped of their culture: those from the same tribe were split up so that groups of slaves would have no common language except that of their masters, and they would be deprived of their musical instruments, particularly their drums. So New Orleans, where the slaves waited to be sold, served as the one American repository of African culture. Until 1830 the slaves were allowed to play drums in Congo Square on Sundays and it was this tradition of African rhythm that informed a black cornettist named Buddy Bolden when he took over the leadership of Charlie Galloway's band during the 1890s and helped to create something that came to be called jazz.

African religion also persisted. In New Orleans, as in Haiti and other French West Indies slave communities, it merged with Catholicism to form a mutant religion known as Voodoo (from the word *vodun* meaning God in the language of the Fon tribes of Dahomey). The Voodoo Museum sports a working Voodoo altar which gives some idea of how this mix panned out. The emphasis of worship shifts from one God indivisible to a focus on the company of saints. On the altar sits a whole array of saints, heroes and villains both. Surrounding them is a selection of the kind of offerings not generally found at the Harvest Festival. Voodoo followers figure that their saints are less interested in ears of corn than in the same little luxuries of life that their earthly followers covet. So the altar is laden with cigarettes and alcohol, dollar bills and candy bars – carnal offerings.

Looking at the Voodoo artefacts mounted on the wall of the next room, I fail to pay attention to the glass case over which I'm leaning. This is just as well, as, when I step back, I notice that it is largely taken up by a boa constrictor. The sight of a large snake successfully puts the hex on me, so I retire to the outer room to examine the selection of Voodoo herbal remedies and take a pinch of gris gris dust for luck.

Next stop is a neighbourhood bar where I drink Dixie beers and check the music listings to find out where to go tonight. Best bet looks to be Charmaine Neville – daughter to one of the Brothers – at a place called Snug Harbor, east of the quarter. Before that I decide to head up to Chez Hélène, a soul-food restaurant north of the quarter. I take a cab up there and, once we head past North Rampart Street, the quarter's northern edge, it becomes clear that while New Orleans may be the Rainbow City, very visibly integrated, in its poorest areas the faces you see are still overwhelmingly black, and not Creole quaint but poverty plain.

It's round here that Congo Square used to be, and round here also that New Orleans experimented with legalized prostitution, in what was known as Storyville. The conjunction of the two is at the root of the perfectly American process by which its great indigenous art – jazz – should have been nurtured in the parlours of brothels. Both Congo Square and Storyville are now long gone, replaced, respectively, by a moderately dangerous park named after Louis Armstrong, and a housing project.

The cab turns into the depressed length of N. Robertson Street to bring me to Chez Hélène. Along the way the stoned immaculate cab driver commends my choice: 'Good restaurant, man, good restaurant.' He shakes his head, and suggests I try the fried chicken: 'Best fried chicken you'll ever eat, man,' he says, and laughs incredulously. Then he cautions me to take another taxi when I leave. 'Bad neighbourhood,' he drawls, back to shaking his head, 'bad neighbourhood.'

Inside Chez Hélène I pass through a bar piled high with cardboard boxes, and enter the dining-room. This is down-home simple: red-and-white checked tablecloths, a jukebox in the corner, and the walls covered with news clippings and stories about Chez Hélène and its chef, Austin Leslie. Turns out that Chez Hélène has lately been used as the model for a TV sitcom, set in a soul-food restaurant and called 'Frank's Place'. They've apparently built a replica of the place as the set. Thankfully neither the food nor the prices appear to have been affected by this success. I blow out on Oysters Rockefeller and soft-shell crab and fried chicken, served with potato salad and okra and fries and some fairly transcendent stuffed peppers. By the time the fresh-baked cornbread arrives I am sufficiently stuffed as to have to remain motionless for some considerable while, which gives me a chance to contemplate my fellow diners. The clientele is an amiable mix of blue-collar locals, mostly black but some white also, and smarter types, again both black and white. The smarter types are all discreetly asked by the genial proprietress, as she brings them the bill, whether they would like her to order a cab. As I wait for my cab to show, I speculate as to the possible connection between the humour of a restaurant and the kind of food it serves; surely the cheeriness prevalent in a place like Chez Hélène must be related to the fact that a condition of entry is that you're prepared to acquire the girth of a Solomon Burke. Anyway, by the time I leave I'm glad to be getting a cab to Snug Harbor, less because of any danger on the street as simply through not being able to walk.

And so, round about midnight, I find myself in Snug Harbor, drinking whiskey sours and listening to Charmaine Neville take flight in her second set. The first half of the show has been solid enough entertainment in the New Orleans groove, featuring some fine piano playing from Amasa Miller, but in the second show she sings whatever the crowd requests. Which, in front of a knowledgeable home crowd, makes for considerable entertainment. Highlight is when someone from the audience hands her a set of lyrics to an old blues, an invitation to 'Meet me with your black drawers on, not your pink ones or yellow ones or brown ones, honey meet me with your black drawers on' – an appropriate enough tune for a city in which gradations of skin colour have long been of enormous significance; New Orleans being the birthplace of such racial micro-definitions as quadroon (a woman with one-quarter black blood), octoroon, etc. Whatever, Charmaine, a slim black woman with Indian cheekbones, sings the grown woman's dirty blues with unusual assurance.

Morning finds me at a car-rental place out near the Louisiana Superdome. What I get is a Ford Coronary or somesuch which shakes like hell as soon as it hits fifty miles an hour on IS 10 heading up to Baton Rouge. I'm on my way west into cajun country looking to hear some music and see a little of the rural South. I've been given the names of two places to check out: Fred's Lounge in Mamou, which apparently sports a remarkable daytime cajun-music session, and Slim's Y-Ki-Ki Lounge in Opelousas, a zydeco hotspot. (The difference between cajun and zydeco might be described in terms of cajun being more shot through with country music and zydeco more blues, but the essential difference is of the straightforward Southern kind: white people play cajun, blacks play zydeco.)

The route I'm taking follows the Mississippi as far as Baton Rouge before heading west to Opelousas. It ought to be a pleasant scenic journey, and if I'd taken the minor roads maybe it would have been, but, as it is, it's like pretty much any trunk route to anywhere. It also takes rather longer than I had expected. I thought driving in America would be done with enormous speed and recklessness. Instead, everyone drives eminently sensibly and keeps religiously to the speed limit – fifty-five m.p.h., except on some of the interstates when it is raised to a whopping sixty-five. So there's plenty of time for idle contemplation of the 'Honk If You Love Jesus' stickers on the backs of the cars and pick-ups in front, and trying to find some cajun music on the radio. The radio, however, seems designed to pick up nothing beamed from more than fifty yards away and it's a blessing when at last a country-music station cuts through the static.

So, listening to Baillie and the Boys singing the marvellously guilt-tripping 'She Deserves You' ('If she wants a man/ who'll take a gold ring off his hand/ and turn around and tell you he'll be true/ then she deserves you'), I leave Baton Rouge and cross a rust-red bridge over the Mississippi. Another hour or so and I'm in Opelousas.

There is not a lot shaking in Opelousas. There's a motel on the main street that looks OK, so I pull in and almost collide with a black wedding party who are gathered taking photos in the car park. Otherwise the place is deserted and it takes considerable sleuthing skills to find someone prepared to check me in. Once that has been achieved and I've watched a piece of a bass-fishing show on the TV, thus confirming that Carl Hiaasen has only to use documentary realism to achieve most of his comic effects, I decide to take a quick stroll down main street Opelousas. After taking in the local black barbers-cum-insurance sales office and the bookstore which maintains a ratio of approximately forty per cent bibles and religious material to thirty per cent cookbooks to thirty per cent Dick Francis/Clive Cussler etc, and attracting a fair degree of curiosity from the local teens, I head back to the motel to pick up the car and make for Mamou.

Forty minutes later I've wound down a lot of country roads and still haven't reached Mamou. My petrol gauge is reading empty and the afternoon is definitely drawing in. And I'm just waiting for the car to stop moving and the funny guy with the chainsaw and the face that looks as if it's made of leather to come by and take me to meet his family. Or, to put it another way, it's getting mighty backwoodsy round here. However, this not being a movie and the car not being packed with wholesome teenagers, instead a sign saying Mamou appears and after that a gas station. So I pull in, fill up and ask the attendant if he knows where Fred's Lounge is. He nods and looks me up and down and says, 'You just turn left.' So I just turn left and soon enough what must qualify as downtown Mamou comes into view. Far from being a hotspot of cajun revelry though, it seems to consist of a closed-down hotel and a closed-down beauty parlour plus, on further scrutiny, across the road a building with 'Fred's Lounge – The Home of Cajun Music' written in faded paint on the side. On closer inspection Fred's Lounge turns out to be at least shut, if not closed down too. So I pick the least intimidating of the two bars that do seem to be more or less open and go in to find out what's happened. Ask a few questions: 'Cajun music gone out of fashion round here or what?' That kind of thing. The bar is dark and cavernous with a huge dancefloor. Nobody's on the dancefloor. Nobody's anywhere much, except for three old guys sat at the bar and a barmaid who is currently about ten yards away across the dancefloor, feeding the jukebox.

A country-and-western version of 'Tell It Like It is' starts playing and the barmaid walks back to the bar. I'm offered a choice between Bud or Bud Light so I take a Bud, and ponder on the question of why, almost uniquely, in America beer brewed for domestic consumption is infinitely less pleasant than licensed versions brewed abroad. Then I ask what's happened to Fred's Lounge. After the old guys have indulged in a little staring at me as if I had just dropped in from Mars, the barmaid gently explains that, as all right-thinking people should already know, the session at Fred's Lounge runs only on Saturday mornings from 7 till 12, and I certainly should have been there because it was quite a time. Quite a time. However, she says, there's a church fete going on just up the road and there's meant to be some zydeco music on, why don't I try that? Which seems like a good idea, so I choke down the Bud and head on up to the fete.

The fete's in full swing and at first sight it's a cute-as-can-be piece of traditional Americana: there are rides and swings and candy floss and hamburgers cooking on the open griddle, laughing children and teenagers holding hands, oh and all sorts. Closer inspection reveals that tradition certainly does run deep at this event. Mamou's population seems to include quite a number of black folks, but integrated it is clearly not. All the black people keep together and so do all the whites; none of them seem to be talking to each other and, when you look at the queues for the rides, well maybe it's just coincidence that all the white kids get on first and then the black kids. Mamou seems to be a place where folks know their place.

What my place might be seems to be a question attracting a little attention. No sooner have I orientated myself, found out where the band are setting up and found out where they sell the beer – Bud or, Jeez am I spoilt for choice, Bud Light – than a guy who looks as if he's been sent from central casting walks over to me and introduces himself as the sheriff. I could have guessed; what else would a white guy in his fifties with a beer gut, red face, cigar in his mouth and a can of Bud in his hand be but the goshdarned sheriff? 'So,' he says in the distinctly Southern tone of voice that could be defined as menacing friendly, 'where y'all from?' I tell him I'm from London, England, giving my accent as much plumminess as it can stand and this seems to placate him a little. 'Well, what brings y'all to Mamou?' I tell him I've come to hear the music. 'Ole Boissec, huh,' he says, waving at the stage where several elderly black men in frighteningly authentic sharecropper gear are tuning up. 'Yep, those nigras like to play for the church, sure are Godfearing folks, play real good once they've had a few drinks, you know,' he finishes, inviting me to chuckle with him at the childlike ways of good nigras. Instead I shuffle about a bit and he walks away in moderate disgust and a cloud of cigar smoke. The band, led by one of zydeco's seminal figures, Boissec Andoine, start playing. The noise they make is so spectacularly unpleasant and hard to listen to that it's hard to believe that they're not doing it deliberately.

Whatever, within a minute or so, another gent with red face, beer gut, cigar and Bud looms up, tells me he's the parish assessor, presumably a local euphemism meaning 'hombre with big nose'. And it is as he too launches into the friendly-as-a-rattlesnake spiel about where I'm from and what I'm doing that the penny starts to drop. Nightfall is coming on apace and funny-looking strangers with an interest in nigra music are superfluous to local requirements. Welcome outstayed, I leave.

Back in Opelousas it's around seven o'clock and I decide to call in at Slim's Y-Ki-Ki. This proves to be on the edge of the town, a big barnlike building with a low ceiling. Inside it's empty this early in the evening, apart from the guy behind the bar, a big, muscular, light-skinned guy who looks a little like Aaron Neville. Turns out he's Slim. He too wonders where I'm from and on hearing the answer nods and says yeah he had some folks from round there before, California he thought. I suspect something of a country put-on and move over to play the jukebox while trying to drink my beer – selected from another choice-that-is-no-choice, this time between Miller and Miller Lite. Slim advises me to come back around ten for the music; Boozoo Chavis is going to be on tonight.

Back at the hotel I collapse on the bed for a while before waking up around ten-thirty feeling terrible. I try to revive myself with a shot of Early Times bourbon, but that doesn't work so I head out in search of food. Food in Opelousas seems to consist of fast-food fried chicken or fried chicken fast-food style or, indeed, fast-fried chicken food. I end up sitting in the car attempting to force down a box of Kentucky Fried quite as unpleasant as that available on Shepherds Bush Green at 4 A.M., which I had previously and naïvely assumed to represent some kind of nadir in the art of the fried chicken.

On reaching Slim's Y-Ki-Ki, though, such complaints are forgotten. Outside the neighbourhood is jammed with pick-ups and a selection of ageing American motors, it being axiomatic that American blacks have greater faith in the American auto industry than anyone else. Maybe because they are the ones whose jobs on the line are on the line. Inside the place is jammed with maybe 600 or so adults of all ages, almost exclusively black and one and all having a Saturday-night country good time. The blondes all look like Etta James and the men range from big guys in Stetsons with the forearms that come only with thirty years or more of manual labour, to young guys in baseball caps, who look a touch more citified. The whole place is moving as one to the music: timeless zydeco – Boozoo pumping out the melodies on accordion and singing in French patois, a bass player with the biggest hands you ever saw, shaking the floors with riffs he could, and on occasion would, play one-handed. Half the floor-space is taken up by tables strewn with the quarter-bottles of bourbon or rum and bottles of Coke that are the bar's stock in trade. Nobody sits at the tables too much of the time; the rest of the floor is given up to dancing. And dance people do, formally in pairs by invitation like country dances the world over. And while in Mamou I had managed to incur the displeasure of the white folks simply by looking as if I came from out of town, in Slim's Y-Ki-Ki, in a part of the country where the Klan still ride, I received nothing but friendliness.

Later at the motel in a state of considerable elation I turn on the TV. There's nothing much on but MTV. Just as I'm falling asleep on comes Madonna with the video for 'Like a Prayer'. In the course of this, Madonna rescues and, more or less, makes love to a Christ figure. Which Christ figure is a young black man with short dreadlocks in danger of crucifixion by a bunch of fat white-racist types. And which apparition here in the heart of God-fearing country seems so implausible as to be a dream (that it is not a dream is soon enough confirmed by the decision of Pepsi-Cola to cancel their advertising contract with Madonna following the outrage the video inspired in the Bible Belt).

Further levels of coincidence are soon added when I call up the Louisiana writer I'm due to be interviewing, James Lee Burke, and he suggests that I visit him on Sunday morning after Mass.

James Lee Burke lives out in the suburbs in a nice house in a nice tree-lined street. His late-teenage-ish daughter Pamela opens the door and then James Lee Burke himself appears. He's a medium-built fiftyish guy with sandy hair, welcomes me with country courtliness and ushers me into the kitchen. He asks me if I'd like a cold drink: juice, soda, Coke, maybe a beer. I say maybe a beer sounds fine so he roots around in the fridge and produces a beer for me and a Diet Coke for himself.

At this point it might be worth mentioning that James Lee Burke has lately, nearly thirty years after he wrote his first novel, come to prominence with a series of books featuring a cajun cop from New Iberia, Louisiana, called Dave Robicheaux, who is among other things crowding fifty, a practising Catholic and an alcoholic, albeit one who has mostly succeeded in giving up drinking. Already some intriguing parallels between writer and hero seem to be appearing. Still and all just because a man drinks a Diet Coke in preference to a beer doesn't mean he's a reformed alcoholic.

Before I can find myself asking intrusive questions about his drinking habits, however, Burke's wife Pearl comes down to meet me. She's originally from China, has been married to Burke for close on thirty years and, like her husband, she seems quietly happy in a way that comes only, I suspect, from having been through a fair share of hard times. As James Lee Burke tells me: 'We had some real hard times but my wife Pearl and my children Jimmy, Andre, Pamela and Alafair have been the greatest; really hung in there. We lived in a garage once, Okie motels, spent a year in a trailer, we bounced all over the country. It's worked out OK but it's a long haul. What a guy has to remember, it's like Kenny Rogers said, it's all peaks and valleys. I've been very successful lately but I could be out of print in five years.'

Through the hard times Burke was always writing, just not making a living from it, and so economic necessity has been the mother of a rich and varied cv: 'I was a social worker on skid row in Los Angeles, I worked on the pipelines, I was a land surveyor for a couple of firms in Colorado, I was a newspaperman, I worked for the State of Louisiana Employment Service, I've been a truck driver, worked for the US Fire Service, taught at five colleges, and I've been unemployed a lot too.'

We chat for a while about the new house that Burke's recent success has bought them. In a few months they'll be moving to a farm at the head of a canyon above Missoula, Montana. A dream home: 'When good people die they go to western Montana,' says James Lee Burke. Then he says he likes to take a walk around this time of day and why don't we talk as we walk. So we set off to stroll for a few miles through pure American dreamland. It is all so pleasant as to be surreal. Burke, a man who seems as genuinely sweet-natured as any I've met, simply enjoys it. As he talks he keeps breaking off to say, 'How ya doing podna?' to passers-by or to comment on cute dogs and beautiful cats. One family's dog is so taken with Burke's charm as to keep us company for a while and all is so serene that it's difficult to believe that there's a world out there where people kill each other for the most sordid and arbitrary of motives.

So we start talking about Burke's early life. It turns out that he does indeed share the same Louisiana roots as Dave Robicheaux: 'I grew up down South in Texas and Louisiana. My family is from New Iberia in Louisiana. I went to school at the University of South-west Louisiana in Lafayette, and later at the University of Missouri. I go back to Louisiana quite a bit. I grew up for a while down on the Gulf Coast. Though I consider Louisiana my home, I was actually born in Texas. My father worked for a Houston pipeline company, he was a natural-gas engineer; my mother comes from a little town called Yoakum, Texas. She still lives in Houston today though we're fixing to move her up to Montana. The Burke family were always either attorneys, school teachers or writers. And guess who's got all the money! My first cousin is Andre Dubus, who I think is maybe the best short-story writer in America, certainly in the top three or four. He's a great writer and his sister is Elizabeth Dubus, or Beth Dubus; she lives in Baton Rouge and she's had quite a success with her novels set in historical Louisiana. Andre Dubus's son, Andre Dubus Jr, has just published his first collection of stories. My father was something of a historian. Writing kind of runs in the family; I think it's Irish loquaciousness.'

Writing may always have been in the Burke family but James Lee scarcely looked as if he was going to follow in the family tradition: 'I was a very poor student in high school, I think I graduated in the bottom quarter of my class, I didn't study and I cut classes, that sort of thing. I graduated so dumb I could hardly write my name. In college I had an elderly teacher by the name of Mrs Lyle Williams, boy she was tough, made me rewrite all my papers. I owe her an enormous debt. At the same time my cousin Andre, who is four months older than I, was writing some very fine stories. He entered the Louisiana College writing contest, it was 1954, and he won first place. Andre and I were always a bit competitive, so I thought I'm going to try that, so I wrote some stories during my freshman year. I entered one in the contest, a western set in the nineteenth century in Texas, and I got an honourable mention. That was really something for me, I was this guy who was so dumb in high school that I could probably identify the men's room, you know, by the sign, that was about it. I published that story in the college writing magazine, I was nineteen years old. And that's all I've ever wanted to do since, and that's been thirty-five years.'

Burke's career started out like a rocket: 'I finished my first novel, *Half of Paradise*, two weeks after my twenty-fourth birthday and I published it with Houghton Mifflin. It took me two or three years to find a publisher, but I felt very proud. I got a six-column review in the *New York Times*, best review I ever had, and I thought that was normal. Of course I thought I was in the door then, but I had a lot to learn. I wrote two more books after that which are still unpublished. My fourth novel, *To the Bright and Shining Sun*, was accepted by Scribners and again I thought big success was imminent and again discovered I had a way to go. Then I published another novel, *Lay Down My Sword And Shield*, with Thomas Y. Crowell. I was thirty-four, I had three novels published, I thought I was cooking with Butane, throwing 11s and 7s every time.'

At this point, in the early-to-mid-1970s, he started work on a book called *The Lost Get-back Boogie*. This prefigured the Robicheaux books, dealt with his favourite territories of southern Louisiana and Montana, and once more focused critical attention upon him. Only trouble was it took about thirteen years to do it: 'It was really a struggle. *The Lost Get-back Boogie* had been under submission in New York for nine years, it had been rejected by fifty-two New York publishers. I finished it about 1973, I spent twenty-five months writing it and I revised it four times. Then, in 1985 LSU press published a collection of short stories called *The Convict* and man, that put me back in business. After that, in 1986, they published *The Lost Get-back Boogie* and, boy, in terms of critical reception I'd never published anything as successful, it just kicked open all kinds of doors. I have a movie contract on it now. It was purchased then by Henry Holt in New York, now

Little Brown want to give it another lease of life. And before, in
the 1970s, people didn't just reject it, they flung it at me with a
catapult. I think that says something about the times: it's a male
novel that deals with the environment. Now we're in the 1990s
and that's what it's going to be about: the environment.'

The *Lost Get-back Boogie*, set in the early 1960s, starts with a
country musician called Iry Paret getting out of gaol in Angola
Louisiana where he's been serving time for killing a man in a
bar-room brawl. Back home in New Iberia his father's dying and
his siblings sicken him, so Iry ends up taking his dobro up to
Montana, to get away from it all. Instead he runs into a whole
mess of trouble. The old prison buddy he's staying with likes to
mix booze and acid, and his buddy's farmer dad is engaged in a
small war with a lumber mill that's polluting the valley. It's a
tough novel, more in the Thomas McGuane western idiom than
a crime novel, but it is also desperately bleak. Its theme is
essentially that a man's gotta do what a man's gotta do, but it'll
like as not not do him any good.

James Lee Burke puts the publishers' lack of interest down to
the fact that it is very much a male novel, set in a distinctly male
world, which chimed badly with the political fashions in publishing at the time: 'During the 1970s it was real tough for male
writers. The country was involved in national self-recrimination.
It was a time when, I don't know, minority literature came into
its own. Which was great because black writers had long been
denied their place, but after the fascination with black writing
had passed in the late 1960s, then Indian writing came into
fashion, then feminist writing and that's all fine, but you have to
wait, to hang in there till the wheel comes around. And I think
that ironically the same social forces that elected Ronald Reagan
are responsible for the return of interest in male fiction. Because
Reagan represents, in a cosmetic way, a superficial set of male
values – jackboots, riding pants, red hunting vest – all that stuff
that makes everybody's genitalia begin to hum! The country
wanted to feel good and they had this fella willing to stand up
there and tell them everything was all right, a kind of innocuous
man in jackboots, a John Wayne without the tattoos. What's
dangerous about these kinds of people is that they vicariously
revise their lives through the suffering of others. And when

countries follow them down the road in some sort of national misadventure it's usually a calamity.'

Burke's love for Louisiana music permeates much of his writing. Country picking Iry Paret, for instance, shares a name with the early cajun star Iry Lajeune whose version of 'Jole Blon' (or 'Jolie Blonde') is repeatedly listened to by Dave Robicheaux. I asked him how far back his interest went: 'I play guitar a little bit. I grew up listening to country music, rhythm and blues. I've known some real good players – Hogman Matthew Maxie, you ever hear him? He was a twelve-string guitarist, he was kind of legendary where I come from. I knew a lot of country musicians. I went to high school with a couple of guys who became big stuff: Tommy Sands, big rock and roller back in the 1950s; Tommy Overstreet, who still is a big star in Nashville. Down South, music is a kind of way of life. I remember in 1954 I went to see Big Mama Thornton. When I was growing up the big R&B singers were people like Jimmy Reed – they used to say "Bring him on out here, yes indeed, Mr Jimmy Reed, the hippy-dippy from Mississippi." He was great. Fats Domino, of course, Big Joe Turner, Ruth Brown, Gatemouth Brown . . . I used to go to the Dance Palladium where Smiley Lewis played; Lloyd Price was real good, great R&B. Sometimes it was called race music, then rock'n'roll came along – Bill Haley and the white guys who were good guys but sanitized. Much of the objection to early rock'n'roll was racial. I remember in 1956 the state of Alabama banned rock'n'roll from the airwaves; fear was so pervasive down South then.

'When I was a kid and you went to a rhythm-and-blues concert, white people had to sit up on the balcony. Everything was segregated and in those kind of instances it was to the detriment of the white people; that's the great irony of it, ultimately its victimization included whites as well as people of colour. I remember one time in New Orleans, about 1960, another guy and I were looking for this great jazz joint, called the Jazz Room. It was a great place to hear progressive bands, black progressive bands. We'd been in there before but when we got in there was plywood nailed all across half the bar, this plywood wall. I said, "What's going on here, where's the band?" The guy said, "It's on the other side of the wall, man." The white people had segregated themselves away from the music; the other side was all black and the blacks had the band. The whites are sitting there listening to Conway Twitty on the jukebox. Which indicates how intelligent an attitude segregation was! That's the advantage a Southern writer has: you grow up in a mixed culture that is deeply neurotic and you never run out of story material, brother,' finishes Burke, spluttering with laughter.

Just around the time he finally made it back into print in the mid-1980s Burke had started work on his first out and out crime novel, *The Neon Rain*. 'I wrote it because I couldn't get back into print. I thought maybe if I wrote within a genre and tried to write a literary novel within a genre I'd really accomplish something. It was the first time I had written a crime novel. Some of my other books had elements of it, but I had never read mystery novels, I didn't know much about them apart from the work of Charles Willeford, my old compadre from Miami. Charles and I worked together for nine years and were friends for twenty. Charles gave me a lot of encouragement with *The Neon Rain*; he was a real good critic. Then bingo, I couldn't believe it, my agent sent it off and I had three companies bid on it. And since then the success of that book and the two that followed has been enormous. I was just dumbfounded.'

The Neon Rain, set mostly in New Orleans with a complex plot linking up the CIA with Latin American drug dealers and the Contras (all this written well before the Irangate revelations), introduced the concerns that continue throughout the series, concerns that immediately separated Burke from the pack: concerns of personal and national redemption. The personal side is centred on Robicheaux's struggle with his bad self, his fight to stay sober; the national side is centred on the corruption of American foreign policy with regard to Central America. And for Burke the character of the one is inextricable from the moral issues provoked by the other.

'He's my favourite character; I think he represents everything I admire in people. He's kind, he has courage, he's intelligent, in many ways he's a moral man living in an amoral world. We must remember that in recent times the United States has been involved in some very nasty things and that fact will not go away. There are too many good people who are unconcerned about the slaughter of peasants in Central America; there's a lot of blood on people's heads in this country – the murder of people in Guatemala or El Salvador with US weapons is not an abstraction, not a matter of interpretation. These atrocities have gone on for a long time and I think they are a direct consequence of the policies of Ronald Reagan. I've said this in interviews several times and those words never show up. There's a lot of factual material in *Neon Rain* that hardly anyone picked up on.

'For example I mention an atrocity that occurred in a small village in Guatemala: the murder of Father Stan Rother, a missionary, and sixteen or so Indians, all killed with US automatic weapons as a warning. That's a true story. I thought there'd be some interest in the book's political content. There's an enormous act of denial with regard to this country's policies. And to my mind this is the greatest country in the world. I believe Americans are people who have enormous social conscience and goodwill, but we've closed our eyes to some very bad things. Dave Robicheaux is a man who has to pay a lot of dues, has to make a lot of hard choices. Also he's a man who has fought the booze for years and these books are meant to be as much about one man's struggle with his demons as they are books about criminals.'

The same unholy conjunction of government and organized crime comes to haunt Robicheaux in the second of the series, Burke's favourite to date, *Heaven's Prisoners*, set this time in the Louisiana bayous, in the course of which Robicheaux rescues a little Nicaraguan girl from the wreckage of a plane that had contained her family and a radical American priest.

In this novel too, Robicheaux is laden with enough bad fortune to destroy several lesser men. Bad luck would appear to be his middle name. In *The Neon Rain* he is pumped up with alcohol and tipped off a three-storey building in a car, when not being almost drowned in a bathtub by ex-Mossad torturers. In *Heaven's Prisoners* a terrible act of violence is visited accidentally on his wife Annie rather than on him, the intended victim. So when in the third book, *Black Cherry Blues*, Dave is fitted up on a murder charge, it seems inevitable that he should draw the meanest judge on the circuit. In *The Neon Rain* someone tells Dave, as he teeters on the brink of being thrown off the New Orleans police force and sinking back into the booze, that this is his dark night of the soul. So far this seems a good enough description of the series as a whole and the religious reference is fully appropriate, because Burke is deeply concerned with upholding Christian morality in a society in which such values are commonly hijacked by criminal charlatans. Robicheaux is perhaps the most explicitly moral agent in contemporary crime fiction.

'I think a lot of crime writing is superficial because it doesn't treat the problem of evil within us. I have a hard time taking it seriously without that. It's the fundamental theological question: how do we reconcile a benevolent God with the presence of evil in the world? I think any novel that treats evil has to address that problem. Every thinking person has to. I believe in God and I believe in a merciful God and I think it's a hard question. When you deal with evil in a book your responsibilities as a writer are not decreased, they are increased. How do you explain pathological behaviour? Do people elect to be evil, are they environmentally shaped? My feeling is probably that people who are genuinely evil elect to be so. I've come to believe that. Most people who do evil things are not intrinsically evil, they're buffoons. As Dave Robicheaux says: take a visit to any county gaol; the guys you meet there have banana peels for fingers and if you turned them all loose it wouldn't make much difference. The guys really doing the damage – the people polluting the environment, the people in the munitions industry, the people who are responsible for the systematic exploitation of the Third World – they're not doing time. But these are the guys I think we ought to be worried about. Forget about the two-bit boosters and the penny-ante crooks.'

Black Cherry Blues has Burke returning to the territory of *The Lost Get-back Boogie*. In *The Lost Get-back Boogie* Iry Paret, on parole in Louisiana, heads for Montana; in *Black Cherry Blues* Dave Robicheaux, on bail in Louisiana, heads for Montana. And while Robicheaux is not a musician like Paret, he is drawn to Montana by the reappearance in his life of a faded rock'n'roll singer called Dixie Lee Pugh; a character who owes something to Jerry Lee Lewis and, for all I know, Tommy Sands. Both books too take their titles from song lyrics Burke has created for his characters. The differences are in tone: *The Lost Get-back Boogie* is packed with calamity and is, in many ways, a bleak and bitter book. *Black Cherry Blues*, despite having a hero who makes Job look like Pee Wee Herman, is a book shot through with a belief that redemption is at hand, that things will get better.

By now our walk has returned us to Burke's house. He and Pearl have decided to take me out for a real heart-of-America lunch. Off we head to a steakhouse, where I eat a pound or so of fine red-blooded American cow meat and we all visit the salad bar which is laden with enough food – most of it related to anything one might reasonably describe as salad in only the most tenuous of ways – to feed most of a small-size country. Burke is sticking to salad; he's on a diet, worried that success might be making him fat.

To combat further this eventuality, when we return to the house, Burke invites me to finish off the interview while he does some weight training. This is somewhat disconcerting, and the questions and answers become a little sporadic until he puts down the weights to tell me about his new book: 'It will be called *A Morning for Flamingoes* and I think it's a smasher of a book. It deals with fear and it deals with black magic in southern Louisiana. It has a number of black characters and also people who would refer to themselves as Creoles, part black, Indian and French, who'd be offended if you called them black – it's an American characteristic that we revise our identities and our point of view linguistically.'

Burke's own memories of the black and Creole people he grew up around are nothing but warm: 'I remember all the people of colour I knew; their kindness and the trust I had in them because you could confide in them in a way you could not to white adults. White adults would drop the dime on you, the people of colour would cover up for you. When we were kids a white person would tell you what you were doing wrong; a black person would say "You boys going to drink that beer, you'd best do it behind my barn where's nobody can see you,"' he says, breaking into nostalgic laughter.

However, he acknowledges that such happy memories of the South are no antidote to the continuing poison of racism, rather just an illustration of the fact that to paint the history of race relations in the South *simply* in terms of the appalling racism is to ignore another part of the story: the real closeness between the races that persisted in the rural South while the notionally liberal North constructed its giant ghettoes. And now Burke feels that it is hard to be optimistic about the racial situation anywhere in America: 'White people of conscience looked the other way and allowed the worst people in our society to have their way, the demagogues and the Klansmen. We kept the black people poor and fearful and oppressed and now we have to face the consequences of that. What's happening with the gangs in south central Los Angeles is just a preview of what's to come.'

James Lee Burke has things to attend to, so I head off to drive around a little and bask in the park for a while. I return *chez* Burke in the evening and we head off to the movies to see the film of Bobbie Ann Mason's *In Country*. Which is a reasonable enough tale of alienated Vietnam vets in a small Southern town twenty years on from what was the forgotten war and has lately become the rewritten war. It's a film marred, though, by a silly, sentimental ending which, as Burke points out, attempts to offer an instant redemption inconceivable in the circumstances.

Later still, back in James Lee Burke's kitchen, Pearl has disappeared upstairs and he finally reveals the reasons for the change of tone between a book like *Lost Get-back Boogie* and his current work: the perhaps unfashionable virtues of faith and sobriety. 'I feel I was given a second chance. I had problems with alcohol for years. I've had twelve years' sobriety now and it's made all the difference. Through my thirties I just became more and more bitter in my view of things, more and more jaundiced, virtually nihilistic. In my prose there was very little in the way of light. I'm not knocking that point of view but I don't feel that way today. I don't keep score any more. But I do like to think that these books might help somebody else.'

As to how Burke does feel today, the last words he had to say on the character of Dave Robicheaux reflect clearly on his creator: 'The amount of compassion and empathy in a person's life is directly in proportion to the amount of suffering he endures. One has everything to do with the other. I've never met anybody who has not suffered who is a compassionate person. Anyone who's ever hitch-hiked down South knows that the people who pick you up are the working-class whites and the Negroes; the middle-class folks don't stop.'

I am fairly confident that James Lee Burke would stop.

3

New Mexico: 'The Uranium Was All We Had'

I drive through the square and park the car in the shade. Isleta Pueblo looks like a ghost town in the noonday sun – the kind of white-painted deserted settlement, built around a church, that Clint Eastwood walks into in every spaghetti western. In which all is silent, too silent, until the church bells toll and the gunfire starts. In Isleta the shops are boarded up and nothing stirs as I walk back across the square towards the church. Suddenly some laughter comes from my left. Down a side alley I can see four Native American guys digging a hole. Now they're taking a little time off to stare at me. Well, while I am hardly the type who becomes a local in every bar he enters, there is at least a basic level of familiarity to be wrenched from most new places. In Isleta Pueblo, high on a hill above the Rio Grande, under the brightest of suns, there is none. No place to hide. No doubt about it, I'm a stranger in town.

It was a map that had brought me to Isleta Pueblo, a map marked Indian Country, that Tony Hillerman had lent me and on which he had marked a route from Pueblo to Pueblo. Tony Hillerman was the reason I'd flown into Albuquerque the night before, frightened to death as the plane bobbed and weaved over the Sandia Mountains. Hillerman has spent the last twenty years engaged on one of the most singular projects in crime fiction: a continuing series of novels that have as their central participants Navajo Tribal Policemen, and as their background, their *mise en scène*, the world of the Native Americans of New Mexico and Arizona: Navajos, Hopis, Pueblos. . .

I'd arrived at Albuquerque Airport the night before, glad to be alive and immediately struck by a relaxation in the atmosphere. Suddenly I was surrounded by laidback cowboy types in faded denims (the one in front of me getting off the plane,

however, was carrying a copy of *Body Art*, a British mag devoted
to tattoos and body fetishism, so maybe cowboys today aren't
the straight-arrow types of yesteryear, but what the hell). The
friendliness here seemed altogether more convincing. I picked up
a map and a rental car – a Chevrolet, my first non-Japanese
motor – drove north and then east on Route 66 towards the
centre.

Route 66 lives up to its billing. All the way through Albuquerque, some twenty miles or so, it is crowded with an assortment
of classic 1950s motels, all with lurid and dilapidated neon signs,
all built around courtyards and, a sop to the 1980s, all offering
cable TV. I chose the Gaslite Motel out of admiration for its
sign. Twelve dollars got me a room with a double bed, a
bathroom and a TV with a picture so dreadful that what I was
watching may or may not have been HBO. The courtyard was
half-full of great American motors in various stages of disrepair
being attended to by Hispanic guys with unruly moustaches.
Mostly the Gaslite seems to house families. Latin and Indian
kids are running around, washing lines are hanging out, and the
room TVs all seemed to be tuned to the cartoon stations with the
volume up to the max.

After a shower, I decided to head on down to Old Town
Albuquerque. This nestles in the shadow of the shiny new
downtown district that has sprung up in recent years. Twenty
years ago Albuquerque was essentially a collection of motels on
the junction of two major roads; now it's a centre of high-tech
industry, particularly military hardware. Hey! This is the one
place on earth with a vested interest in the Star Wars programme. And its average age is twenty-eight. Old Town Albuquerque looks as if it has been remodelled to provide a place for
the nuke employees to buy western stuff for the folks back home.
It's old but it feels fake. It's made up of a collection of adobe
buildings grouped in a square, almost every one selling upmarket
Indian souvenirs: Navajo silverware, rugs, jewellery, dolls and
pottery, mostly generic folk art, designed to appeal only to
tourists, and with an ever weaker connection to anything resem-
bling a tradition.

Most of the shops and restaurants were closing up and a high
wind was blowing dust up in my face as I tried to find somewhere

to eat. Down a side street I caught sight of the High Noon
Saloon, an old white adobe structure. Covering my face with my
jacket to keep the sand off, I made a run for it. Inside, it was a
severe culture shock. I passed through a deserted lobby into a
small and elegant bar, empty apart from two Indian guys sat at
the bar silently drinking bourbon. From the bar I emerged into
a ritzy restaurant. It was surprisingly full, but they found me a
space and I ate a great salad and giant enchilada while being
buffeted by some of the most over-the-top service I've ever
encountered. One waiter took my order, one set the table,
another assisted me in ordering a Mexican beer, a waitress
brought me iced water and two of the waiters combined to bring
each dish to me. Then each of them would come by in rotation
to ask how I was enjoying the food and to refill my glass after
each sip; the iced-water waitress seeming particularly unimpressed by my rate of water consumption. All this parody of
European restauranteering seemed peculiarly surreal in this
eighteenth-century adobe building whose defining architectural
feature is its asceticism.

After this it was time to find a regular bar. I drove back down
Route 66, past the hotel, till I saw a place with neon beer logos
in the window, called the Fat Chance Bar and Grill. Walking
towards it I half-registered the number of bicycles locked up. I
entered and realized that, of course, I've walked into a student
hangout. All around, fresh-faced types were sitting animatedly at
tables around pitchers of beer. There was a small stage where a
girl with long blonde hair tuned her guitar. Presently she would
sing Bad Company songs in a high clear voice. Meanwhile I sat
at the bar drinking Dos Equis and talking briefly to a black guy
who says he was born in London. He wants to go back one day,
look up his relatives. This seemed like reason enough to drink
some more and by the time I left I was glad it was a short
distance and a straight empty road that took me back to the
hotel.

Next morning I took my sore head to the Gaslite's diner and
read the paper while tentatively wading into coffee, eggs, hash
browns and bacon. The paper revealed a level of crime more
appropriate to an English local paper. The nearest thing to
violent crime seemed to be a man trying to rob a bank by holding

his hand in his pocket so as to simulate a gun. This devilish ruse apparently failed to convince the bank staff and the man ran off empty-handed. By this time I was starting to feel up to looking about me at my fellow diners. These were a motley crowd of working stiffs of all races, the kind of guys who would get roped in as extra villains in a western, but here, up close, this seemed like a palpably easy-going society: black, white and red men all with hard work and dodgy pick-up trucks in common.

Wrenching myself from this reverie, from the feeling that maybe here was the American heartland, the place where the American Dream and the Levi's ad campaign came together and found themselves melded into real life, I paid the bill and headed off to see Tony Hillerman. Hillerman lives on the outskirts of town in a family house in a quiet street with the obligatory pick-up parked outside. He's a big man, running to fat in his sixties, but this seeming to be less a symbol of complacency than simply of satisfaction. The tough, sharply defined, reporter's face familiar from his old book jackets has been softened into jolliness by the addition of a double chin. His glasses now look amiably studious rather than interrogative. He'd had to go to the hospital for some tests that morning. He wasn't feeling too good and, besides, he had an article to write for the *New York Times*. So we talked briefly and then he gave me a map and showed me where to head to see something of Indian Country; we'd talk some more on my return that evening. So that's how I came to be in Isleta Pueblo. And why, really, I'm not too worried as I step alone into the noonday sun, and start to cross the square towards the church.

Halfway across the square, I'm not so sure; the silence is broken only by insect noises and the workers have stopped working and started staring at me. Feeling like the guy who's been sent out unawares to test a minefield, I keep on going towards the church, thankfully find it open and enter. Inside it's spartan, white and, inevitably, empty. It's affecting, too, familiar and not, a Catholic church with a simple Christ at the altar and whitewashed walls dressed with rainbows, painted in bold Indian colours; the effect cool and moving, redolent of a transplanted piety.

Somewhat renewed, I head back out into the square and

immediately things are changed. I wander around a little and one of the working guys comes over, turns out to be dead friendly, insists on opening up his sparsely stocked souvenir shop for me, turns the radio on to a pop station. I buy some chillis and some postcards, walk back to the car and head on to Acoma Pueblo: the oldest continually occupied site in the States, settled around 600 A.D. The drive is remarkable, through what Hillerman calls 'empty country'. You can see for miles across scrubland and near-desert; through the middle of it all runs the Santa Fe railroad. A goods train passes through. Suddenly a sign announces the Rancho Mesa Bar. I drive down a track, only to find a trailer and a man digging a hole. I ask him about the bar, of which there is no sign. He says, 'Well . . . it s'pose to open yesterday but . . .' He shrugs and laughs and goes back to digging the hole.

Approaching Acoma, just off the road there's a huge rock escarpment; it's oblong, sheer-sided and flat-topped, rising dramatically out of the desert landscape, what they call a Mesa. At Acoma I learn that this is known as the Enchanted Mesa, 'Katzimo', and legend has it that this was the ancient home of the Acoma people until one day, when all the able-bodied people were down below the Mesa working in the fields, a great storm washed away the rock formation that had allowed access to the top of the Mesa. All those left behind on the Mesa starved to death, and those in the fields moved to the nearby Mesa that they inhabit today.

At the foot of the Mesa is the Acoma tourist centre, where you pay your money and wait for a minibus (the 'Sky City Shuttle') to take you to the top of the Mesa. There's a scale of extra charges for taking pictures. The charges are made in ascending order for camera, camera with tripod, video camera and, top of the range, sketching or painting. The Acomas have clearly woken up to the value of cutesy sketches of 'primitive' places. While I wait for the bus, I have a look round the centre's cultural display. This is solidly informative of Acoma Pueblo's long history. Then, as you come to the end of it, you are suddenly confronted with a display of pictures of the Miss USA pageant, which was partly filmed in Acoma in February 1987. Apart from the usual beauty-contest tackiness, these pictures approach the surreal by attempting to incorporate nods towards Native American culture and thanks to the fact that February in Acoma is clearly bloody freezing. So there is a remarkable photo of several contestants lined up outside the tourist centre, surrounding a specially chosen Miss Acoma. Miss Acoma is a retiring-looking girl in glasses, sensibly clad in several layers of traditional clothing. Misses Delaware, Oregon, Florida etc, however, are all wearing swimming costumes, elegantly topped with fur coats, or, in the case of Miss Florida, a tall black girl, a leather car coat with tiger-stripe lapels. The effect is alarmingly like that of a sudden outbreak of big-city prostitution on the reservation (the Hopi Hookers maybe?). Final icon, also available as a postcard, is a picture of All-American blonde Miss Illinois, sat on top of the Mesa in her swimsuit, her right leg extended in the direction of a piece of pottery, and grinning like all hell beneath a clear blue sky. Only trouble is the ground's covered in snow.

Up on top of the Mesa, at Sky City itself, I trail round after an Acoma guide who has a disconcerting habit of bursting into fits of giggles as she explains the culture and history of the place. There's a church similar to the one at Isleta but larger and additionally decorated with peeling reproductions of Old Master-ish pictures. Later on Hillerman explains to me a little of how the Catholic and the traditional religions have meshed together. 'The Pueblos are pretty much one hundred per cent Christian, mostly Roman Catholic. At Acoma one of the big ceremonies is St Stephen's. That's open to the public; they close the pueblo when they're conducting their Kachina cult dances. Their traditional religion involves the Kachina spirits. I don't know how you'd describe them, there's a million of them.' He points to a couple of figures on his study wall: 'There's a couple of them on the shelf behind you – that's Mudhead there. They represent various kinds of benign friendly spirits who bring rain and so on. It's not so difficult to merge with Christianity. They believe in one God, he's benign, he's interested. They believe in life after death, and something like the community of saints, the Kachinas are like saints in a way. They're matrilineal, matriarchal; the idea of the Blessed Virgin was appealing to the Pueblos. They believe in good rewarded in a future life – all these were the same things the Franciscans were preaching. So they took readily to Christianity. If the Spanish military would have left them alone

there would have been a very peaceful melding. But they didn't
. . . Still they became Christianized. In Santa Domingo, one of
the really big pueblos, when they do the deer dance which
reestablishes their rapport with the animals; straight after this
dance they dance right into the church for midnight Mass.'

Leaving the church, as we pass each building in this remarkably authentic desert medieval village – the houses up to a 1,000
years old and the older ones often three storeys high – a woman
strolls out and half-heartedly markets some pottery to us. Suddenly I'm struck by the notion of this being the oldest place in
America: a cluster of pottery vendors stuck on top of a mountain
that was finally connected to the outside world thirty years ago,
our guide tells us, by Hollywood. Acoma was scouted out as a
location for a 1950s western called *Sundown* and, as part of the
deal, Hollywood money built a road connecting Acoma to Route
66.

Now they're planning to transfer Tony Hillerman's work to
the big screen, and Acoma may find itself back in the movies.
'All of the books have been optioned by Robert Redford's
Wildwood Films. There's a couple of women hired as producers;
they're coming out here next week. A script's been written, based
on *A Dark Wind*. He's planning three movies on the reservation,
using Navajo actors as much as he can. And, who knows, maybe
he actually will. They might use Acoma rather than Hopis. The
Hopis are very difficult to work with. They have a schism within
the pueblo between the traditionalists and the moderns. The
tribal council are modern but the traditionalists are very influential, so they're very suspicious about anything that involves
the outside world, and especially their religion. The Acoma, as
you saw, are perfectly willing to make a buck. And I don't blame
them.'

Heading out of Acoma I pass the inevitable aircraft-hangar-
style bingo hall and stop at the reservation with its enormous
stocks of duty-free cigarettes. And head on to Laguna Pueblo. At
Laguna I park by the trading-post-cum-gas station, eat a Native
American tuna sandwich on wheat, and take a look around the
store. There's a poster on the wall explaining the principles of
community to the customers: 'We cash your cheques. We help
you out in your hard times. So do your shopping with us.'

Weirdest thing is the video section, complete with *Blazing Saddles*, a pile of westerns, a porno movie called *Indian Lady* and a selection of teach-yourself elk-hunting videos. Still, number one in the rental charts is *Die Hard* with Bruce Willis, just like every other video store in America this month.

Standing outside, eating my sandwich, I get to talking a little to the guy who runs the store. He says that times have been hard for his people lately, since the uranium mines closed down: 'Damn well-paid employment that was: seventeen, eighteen bucks an hour.' Of course he understands environmental objections, but the discovery of uranium on the reservation had come as a godsend – reservations having generally been chosen for their lack of resources. So to have their one source of a decent income removed on environmental grounds, by the very people who have destroyed their old, environmentally-conscious way of life, is galling indeed.

Hillerman's name crops up in conversation soon enough, as the one ray of light on the employment front is the possible filming of his books. Already Hollywood types have been nosing about and maybe there'll be work as extras or in servicing the film folk. Who may, ironically enough, be filming Hillerman's *People of Darkness* which has, as a central element of its plot, the long-term dangers of uranium mining.

Hillerman understands the Native American ambivalence to eco-politics. As he observes, talking about the Navajos, 'They're about like the rest of us. On the one hand they hate to see their reservation despoiled; on the other they badly need a job or the revenue from the drilling royalties. So they're sort of torn. You look around; we're exploiting Alaska for oil and now we've got this horrible oil spill. We want to shut the whole thing down in Alaska, but we know it's going to cost us a dollar a gallon if we do. So we let our appetite overpower our conscience; Navajos do the same thing. So there isn't much of an ecological movement as yet. What there is tends to be stimulated from the outside, from white folks, mostly, who believe that the Navajos ought to feel this way and prod them into it. They get some followers and some Navajos, but not too many, and for one reason and that's economics. You have in the general population a substantial number of people who are affluent and, being affluent, can set aside greed – having satisfied it, right – and be pure ecologists. You don't have hardly any Navajos who aren't either needy or just barely across the line. They tend to put eating first. I think that's why. I think if you had an affluent Navajo society, then you'd have a higher percentage of environmentalists than you would among white people. Because I think they are more sensitive to beauty than we are.'

One Native American who has a well-developed concern for the ecology is a guy named Greg, a silversmith whose parents came from Acoma to Laguna and who has a little shop behind the Laguna Store. He has sent off samples of local earth for examination, says he fears for his children's health. His shop has new-age music tinkling in the background and art photos of the desert on the walls.

Back on the interstate I head west to Grants. Grants is Albuquerque in miniature: a long strip of motels, thrift stores, western stores, liquor stores and bars. It's a half-closed town, as ephemeral a place as I've ever been, a place for Indians to come and get drunk. 'It's a terrible problem among Native Americans off the reservation,' says Tony Hillerman when I arrive back at his place in the early evening. 'They have the highest alcohol death rate in the US by far. There are people who are believing more and more, though it used to be anathema to say it, that there might be some racial, genetic connection, in addition to the economics and the problems of being caught between two cultures, because so many Navajos . . . I don't know any Navajos who drink socially. My Navajo friends do not drink at all. You don't find Navajos who'll drink a beer or two beers with you. You find Navajos who'll take their monthly cheque and go to a bar and get absolutely drunk as quick as they possibly can. It's strange. A lot of Navajos hate the stuff. It's prohibited on the reservation, maybe all the reservations, though there's a suggestion now that that may be a bad idea. The reservations are losing the revenue as they'll drink anyway in Gallup or a border town, get terribly drunk, maybe get robbed or die of exposure. So perhaps it'd be better to have it closer to home.'

We talked over German beer in Hillerman's study, a room bedecked with maps of Indian Country, Pueblo Kachinas on the mantelpiece, and a plaque on the wall. The plaque turns out to be Hillerman's proudest possession: 'That plaque . . . the Navajo tribes have a fair each year at Winter Rock, their capital. I got a call asking me to take part. I said OK and I heard they wanted me to ride in their parade. When I got there it turned out they wanted me to ride a horse and lead their parade. I said I'd be willing if they found an old fat horse. They found a young frisky one . . . Then they had me come to their fair in the evening and they called me up to the grandstand and, to my delight, the tribal council chairman read this piece out, declaring me to be a special friend to the Navajo people, and gave me that plaque. A high point.'

Hillerman's involvement with Indian culture goes back to his childhood: 'I grew up in a tiny farm community in Oklahoma where most of our neighbours were Native Americans – Pottawottamee, Seminoles, some Blackfeet – most of the children I played with were Indian kids. It was a segregated state but we were so far in the country that we segregated blacks, but I went to an Indian school for the first eight grades. So I learned, I think, early on that Indians were no different from other people, certainly no different to how I was. We shared a lot. Poverty for instance; it was a very bad time and a very poor part of the country.'

Hillerman's parents, too, were instrumental in developing his loathing for discrimination. 'My father was German, second generation. He was also a pacifist socialist. He hated National Socialism. He took great pains as us kids were growing up to ensure that we were not infected with that sort of thing.'

Living so far out in the country also led to Hillerman having an involuntarily Catholic range of reading: 'You'd order three books at a time from the state library. You'd order *Captain Blood*, *Death on Horseback* and *Tom Brown's Schooldays* or something. Then, about a month later, you'd get a box and there'd be a letter on top saying, "We are sorry the books you ordered are not on our shelves, but we have selected three others we hope will be of interest." And you'd get *Conquest of Granada*, Washington Irving maybe, and Lord North's translation of Plutarch's *Lives*. Or a history of the Masonic Order in Oklahoma; but if you're a reader you read anything.'

Hillerman's route out of the backwoods took him first into the army. He fought in Europe in World War Two. 'I was a PFC. I made that rank twice as I got busted down, then I was wounded.' It was while on a convalescent furlough that Hillerman first ran across Navajos, the Native American tribe with the largest role in his fiction. 'I'd got a job driving a truck with oilfield equipment from Oklahoma City to Crown Point, part of the reservation. It was towards the end of the war and a lot of Navajos had been in the marine corps in the Pacific. They were coming home and their families were having curing ceremonies for them and I blundered into one of those.'

His war wounds were influential in pushing Hillerman towards writing for a living. 'I had come out of the army with a bad limp and a bad eye. I didn't know what I wanted to do, but I was limited. During the war a reporter had written a feature about me and she'd read some letters that I'd written home to my mother. She told my mother she wanted to talk to me when I got home. So I went to see her and she told me I ought to be a writer. So I went to journalism school. From there I became a police reporter, then a political reporter, and eventually an editor. After seventeen years of that I decided I wanted to get serious. So I quit a job as editor of the paper at Santa Fe and came to the University of New Mexico as a graduate student, with a part-time job, and started to try my hand at writing non-fiction and other forms . . . fiction.'

His first novel was called *The Blessing Way* and it introduced the character of Joe Leaphorn, a Navajo Tribal Policeman. Leaphorn is a hard-bitten man, he's approaching middle age and is integrationist in a low-key way. He's sceptical of his people's traditional religion and married to a white woman. In *The Blessing Way*, though, his is a supporting role. 'I'd planned to write a mystery as my first book as it seemed to me it would be short, it would have a form and it would lend itself to narrative which I had experience at, thought I was good at. I decided I'd use the Navajo country as a background because I knew it, I thought it might be an interesting stage setting. I didn't plan to write about the Navajos. When I started to write that book the only central character was going to be the anthropologist, a white man, and I was going to set it on an Apache reservation, as I'd known an Apache Tribal Policeman who was killed, who interested me.

Then I found that the Apaches were not as interesting, certainly not as complicated, as the Navajos, plus I knew more about the Navajos. But in the first draft the policeman was a minor character, then Harper and Row said they were interested. But could I change the final chapter? So I rewrote that and I also beefed up the character of the policeman.'

His next book was intended to be the big book. It's a tough political thriller called *The Fly on the Wall*, which draws on Hillerman's newspaper experience and is his one book not to feature an Indian backdrop. 'I'd wanted to use my experience as a political reporter. The novel takes a reader into a situation where the reporter is investigating corruption. It confronts a question that always occurs in a democratic society: where you draw the line in what you report. In the final analysis publishing the story he worked so hard to get did more harm than good. I wanted to do something with that sort of ambiguous situation.'

Fly on the Wall did well, but his next novel saw Hillerman returning to Navajo country. 'Even while I was writing *Fly on the Wall* I was troubled by the fact that I hadn't done the Navajo book well. I wanted to get back and do it right. So, as soon as I finished it, I started writing a second book using the Navajo Tribal Policeman. Thinking that if I started out knowing I was going to write a book in which the Navajo culture was pre-eminent and a Navajo was the central character, as was not the case in the first book, then I could get the job done. Well, I didn't. It was a pretty good book, it had some good stuff in it, but I thought well, I'd better try it again . . .'

And so a series character was born. Leaphorn appeared in all Hillerman's 1970s novels. Then, for 1980's *The People of Darkness*, Hillerman introduced a second Navajo policeman, Jim Chee. Chee is younger than Leaphorn and far more committed to the traditions of the Navajo community. He's a product of the post-civil-rights resurgence of pride among minority populations. Hillerman's reasons for creating Chee, however, are mixed: 'There were two reasons; one was greed and one was artistic. I wanted to set a story in the so-called checkerboard reservation, where the Navajos are all mixed up with various kinds of white people and white reservations. So I started this book thinking I'd use Leaphorn, who I'd used in three books by then. But I felt like I knew Leaphorn and it was sort of out of character for Leaphorn to be as fascinated by white people as I wanted this fellow to be, when he'd been around them for years. Nor would he have the protective attitude I wanted this fella to have to the Navajo trad religions. So I thought well I'll skip him back and make him a young Leaphorn. But it didn't work – my imagination wouldn't allow it, I couldn't conceive of him as a young man – so I thought I'd better start me a new one. At the same time I'd signed a movie contract, a complicated document with a low price for TV rights and a higher one for film. The option was renewed three times, which was enough to pay for the TV rights, but the deal included continuing rights for the characters. Well Leaphorn was the only continuing character. So I realized I didn't own TV rights to Leaphorn any more, so I had double motivation for starting a new character. Maybe I'd have done it anyway, who knows. I have now bought back Leaphorn from the TV people. It cost me 22,000 dollars to buy back my own character.'

I asked Hillerman how he coped with the difficulties of, in effect, writing as a Navajo. 'First I don't believe racial differences exist; we're all one species. The differences are cultural and, more important, economic. Plus you tend to form in your early years and in my early years I was very much like your average Navajo. I was rural, I was poor. We pulled our water out of a well. We didn't have indoor plumbing, we depended on the weather, being farmers, and we had a feeling of being second-class citizens. We had a feeling that when we went to town we were looked down on. I felt that way; the boys I played with who were Indians felt that way, like we were outsiders. When I go on to a reservation and sit around and talk and watch I see the same things that I saw when I was a child, same attitudes. I would have much more difficulty, for example, writing about the kinds of people John Le Carré writes about; people who went through the English public school, or the Ivy Leaguers, the rich people, the privileged class that most people write about. They're strangers to me, they're very exotic and interesting, but I don't know them and I don't understand how their minds work. But the Navajos, from the beginning I've found a rapport with them and a sympathy for them. It's very difficult for them to get an education, and it was very difficult for me to get one.'

To write the books Hillerman uses a mixture of academic research and more informal research built up over his years of living adjacent to Indian Country. 'When I started writing *The Blessing Way* I found I didn't know nearly as much as I thought I did, and there were things I knew but didn't understand. We have at the University of New Mexico a remarkably good library collection of Western Americana or Native American stuff. There are a lot of oral-history tapes; a senator who spent his life collecting this stuff gave it to the university. So I have easy access to the finest collection of research about the Navajo culture, and I live close enough to Navajo country. I have a lot of friends there, and so forth. I combine what I know about modern Navajos with what the anthropologists tell me about the metaphysics and so forth. I don't know the big shots in the Navajo tribe. The Navajos I know are the plain old people: the guy who has a hogan over at Caroline, Arizona; a kid over near White Horse Lake who's trying to get through school; a sheep herder – just average people.'

And it's these casual, friendly relationships that give Hillerman his easy personal perspective on Navajo culture. 'Say I've got a scene in a book that takes place at a trading post and I want to hang out at a trading post for a while just to see if there's anything about it that I'm overlooking. So I go to Two Grey Hills, which is a fairly isolated trading post, and I go in and buy a cold drink and start talking to the guy behind the cash register and someone comes in and we include him in the conversation and before long you find out that he knows someone you know in Utah; it's a small world out here and 'fore long you're friendly, he looks you over, you're a white man but you're . . . nothing much particularly. And before long you kind of know him. And you see him again some time, see I'm sixty-three years old. I've been out here a long time. You see him and you remember him and you're talking about a ceremonial and you say I'd sure like to get invited to one of those and he says, "Well, I've got an aunt who's got a sick kid and she's going to have a 'Wind Way' or something, I'll see if it'll be OK I bring you."'

I wondered what the reaction of Native American readers to

Hillerman's fiction has been. 'First of all I got that plaque. I also get letters from high-school kids asking me to be their commencement speaker. I get letters from Navajo kids; they use me in the schools a lot, so they have to read me. They are very polite people so they may hate my stuff but they never tell me that. Generally speaking I get a lot of good feedback. I've had people tell me that they couldn't get their kids interested in the Navajo way. They thought, "That's old stuff, I want to get off the reservation and get me a hot car," then they started reading me at school, and here they're seeing their culture dealt with in a real book, not as characters in a text-book, but with Navajos as central characters and their religion treated with respect. So they go back to their parents and ask questions. I've had dozens of parents tell me that. There's a Navajo woman who is a librarian on the Pima reservation in Arizona; we were talking about native American writers, about James Welch, Scott Momaday, Leslie Silko and others. I was asking how Indians react to them; she says, "We read Welch and Silko and we say, 'That's us, they really understand us, that's us and it's beautiful, but it's so terribly sad.' Then we read you and we say, 'Yeah that's us too, and we win.' And of course kids like to win."'

By now it's getting late; one of Tony's kids has dropped round with his wife. We chat a little about Albuquerque and where to get a good steak. Then it's time to go. As I leave I ask Hillerman whether he thinks his books have succeeded in changing the way the majority community regards Native American culture. 'That's one of the disappointments. Each time I have the ambitious notion that I'm going to teach quite a bit in this book. But then you have to consider the fact that the reader – if he really wanted to know about Navajos he'd go to the library and get a book – you can't really force the guy to learn about Navajos. He bought the book to be told a story. So you restrain yourself, and after you've written it you cut out a lot of stuff. So you don't do much, but at least each time it gives people, white people, the idea that Indians are human beings, you know.'

Next morning there's a couple of hours to kill before catching my plane. I head back to Old Town looking for some souvenirs. In the tourist shop the guy behind the counter is bemoaning his lack of stock. 'It's the Japanese,' he says, 'they're crazy for western gear, they come over and buy everything.' In next door's shop it's the same story, apocryphal stories of Japanese extravagance are being cobbled together – 'Why of course it's a reasonable price, ma'am, do you know what the Japanese pay for this kind of quality' – that kind of stuff. Depressed by the over-manicured merchandise on offer, I head back into downtown Albuquerque, thinking about Hillerman's dismissive thoughts on the contemporary vogue among new-age types for 'Navajo culture' – a selective pot pourri of half-grasped mysticism and pretty artefacts. 'There's been a lot of romanticism about Native American culture,' says Hillerman. 'You can go right back to Tennyson. Then it came up again in the 1960s with that awful German writer, Herman Hesse. Now nobody in his right mind would read Herman Hesse, but the interest has revived again. These things are cyclical. The interest in esoteric religions, magic, mysticism, shamanism, rises and falls. But there's a lot more to Navajo culture than shamanism and mysticism; there's some deep-rooted philosophies that the culture's built on.'

I turn into a parking lot along from the seediest parade of shops this somewhat shining new city has to offer. There's a snooker hall and a sex shop, the kind of amenities which normally accompany a Greyhound station. Also a second-hand bookshop and a row of three excellent establishments. First an old-style hat shop – the kind of place Doc Holliday would have been proud to patronize, filled with voluminous Stetsons and rakish straw hats. Making a mental note to return here if I ever decide to embark on a career as an itinerant poker player, I gravitate next door. This advertises western utility wear and sells clothes for real cowboys: unshrunk Levi's in giant sizes, khaki shirts and tasteless T-shirts. Also on offer, Albuquerque Police Department uniforms. Useful for under-cover work no doubt but aesthetically less than tempting. A couple of doors further down is the Sandia Pawn and Gun Shop. Entering ahead of me is an Indian guy; he's got some jewellery to pawn. The charming old gent behind the counter appraises it, quotes him a figure, and the guy wanders towards the glass case of guns, starts debating their merits with another assistant.

The jewellery here is altogether more authentic. Old Navajo silver and turquoise, bracelets, bolos, brooches. The bolos are particularly striking: men's jewellery, stark ornamentation mounted on a leather bootlace, a tough guy's affectation. And here in the Sandia Pawn and Gun Shop is something of the old west – a man invests his savings in gold and silver, wears his money and, when it comes to the bad times when he's gotta do what he's gotta do, then he can sell the gold and silver, buy a gun and make some more money. A simple life. The Indian guy is picking up a serviceable-looking pistol for 200 dollars, he asks the guy if they sell ammo. 'No, K Mart just down the block.' I take a look at the gun case. Cheapest item is a lady's gun, a handbag-sized Derringer, just seventy-two bucks plus tax. A Smith & Wesson, an ugly snub-nosed thing, nothing like the toy models I played with as a kid, just a tool for killing with, pure and simple, is $300. A pretty Smith & Wesson, like they use in the movies, is $495. For a hundred bucks less you could buy something a little more modern, a semi-automatic machine pistol, a weapon whose only apparent domestic use is for going berserk and killing indiscriminately at your local McDonalds or primary school.

I end up just buying a bolo and leave wondering about the guy who bought the gun, pushing middle age, and his luck not looking to be of the best, a prototype Hillerman villain. Or victim; Hillerman is reluctant to see even his most vicious characters as evil; 'I have never known any really bad people. As a police reporter . . . for example, the murderer in *People of Darkness* was modelled after the last man executed in New Mexico – we've repealed the death penalty – I was a reporter and I spent a lot of time talking to him. He was being executed for killing about five people. One time he was hitch-hiking and some newly-weds picked him up. He decided he wanted their car so he killed them both and stuffed them in a culvert with not a bit, as far as I could find out, of repentance. Nobody knows how many people he killed. Anyway, when you got acquainted with him you could understand why, and you understand why when you read *People of Darkness*. A perpetual search for his mother – that was this guy's problem. He'd come home from school when he was eleven, and the trailer was gone, there was just the blocks left – his mother and the guy she was living with had upped and gone without so much as a note. And that started him on this lifelong quest for his mother, killing people along the way. No matter how villainous what people do might appear, they tend to have rationalized it, they can justify it some way or another.'

Which outlook clearly suggests that Hillerman has considerably more in common with the Native American worldview than that of the born-again death-penalty groupies currently proliferating across the States. And sucking on that I head back to the car and on out to the airport.

4

Los Angeles: Looking for the Big Nowhere

Los Angeles is a place it's almost compulsory to dislike. Expressing a fondness for it is tantamount to saying 'I'm going to make it in the movies,' 'I'm addicted to cocaine,' or 'I like to watch drive-by killings.' The twin images are Beverly Hills boredom or ghetto gunfire. The other thing you hear, and which is more like it, is that there's nothing there: a bunch of suburbs in search of a city, a gigantic freeway interchange, etc.

Certainly it's a hard place to grasp. Lee, a friend of a friend, met me at the airport and drove me across most of LA to her flat in east Hollywood where I'd be staying while I was in LA. The strangest sight along the way was the oilrigs next to the freeway – oilrigs, cars and smog, the one feeding the other – that's LA. And a little unfair; the smog is not what it was, everyone drives unleaded now. Then we cut through crowded Koreatown, which looks like any busy twentieth-century cityscape, and arrive at a quiet street just a block off Sunset Boulevard on the borders of Hollywood and Silverlake.

Sunset Boulevard is inevitably anti-climactic, neither glamorous nor even spectacularly seedy. Instead, it's seedy in a drab and dusty kind of way. All that's on it around here are a couple of supermarkets; LA, I quickly discover, is a city in which giant supermarkets are the familiar reference points. Ask where some place is and you'll be told, 'on Sunset, next to Von's', or 'on Hollywood, near Ron's.' Best time to visit them is around 4 A.M. when the weird go shopping. Otherwise all this end of Sunset has to recommend it is a hot-shoe motel offering waterbeds and adult movies in every room, a couple of twenty-four hour porno stores and a diner or two, plus the usual complement of gas stations, drive-thru McDonalds and Korean fruit stalls that every American thoroughfare possesses these days.

After sitting and drinking herb tea with my hosts – hey, this is California – I try to explain what I'm doing in LA. I've come to talk to a guy called Gar Haywood who writes PI novels set in south central LA, the ghetto home of gang warfare, and to look for James Ellroy's LA – this is a guy who writes books set in LA over the past forty years which are filled with homicidal madness. Oh, right, how interesting they say, and I have a sense of the perversity of what I'm doing, here in the quiet flat of nice leftish, post-hippie types, a smoke-free zone. In a place of intended harmony I've come looking for sickness and violence, and I will be disappointed if that's not what I find.

That's James Ellroy's mission. After a series of thrillers set in contemporary LA, he's now embarked on an epic series of LA life in the 1940s and '50s, novels designed to rip apart the cosy nostalgia that surrounds 1950s America. 'The 1950s to me is darkness, hidden history, perversion behind most doors waiting to creep out,' says Ellroy. 'The 1950s to most people is kitsch and Mickey Mouse watches and all this intolerable stuff . . .'

My first couple of days in LA give no handle on the place, though I do nothing but travel around it. Anyway it's a fool's errand looking for James Ellroy's LA, it's like trying to find his childhood, it simply isn't there any more. Ellroy, perhaps more than any of America's crime writers, is fascinated by the extremes of crime, the grotesque, the savage and the mad. And more than any other writer he is identified with his work. Ellroy has acquired a reputation for strangeness; American crime writers are generally a fairly clubbable bunch, eager to say nice things about their fellow writers. Someone like Tony Hillerman is known and loved by all; when Sara Peretsky in Chicago says she's heard Tony's a lovely man I laugh, having heard the same thing from so many mouths. Mention James Ellroy, anywhere except New York, though, and there is a general coolness; barbed compliments suggest that this is a man a little too big for his boots, a man who has long proclaimed his desire to be 'the best writer of crime fiction, ever' and is generally dismissive of other writers. He is also reputed to be a little too close to the madness of his books.

This first time I met James Ellroy he was playing the angles. An inordinately tall man with glasses, a receding hairline and an

Ivy League outfit, with gold buttons still cased in dry cleaner's tinfoil, he delivered what is clearly and unashamedly the James Ellroy rap, a journalist-friendly life story taking in events like his mother's murder and his own life of petty crime, culminating in salvation through brutal fiction writing. If the professionalism with which this was delivered undercut the message to some degree, at the same time its very offhandedness combined with the fact that he delivered it while staring relentlessly at the breasts of a woman sat at the next table, had a certain chill of its own.

I was born in Los Angeles in 1948. My father was a womanizer, a minor hero in the First World War. He was briefly Rita Hayworth's business manager in the late 1940s. He would jump on any woman that moved, he was a raconteur, a bon vivant. My mother was a registered nurse; they were divorced when I was six. I was an only child.

I grew up very tall and I was a very early reader. My father taught me to read when I was three and a half. It was the only evidence of precocity that I ever evinced. I couldn't tie my shoes too well. I couldn't tell the time till I was eight or nine, but, boy, could I read. Hence I escaped into books at an early age. My parents were divorced when I was six and I went to live with my mother, saw my father on weekends. June of 1958 my mother was murdered; a man picked her up in a bar, strangled her, did not rape her, dumped her body in the bushes outside Arroyo High School in El Monte, a sleazy, very lower-middle-class, white-trash and Mexican neighbourhood in East Los Angeles.

I went to live with my father. My reading then took on a distinct focus – crime books – anything to do with crime. I was much closer to my father than my mother, hence it wasn't quite the bereavement one would normally think. My father was much better to me. My mother wasn't an abusive woman; I simply loved my father more. I was very curious. I wanted to know why. Sex fascinated me at an early age. At forty it continues to: aberrant sexual behaviour is a real fascination even though I was, at that time, pre-pubescent. During that summer I lived with my father in a dingy small apartment at the edge of a rich neighbourhood in Los Angeles, and I took to breaking into places – this was the 1950s and people didn't lock their doors – I would go in, prowl around and steal some trinkets, make myself a sandwich out of the refrigerator. I enjoyed being in other people's houses. So . . .

. . . So I grew up bookish and strange and tall and frightened and volatile and . . . And for my eleventh birthday, 1959, my father bought me a book called The Badge *by Jack Webb, which was a stupefyingly right-wing paean to the Los Angeles Police Department and it contained, among other things, a haunting ten-page summary of the Black Dahlia murder case and I became obsessed, because it was all the horror of my mother's death plus a lot more. It was a much more explicit crime, a brutal, awful sex crime and it, like my mother's killing, was unsolved. I became sexually obsessed with the Black Dahlia victim Elizabeth Short. I had fantasies of going back to 1947 and saving her and, uh, enjoying sexual adventures with her. I speculated in my mind and with a friend I made at that time, Randy Rice, endlessly. Who killed the Dahlia? How did she come to die? And on and on and on.*

Well, my father was old. He was fifty when I was born and he got sick fast. I sort of went crazy. I was kicked out of high school, I drank and used drugs, I joined the army and faked a nervous breakdown to get out. I was seventeen and came back to Los Angeles and caught the 1960s dope revolution in full flow. So for the next twelve years I drank a lot of cheap wine, smoked a lot of marijuana, took a lot of pills, slept in parks, broke into houses, stole things, shoplifted, uh, went to gaol a lot. Not for any great length of time; I was only arrested for misdemeanours, thirty days here, thirty days there, ten days, twenty days, drunk, drunk, drunk, drunk. I slept in parks, I was homeless before it was in vogue and I almost died from a series of booze-related maladies and in early 1977 I got sober and realized 'no more booze, no more drugs or you will die'.

Throughout this time I'd been reading many, many, many crime novels. I loved it, it was my raison d'être. *I read and I read and I read and harboured dreams of being a great novelist. So . . . I got sober in August 1977 and I stayed off the booze for a year and a half, and for a couple of years I worked as a golf caddy and got an idea for a crime novel.*

A footnote to the story. I ran down a copy of Jack Webb's *The Badge* and here is the description of murder that burned itself on to Ellroy's brain.

The Dahlia had been roped and spread-eagled and then hour after hour, for possibly two or three days, slowly tortured with the little knife thrusts that hurt terribly but couldn't kill. She had made the rope burns on her wrists and ankles as she writhed in agony. Finally in hot rage or *coup de grâce*, there had come the slash across the face from ear to ear, and the Dahlia had choked to death on her own blood. But the killer had not done with her body. Afterwards, he (or she) drained the system of blood, scrubbed the body clean and even shampooed the hair. Then it was neatly cut in two and deposited at 39th and Norton.

God knows what kind of a gift that was to the fantasy life of the tall and strange young Ellroy — tales from the morgue, the pornography of an authoritarian time.

It took Ellroy seven books to get famous. He'd got sober in 1977 and the first novel, *Brown's Requiem*, came out in 1981. Seven years later *The Black Dahlia* made it into the *New York Times* bestseller lists. In between he's written three novels featuring an LA cop called Lloyd Hopkins, a book called *Clandestine* which uses his mother's murder as a starting point and a book called *Silent Terror*, a novel in the shape of an autobiography of a serial killer with a discomfiting amount of Ellroy's own background.

This is the problem with Ellroy: there is a temptation, which he has done little to discourage, to view him as another Jack Henry Abbott (the convicted murderer who wrote an autobiography, *In the Belly of the Beast*, while in prison, which led Norman Mailer, among others, to campaign for his freedom, on receipt of which he promptly killed again), a man who has been to the abyss and lived to tell, a tame psycho. What is muddied is whether Ellroy is interpreting his past or his nightmares, or whether he is consumed by them. His first novel, *Brown's Requiem*, has a central character, an ex-cop turned repo man and occasional PI named Fritz Brown who has more than a little in common with Ellroy. A tall ex-alcoholic with a love of classical music and a distaste for counter-culture types, he has a best friend named Walter who likes to talk about the Black Dahlia, just like Ellroy and his buddy Randy Rice: 'Walter was a sort of spin-off from Randy Rice, though Randy didn't kill himself. He's a guy I grew up with, we got drunk together, got sober together, did all kinds of crazy stuff. He's got light-blue eyes so light it looks like he sends them out to be bleached. He's a book scout now, lives in Venice Beach.'

Much of the book is set in the surprisingly lowlife world of the LA golf caddie, again a throwback to Ellroy's lost years. 'I used to know a caddie who later drank himself to death. He got me a job as a caddie at a country club. It was great; tax-free cash every day which encourages behaviour such as alcoholism, drug addiction, compulsive gambling . . . absolutely no responsibilities, good cash flow. I loved it.'

This time, the second time I meet James Ellroy, he's in Ivy League casual mode, button-down shirt, loafers and Levi's just barely long enough for his legs, faded and fraying at the bottoms. This time, like the first time, I won't have much time with Ellroy; he's hot right now and seriously busy. Though it doesn't seem to matter; Ellroy is the reverse of the normal interviewee – the longer you spend with him the less there seems to be to say – he has mastered the art of the interview as publicity and seems largely unwilling to allow an interview to move off into uncharted regions that might reveal anything more than what he wants revealed. His answers are either off pat, or general to the point of evasiveness.

He has a new book out, *The Big Nowhere*, far more ambitious than anything he has previously tried and he's keen to impress me with the extent to which he's a serious writer, not some psycho who writes slasher novels. He wants at least to be seen as some psycho who writes *Dostoyevskyan* slasher novels. He's intent on pulling back from his carefully constructed persona, talks about how marriage has changed him ('I got married in December, you know . . . we've got a dog now.'). He claims to have found a new maturity; 'I think *The Black Dahlia* was my last book as a young man. I was thirty-nine when it came out. I think *The Big Nowhere* is my first book as a mature man.' He goes on to poke fun at the 'I've been there' *schtick*. 'I think there are people like myself who are now morally appalled at the way they once lived and get a vicarious kick out of reliving that and taking it much further. Yeah, I was a drunk, yeah I slept in parks, yeah I rolled a drunk maybe two times in my life and did maybe eight months of county gaol time, but I like writing about pervert killers who wear wolverine teeth, you know . . .'

Ellroy's writing is jammed with contradictions: *The Big Nowhere* is more serious than previous books, has an extraordinary scope but it is also full of hack cartoonery, horror-comic stuff (wolverine teeth??). The gore is increasingly the least interesting aspect of

Ellroy's work; what grips is the sweep of his re-creation of 1950s LA.

As he was born in 1948 I wonder what he remembers of that time. 'I remember it in many different ways, I remember it inchoately, right on the edge of memory. Also, as with a lot of writers, I don't know what is actually my memory and what is memory I've created out of my imagination. I remember Mickey Cohen [celebrated 1950s LA gangster who makes an appearance in *The Big Nowhere*] . . . I remember meeting Mickey Cohen in a barbershop on Fairfax Ave; he had a bulldog named Mickey Cohen Jr. I remember LA back then as a time when men cut deals, travelled in packs and cut deals, talked about women openly and blatantly, and ate steak a lot and went to the fights a lot. And frankly I miss that time. Writing about the 1950s is very much a way of reclaiming my past, though it's not my literal past, it's one I'm re-creating out of my imagination.'

Prior to *The Black Dahlia* Ellroy had used contemporary LA as the backdrop for his series of novels featuring LAPD rogue cop Lloyd Hopkins: 'What I wanted was to create my antidote to the world-weary, beer-drinking, woman-yearning, predictable private eye. You know, the private-eye icon/hero who has become such a ritual, such a cliché. He hates authority, he has such a distinct past, he'd really like to be with a woman but no woman would go with him because of the violent lifestyle he leads. He gets weepy over lost dogs and little kids, he hates authority, he hates big money. He has a witty riposte and an astute sociological observation for every situation that comes his way. I think that the character that Raymond Chandler created and which has spawned so many imitators is essentially bullshit. So I wanted an antidote to that. I wanted a real, repressed, violent, right-wing – though not particularly right-wing ideologically – LA cop. I wanted a man who is obsessed with order because he has no order in his own life. I wanted a man with more than his share of hypocrisy, full of ambiguities and contradictions. Heroes don't interest me in the least and I don't think Hopkins is a hero. I think he's efficacious in that he puts evil people away and I love and respect him for that, but the price, of course, is great.'

I wonder if he intends writing again about contemporary LA: 'I may set other novels in LA in the present. But not in the foreseeable future. There's a great deal I don't know about LA today. When I grew up it was a white man's town; now it's largely oriental and Latin and there are entire pockets where they don't speak English at all. My old neighbourhood is now Koreatown. I've gotten away from LA, I've lived there in the past to such an extent that LA now eludes me. I come back to LA and I want to eat in places that used to be there. I want to stay in the mindset of LA in the past.'

Ellroy has to go; his agent has someone for him to lunch with. He gives me his number in Connecticut, the American dream home the books have bought him; 'Let's keep in touch.' And he's gone. Meanwhile, I keep looking for LA. Word has it that Melrose is the hip place to be these days, where the chic go shopping. Deployment of the not entirely appropriately named Rapid Transport System (i.e. a rather slow bus) lands me on the Melrose strip, and it does indeed have the requisite complement of boutiques, eateries, record, book and sunglasses emporia that mark it out as a happening youthzone. But it is depressingly like anywhere, a sunny version of London's King's Road, for instance. Most alarmingly, its dominant theme is retro: 1950s America. There are mock-1950s diners, American classic clothing stores and places selling tarted-up 1950s kitsch at alarming prices and I have the strong sense that this is symbolic of a huge failure of nerve. Fetishizing your recent past used to be the preserve of faded European nations; the American dream has always been of a better future. This mass flight to get back to the future, to an imaginary 1950s wonderland, is perhaps the most depressing legacy of the Reagan 'let's feel good about America' ethos. Certainly this sanitized version of the 1950s is savagely contradicted by Ellroy's work. As he comments: 'The 1950s to me is darkness, hidden history, perversion behind most doors waiting to creep out; the 1950s to most people is kitsch and Mickey Mouse watches and all this intolerable stuff . . .'

Melrose, then, sure as hell isn't Ellroy country. Undaunted, though, I head back over to the eastern end of Hollywood and take a walk west up Sunset Boulevard. Things don't look up too fast; for miles it insists on looking like the outskirts of any place – not the suburbs, just the motley developments that cling to the main drag out of town. For about a mile past LaBrea there isn't

even a place to eat. Finally there's a Jewish deli which turns out
to be run by Koreans but serves up a passable tuna on rye.
Sitting down, I listen to a woman too old to be talking about
slumber parties trying to impress a bloke who doesn't need
impressing.

Further on down the road I at last encounter something.
Something is in the shape of Rock World, a glorified instrument
shop with the handprints of heavy-metal drummers embedded
into the marble-ette pavement outside. Inside are a bevy of guys
with blond corkscrew perms and leather trousers. Neat.

Finally I'm getting close to the Sunset Strip section of Sunset
Boulevard. This is signalled by the appearance on my left of a
shop selling rock'n'roll cowboy boots and on my right by the
shadow of the Chateau Marmont, a hotel popular with rock'n'roll
stars of the hotel-room-trashing era. It is of course 'legendary' –
legendary being a specialized rock'n'roll term meaning 'vaguely
connected with Jim Morrison' (incidentally, one exception to
Ellroy's blanket hatred of the counter-culture: Ellroy's own title
for his serial-killer novel *Silent Terror* was *Killer on the Road*, a take
from Morrison's 'Riders on the Storm'). The Strip itself looks
like the fag-end of the King's Road: second-division designer
stores and pot-plant-festooned brasseries. It seems like a stopping
place on your way up to Beverly Hills or a place to go for the
bored offspring of those who already live in Beverly Hills.

A fast Dos Equis and back on the bus to Hollywood Boulevard.
Past Mann's Chinese Theater, the classic cod-oriental movie
palace currently showing *Dead Calm*, a movie made from a fine
book by Charles Williams, a great crime writer of the 1950s and
1960s who killed himself in the mid-1970s. Past Frederick's of
Hollywood, a deco institution decked out in purple and pink, the
place where countless travelling salespeople have come to buy
crotchless undies and baby-doll nighties for their loved ones. On
Hollywood Boulevard there are stars on the pavement, each one
dedicated to a Hollywood legend – allowing for a definition of
legend loose enough to include the likes of Leif Garrett.

Coming up to the junction of Hollywood and Vine, the one-
time key corner of the movie world, there's a bunch of street
vendors, a few places selling genuine English new-wave gear,

even real Dr Martens for LA skinheads. And there's a cluster of sex shops.

The sex trade has long been a standby for thriller writers looking for a nexus of evil. A rash of novels – Robert Campbell's *In La La Land We Trust*, for example – suggest that you need only walk into a sex shop to be asked which variety of snuff movie tickles your fancy – 'Would sir be interested in the strangulated Latina or perhaps something a little harder, a brace of dismembered pre-teens mebbe?' The truth is thankfully less lurid. Inside the delightfully named Le Sex Shoppe, about the first thing you see is a bunch of disclaimers: ALL MODELS OVER 18/NO ACTS OF VIOLENCE/ALL CONSENTING ADULTS. Next thing you see is a range of luridly packaged videos and then a vast array of magazines whose titles seem designed to discover every possible permutation of the following words: sexy, cum, lesbian, orgy, whoppers, anal, wet, fantasy, blonde, big, black, tits, hot, oral, ass, suck and oriental. Often in the most implausible combinations (anal lesbians!!). Noticeably absent, though, are words like torture, pain, alsatian or snuff. Another side of the shop is devoted to the same again, except delete lesbian and tits and replace with dude, gay, honcho, cowboy and meat. In between is the really strange stuff. This is a rack of contact magazines and newspapers. Magazines like *Cocoa'n'Creme* for inter-racial swingers, which is made up of polaroids of black and white individuals and couples in explicit poses attached to brief résumés of sexual peccadilloes and contact addresses.

Which invites speculation on two counts: first as to whether placing such advertisements is conceivably safe in the homeland of the serial sex-killer. Maybe, as with British football hooligans who disdain to attack fans actually dressed in the colours of an opposing team (preferring to wait for the greater challenge of identifying opposing hooligans who will be spotted by more arcane details like the brandname of their footwear), they are seen as simply too easy, soft targets, clay pigeons. Second, on the sex shop as an underground index of what used to be called the race question. As with most areas of American life, there is the evidence of segregation in porn: slick white magazines for white folks and slightly old-fashioned-looking, cheaply produced, black porno for black folks. Then in among the white-folks mags you have a selection of titles catering to one of America's most potent and thus most repressed fantasies: the black man with the white woman. As ever, as must be, in this fantasy the black man has a huge dick and the girl is blonde. But in the porno version, unlike *Birth of a Nation*, the white girl isn't screaming rape, she's loving it. That this fantasy should, still, be saleable to an audience, presumably, of white men, seems to point to some sexual equivalent of *in vino veritas*. Certainly a country in which white couples place ads in magazines for 'well-hung black men' to come round and fuck the wife while the husband videos the event is not one in which the race question might be said to have been answered.

Not that, in LA, there's much danger of suspecting that it has been. Riding the bus back to where I'm staying, a man and his mom get on the bus. Mom is a middle-aged black woman, definitely respectable, who sits down with a huge handbag balanced on her knees. Son is altogether funkier, wears a burnoose and torn sneakers hanging off his feet. He sits down next to me and gives me his hard-luck story, an epic that starts in the Detroit ghetto, moves to Vietnam, takes in an ankle fucked up in an industrial accident in Florida and leads, via Detroit once more, to the streets of LA. At the end he asks me to lend him two dollars. I do, wondering all the while why I care whether the story is true; obviously it's true enough in spirit, and surely it must be more interesting to embroider a story you're going to have to keep repeating all day long. Maybe he should write a novel, I think, wondering what the hell I'm doing: a tourist not simply confronted incidentally by other people's misery on holiday but actually seeking out that misery, soliciting stories of violence. Maybe he will write a book himself; he took enough interest in the book I was reading, Anne Rice's *Interview with a Vampire* – 'Hey, you're lucky to have that book, man, my family told me about that book, that's a hard book to find, man.' Then he goes over to mom, gives her the money. She smiles at me, puts it in her handbag.

Were the man in the burnoose to write a novel he'd have few enough precedents. Even in crime fiction authors tend to have had at least some advantages in life. Even Ellroy had a starting point above zero from which his life fell to pieces. The names of black American crime writers you can count on one hand: Chester Himes, Clifford Mason, Donald Goines, Walter Mosley and the man I'm going to meet next, Gar Anthony Haywood. And even of these, only Goines really came from the streets (Himes spent a long period in prison after a short and incompetent career as a jewel thief but came from a relatively middle-class background). As such, too, Goines's life followed his art to the extent that he wound up dead at thirty-eight, shot repeatedly in the head by two white men, perhaps drug-business associates. The killers were never found; Goines's two daughters, who saw him killed, were too young to be much help as witnesses. At his funeral he was placed in his coffin with copies of two of his paperback originals, *Daddy Cool* and *Never Die Alone*. Sometime during the funeral the copy of *Daddy Cool* was stolen. Which is about as grim as funny stories get. And too appropriate.

Gar Haywood, however, proves to be hardly in the Goines mould, when he shows up next morning at the place where I'm staying. He's a tall, lightly bearded, light-skinned guy wearing jeans, a leather jacket and an LA Lakers T-shirt. Which last detail, in the labyrinthine world of American race relations, is pretty much a statement of aspirational blackness. LA Lakers are the supreme basketball team of the 1980s, longtime home of major black hero Karim Abdul Jabbar and now of Majic Johnson. The Lakers have taken over the space once occupied by the the Harlem Globetrotters. By contrast, among the homeboys of South Central the major allegiance is not to the Lakers but a football team, the superbad LA Raiders. On the dispossessed side of the street there are three acceptable logos for your baseball cap: two are drawn from the world of hiphop – Public Enemy and NWA – and the other is the LA Raiders, even among the Times Square posses a continent away.

We decide to go and get some breakfast. Haywood has stopped off on his way to work. He's a roving computer troubleshooter for a firm called Control Data and his van is parked outside. He clears away a pile of *Sports Illustrated*s and we drive down Sunset into Silverlake, stopping at a place called Millies that takes the truism about all LA waiters being resting actors a step further. In the case of Millies the whole place seems to be a resting sitcom: premises, staff and customers all seem to be in a state of perpetual audition, waiting for a peckish producer to drop in and suddenly exclaim, 'Hey, you guys are funnier than Alice's Restaurant any day. Let's rebuild this place on the Universal lot; you're all hired.' Wisecracks fly somewhat faster than the service, which is a little trying at nine in the morning, but still, once the eggs and coffee kick in we get down to talking.

'I, uh, don't generally go into places like this,' says Haywood, casting a somewhat bemused eye over the bohemian clientele and pop-art-inflected decor. This isn't because Haywood is any kind of ghetto product, unused to the society of white folks, but rather a reflection of his fairly straight-arrow background as a product of the black American middle class. As Haywood comments when I ask him about his political background, 'I always thought of myself as a good all-American guy, right up until I was thirty years old.'

Haywood is now thirty-three and his first novel, a private-eye tale called *Fear of the Dark*, set in the giant ghetto of South Central LA and infused with a good deal of cynical political awareness, has just come out. His father, Jack Haywood, is an architect and, when Gar was six, was one of the first blacks to move into the middle-class suburb of Baldwin Hills. 'We moved there in 1963; it was a predominantly Jewish area at the time, so I was there for the evolution of the community from an all-Jewish one to an all-black one. That was quite an eye-opening experience, to see most of your friends migrate out of the neighbourhood.'

So Haywood grew up in black suburbia, part of a social world largely ignored by whites, who tend to see black communities as inevitably deprived ghettos, turning a blind eye to the fact that segregation in American life does not operate only at the bottom of the economic ladder. Blacks who achieve middle-class status have black middle-class suburbs to live in behind their very own white picket fences, black colleges to send their kids to, *Ebony* and *EM* to read instead of *Harpers* and *GQ*, a kind of separate-but-equalish-up-to-a-point-and-given-the-breaks policy.

Haywood went to a mostly black high school, upscale enough to be clear of the gang rivalries that make school an urban battlefield for most black Angeleno kids. 'All the colour lines I had to deal with were racially drawn, black and white, not red and blue,' he puts it. At school he was a comic-book obsessive, writing his own comics with a couple of friends. From his father, meanwhile, he acquired both a fondness for sci-fi and a dauntingly high set of expectations. 'My father's expectations were always pretty great. He's one of those guys, no matter what you accomplish, rather than applaud you for it his approach is to say, "That's great but if you had done this much more then . . ." I often think that one day I'll bring home the Pulitzer Prize and he'll say, "Only one, huh, you should have tried, you could have got two." That's the kind of guy he is. His expectations for my writing were, like, if I was any good I'd be published by the time I was twenty-two. I recall a conversation when I was about twenty-two or -three, I showed him something I'd written and he said, "Yeah, this is OK, but let me show you some good writing," and he showed me *The Andromeda Strain* and said, "This is what you could be doing if you really put your mind to it." And the fact of the matter is that given my age and background there was no way I was about to write *The Andromeda Strain*, not just the subject matter but that quality of writing.'

Unsurprisingly intimidated by this pressure to succeed, Haywood drifted for a while after school. He toyed with becoming an architect in his father's footsteps, attended a series of junior colleges and finally, at twenty-one, started working for Control Data. Now he's married, to Lynette, they have two small daughters and live out in the San Fernando Valley in Sherman Oaks, a pleasant, and mixed, middle-class community. However, he has clearly internalized his father's drive. Where many people would feel pleased to have continued writing while establishing a money-earning career and starting a family, then having a first novel published at thirty-two, Haywood sees himself as a dawdler: 'I always felt I should have developed quicker than I did.'

Through his twenties he was writing sci-fi: 'I read a lot of Larry Niven. My biggest influence as far as motivating me to write was Robert E. Howard and the Conan books – they were really really good, I think. Failed sci-fi stories was what I concentrated on up till the last five or six years.' At which time his reading tastes were moving away from sci-fi: 'By my mid-twenties I was reading a lot of mysteries. Everyone starts with

Chandler and I guess I did too. I got into John D. MacDonald. Science fiction was growing more and more technical, getting into hard science, and I wasn't qualified to do that. One of the reasons I moved towards mystery writing is that there are very few rules. You set a guy down in a situation and how he reacts is how he reacts.'

So Haywood switched from a kind of writing as far removed from everyday reality as possible to one that is positively mired in it; from writing as escapism to following the familiar advice to 'write about what you know'. What Haywood knew was LA; the first time he left southern California he was twenty-five and Control Data flew him to Minneapolis for a training course. Writing about what you know is, of course, a highly selective process. Haywood has chosen to write about the streets of South Central rather than, say, a family drama of black suburbia, though he is concerned to stress his distance from those mean streets. Talking about South Central, he jokes, 'I cruise the neighbourhood, you know, eighty or ninety miles an hour.' This is the reverse of most crime writers, who are desperately keen to impress on you just how streetwise they are and, at worst, end up coming over as the kind of people who desperately try to think of black acqaintances they can invite to their barbecues to impress their friends on the university staff. Haywood has far too much of a sense that there but for fortune he could be to want to play the part of an Uzi-toting, Tyson-cropped, urban guerrilla novelist. Not for him the Ellroy route of giving the people what they want.

And, in fact, Haywood is connected to South Central far more directly than any white liberal novelist trying to dress up sociological theses as crime fiction: 'I scouted some locations, others I made up. I don't want anyone to say, "That's my bar he's talking about." I may have moved the odd gas station, but I know the neighbourhood pretty well. I've never actually lived there, but I have friends there, some members of my family live there. I've spent enough time to know what it's like. This might sound very shallow but I think the fact of the matter is that being black you feel kindred with other black people. So even though I've never experienced genuine poverty, I think in some way I can relate to it. The factors that are holding black people down in the ghetto are the same pressures that apply to all of us. All you're talking about is a difference in degrees. I don't feel that I had to fabricate any of the emotion.'

Fear of the Dark's protagonist also reverses the familiar relation of the crime writer and his/her fiction. The private eye is conventionally some kind of wish-fulfilment alter ego for an author, younger, stronger, better-looking, sexually irresistible etc. Haywood's Aaron Gunner is older, shorter, balder and generally unhealthier than his creator, and his love life is disastrous. 'I wanted to create a black PI in LA who was not going to come off as John Shaft, who was not going to be a typical soul brother. And I knew that somewhere along the line he was going to quit. That was one thing I was determined about. We've seen enough heroes who just deflect everything that comes their way – I wanted someone who was capable of saying, "Hey, this is getting very heavy, I don't know if I can cut this, let me quit now, while I'm ahead."'

Gunner is an army veteran and failed cop, just barely making it as South Central's lone freelance operative, constantly under pressure from his cousin Del to take a proper job as an electrician. He's a man whose energies are taken up with keeping his head above water: 'I'm as apolitical as a guy can get,' he tells Verna Gail, the woman who shows up to ask him to investigate the murder of her brother, Buddy, a black nationalist militant. It's money not political commitment that drags Gunner into the middle of what looks like an approaching race war between the black nationalist group, the Brothers of Volition, and the forces of reaction being whipped up by a right-wing congressional candidate. By the end of the novel Gunner is still in the middle and finding it a mighty lonely place to be. But by now he is not in the middle simply through apathy, but through consciously believing that, for all its disappointments, the integrationist tradition of the civil-rights movement offers the only real chance, that fantasies of war on whitey may be satisfying, even necessary, as daydreams, but could only be suicidal given the realities of power in corporate America.

Other writers, Ellroy among them, disparage the private eye as a protagonist, arguing that cops are infinitely more believable. For Haywood though, to make his character a cop would be to embroil him in such overwhelming contradictions as to prevent him functioning. The desirability of law and order may be a given for most crime writers; for a black writer, however, it must be open to question. 'Law and order is definitely more of a grey area for black people, especially the underprivileged, than for the rest of us. You can't expect the cop on the beat to change the system, you can't expect the homicide detective to change the system. The changes that have to be made to make law and order mean something in this city have to come from a lot farther up.'

Even as a PI, Gunner is distinctly unconvinced as to the value of his work: 'He didn't have to spend many nights in motel parking lots, waiting for one client or another's stray spouse to cut an incriminating pose for his Polaroid, to understand what he had become and where he was headed,' and the law is only a support in the absence of anything better: 'He was living in an age in which conviction to causes was out of vogue and apathy was often confused with open-mindedness. The only line that remained indelible between men was the law. Corruption was blurring that line more every day . . . but the illusion of just men waging war against the forces of darkness was still intact in the realm of law enforcement, and for Gunner the lost lamb, an illusion seemed good enough.'

It's a difficult illusion to maintain at a time when the US administration seems to have a crudely literal interpretation of what kinds of peoples constitute 'forces of darkness'. As Haywood observes; 'Somewhere in the last four or five years I became aware of the shift in American politics since Reagan came into office. The greatest damage that he has done is to repopularize the approach to American capitalism that says as a business man you have a God-given right to call your own shots. Meaning that in the interests of free enterprise you can go ahead and discriminate as you see fit. "Whatever is most profitable, this is what we endorse as an administration," that's the Reagan line. It was suddenly OK to come out of the closet and call a black man a nigger if you wanted to, have the freedom you used to have in the good old days – Happy Days. All your blemishes and pimples – it was OK to have them back out in the open.'

The rebirth of black-militant groups, like the book's Brothers of Volition, seems to Haywood to be the inevitable consequence of the changed political climate: 'I was sitting there thinking, where are we going? There's a lot of pressure on black Americans to get the movement back in gear. In the last few years it seems we've let the battle go. We felt we'd got all the rights we wanted and it's OK to put the picket signs down and enjoy our lives, and the fact is that we've allowed right-wing politicians to reverse the process. Now we're reliving history; the same forces that produced the Black Panthers are coming to the fore again. Americans have been lulled to sleep as far as the civil-rights movement is concerned. In the 1960s we had no illusion as to everything being all right – we knew it wasn't – but now black people have had a little taste of what it's like to get a job without being discriminated against, they've moved into a neighbourhood they might not have been able to before. And these people are going to be harder to get excited. So I think it's still some years ahead before we reach that point of frustration again where we have enough self-awareness to see that we've got to go back to work, pick up the picket signs – and the guns – and whatever and go back to work.'

For the moment, though, the quotidian reality of life in South Central is not dominated by thoughts of militancy but simply by concerns of staying alive in the midst of a terrifying escalation of black-on-black violence. This is gangland; the territory that is fought over by the Crips and the Bloods. Here young black males are faced with a choice that is no choice: whether to stay out of the gangs and be fair game to all, or to seek the protection afforded by joining one gang while accepting the increased possibility of being shot by the other.

The gangs aren't new. They were around in the 1940s when LA exploded into racial violence during the Zoot Suit Riots, so-called because of the fondness among young black and Hispanic gang members for the hugely oversized 'zoot' suits as worn by the likes of the bandleader Cab Calloway. What has changed is that the gangs are now heavily armed and are in control, at street level, of the hugely popular crack industry. It's a story familiar from a heap of hand-wringing magazine articles and the movie *Colors*: ten-year-old kids earning a fortune as lookouts for the dealers, addicted mothers bearing addicted babies, random drive-by killings.

For his new novel, *Not Long for this World*, Gar Haywood has turned his attention to the gangs, looking to go beyond the dominant common-sense perception that deprivation plus some kind of black pathology equals madness and violence. 'I think the gangs exemplify how easily black problems and black concerns are written off by the general public. I think if you were to take a poll of the Los Angeles people who read an article about one of these killings you'd find about eighty per cent saying these people are nuts, they're sick, they should be put in a camp and gassed – I'm not just talking about white people, I mean black people, everyone. That's just the general attitude.

'But it's a lot deeper than that. If they are crazy there's a whole lot of things to blame for that. And essentially I wrote the book because I realized I had this hang-up that I couldn't relate to these kids who are aiming Uzis out of a moving car and firing into a crowd. I can't relate to that and my first reaction was "This is insane." But I think what we're losing track of from the beginning is that the majority of these kids think it's all a game, they have no concept of the value of human life because of the kind of life they've had to lead. We're talking about kids that from day one have had no hope of anything, they have totally lost all faith in their own future. They are surrounded by people who don't have anything, never had anything and are convinced they never will have anything, so how do you motivate these people to care for themselves? Your concept of life and my concept of life is going to differ totally from that of someone who lives in that environment. Their idea of life is hell on earth, being forced to dodge bullets going to and from school, coming home to see your mom doing crack and your father deal whatever. What is the value of that and what are you doing when you kill this sixteen-year-old kid because he's wearing the wrong colours except sparing him a few more years of this?

'These are the kind of things I wanted to explore. I wanted Gunner to take the attitude from day one that was my original attitude: these kids are crazy. So when the case first comes along for Gunner to work in the interests of a gang leader who is accused of killing an anti-gang figure, he doesn't want anything to do with it. Gunner's sense of frustration and self-hatred and whatever is far greater than mine because he has to live in South Central. I don't, I live in Sherman Oaks, I might have to drive through it once in a while. He sees it daily. Like he says in the book, "I don't have to read about it. If I want to see a shooting all I have to do is go to the nearest mall and sit around in the parking lot for a few hours." So what I'm trying to do is take Gunner from point A of not wanting anything to do with it to point B where he realizes that these kids are lost from day one. The title *Not Long for this World* comes from a preacher describing these kids. They're born not long for this world. These kids come into this world with a life expectancy of zero and it doesn't go up from there. Maybe I'm painting an overly bleak picture but I don't think so.'

Politicians like to deliver little homilies to the kids: put down the guns, get educated so one day you can work for minimum wage at McDonalds. For the kids themselves, Haywood points out, such talk is a tired comedy routine: 'I have a friend who lives in that neighbourhood, he's educated, got a job, most articulate guy I know. And people will point to him and say "Why can't you all be like this guy, pick yourselves up by your bootstraps, ignore the gangs, just say no." You got to understand that there aren't many people like that born every day. There are certain tools that this guy had from birth; not everyone has them. For each one who has the strength and determination there's another kid who doesn't, and first time he comes under a burst of shotgun fire he thinks, "That's enough, I'm going to attach myself to a gang." That's not an offensive manoeuvre, that's a defensive manoeuvre: like, "If I'm going to get shot at I could use a little help!" These kids are not angels, none of us are. And a lot of them are lost; you can't just pat them on the back and say, "We love you, chile, let's get our act together." But you can't ignore their environment and their economic outlook.'

So what does Haywood hope to achieve by writing about this all? 'In the end the biggest uplift for me is in that Gunner has come from point A to point B. Next time he reads about two kids killing each other he's not going to write it off as a couple of nuts, he's going to have a little more awareness. And that's where it all begins. We as a society have to realize that these lives do have value, that we're throwing away potential there, otherwise it's never going to change.'

Haywood is by no means exclusively interested in writing for a black audience. He recognizes that the mass audience is white, and on one level would simply like to add a believable black PI to the crime-fiction canon. However, to reach a black readership is important to him and here he feels frustrated by the same forces that are the bedrock of his subject matter: ghetto economics. 'One thing that upsets me is you won't find my book in any of the bookstore chains. They tell me that's not unique to my book and that may be true, but the fact of the matter is that the black readership on the south side don't have mom-and-pop bookstores to go to down the street. If it's not in the one Crown Bookstore within a sixty-mile radius they're not going to find it, if it's not at the mall where they gonna go? So I don't think that many black readers have had access to it.'

The interview is winding up now and we start talking about this and that: the role of crime fiction as social commentary, something Haywood passionately believes ('the problem is that crime fiction is viewed as pseudo-literature. I think we have to move away from the idea that because a novel has a dead body in it, it can't say anything about the world we live in'); the fondness of publishers and reviewers for pigeonholing novels ('they always want to call my book *gritty*. Like before they've read it they're saying, "Hey, this is about a black PI in South Central LA. Hm, gotta be gritty!"'). Haywood says his next novel won't be a private-eye book but something in the ultra-realist style of Elmore Leonard, the one white writer whose black characters Haywood feels ring true. And then, having consumed more coffee than the Surgeon General would advise, we leave.

Talking to Haywood about his research for *Not Long for this World*, he mentions the lack of any modern reference work on the gangs. As it happens, I've been given the number of a man called Mike Davis who is engaged on more or less that project. Later in the morning I call Davis up and he suggests taking a trip that night to what he describes as 'the last blues club left in South Central'. We'll meet at his place this evening.

Beforehand I read an article Davis has written about the gangs. Called 'Los Angeles: Civil Liberties Between the Hammer and the Rock', it details the awful lack of considered response to the gang violence. Mostly there is repression: the hard-line Police Chief, Daryl Gates, has launched Operation Hammer, in which more black youth were arrested in one weekend than at any time since the Watts riots of 1965. The city attorney James Hahn has invoked all manner of arcane laws in an attempt to rescind the civil liberties of gang members. This is seen as both going too far and not far enough. The charge of not far enough can be heard, surprisingly enough, from black groups who see the gangs and drug dealers (referred to by the novelist Ishmael Reed as 'crack fascists') as destroying the fabric of an already economically embattled community. Thus the former Black Panther Minister of Propaganda, Harry Edwards, calls for crack-dealing teenagers to be imprisoned indefinitely. Too far in that the notoriously racist LAPD is not the ideal organization to be let loose on the black community, if you're concerned that only the bad guys should be arrested. As it is there have been incidents such as LAPD officers shooting innocent teenagers on sight. On one occasion a supposed crack house was stormed and its inhabitant shot dead. Unfortunate that the inhabitant should have been an eighty-one-year-old retired construction worker. No problem for the LAPD; despite the complete absence of drugs on the scene they put out a statement saying that the gangs are paying the elderly to use their houses. This is no less than you would expect from Chief Gates, a man who explained a rash of deaths among young blacks, resulting from chokeholds put on them by police, by telling the world that black people's arteries fail to open 'as fast as they do on normal people'. Ah.

Meanwhile liberals and the left have not even the beginnings of an alternative law-and-order strategy. The eminently concerned leftist types I'm staying with are all heavily politically involved in Latin American politics, helping refugees, campaigning against US involvement in El Salvador and Nicaragua, but mention South Central and they just shake their heads and say, 'Oh, God, it's terrible.'

Finding Mike Davis's place is something of an adventure in itself. After negotiating a series of LA freeways – an operation which, at night, is something like being part of a giant video game with the disadvantage that when you crash you crash – I wind my way up a hill and the road turns into a kind of country lane. Eventually I find the address; my directions tell me to go through the door at the side of the house and round to the back. The door, however, is locked. So I figure, time to ask the neighbours, check I've got the right place. Out in the lane some guys with torches are working on a car. As I approach they walk into the house opposite. I follow them, passing the car, which looks as if it's auditioning for a part in *Mad Max Goes to Hell* and seems in need of resurrection rather than repair. Through the window of the house I see two guys who look as if Charles Manson would have thought twice before letting them meet his family. The room is empty apart from a vast quantity of dime-store religious icons – dayglo madonnas and 3D-effect pictures of Jesus. Maybe the guys're looking to invoke the miracle of the dead automobile. Anyway, I'm already so irritated by not being able to get where I'm going that rationality is not playing too great a part in my thought processes, so I bang on the door and ask if I can use their phone. The first guy laughs, then the second guy laughs, the first guy splutters, 'We don't have a phone, hur, hur, they took it away, ha, ha,' and the second guy manages to get a grip on himself; 'Maybe we'll get one for the *car*, hur, har, hur, har.'

I quit while I'm ahead and they're still laughing and try next door. The entrance to next door is round the back. I knock and the door is opened by a young woman wearing a bath towel who was evidently expecting some person else. I explain what I'm doing, talking very fast, and she suggests I drive back a few miles and use a payphone. Which I do, and Mike Davis says, 'Oh yeah, I thought everyone knew how to unlock those kind of doors. Well everyone from California does anyhow. It'll be open when you get back.' It is and I meet Davis and a couple of friends drinking wine and discussing gang warfare. The friends are a woman from some Mid-Western, I think, university who is also researching a book on gangs and Davis's next-door neighbour, a Latin guy who's a social worker in east LA. It's a strange conversation I've walked in on: they're all talking about gang leaders as other people talk about baseball stars – 'Hey one time I interviewed this guy in Saint Quentin, killed twenty or thirty dudes before they put him away, now he can quote whole pages of Frantz Fanon'; 'Yeah, well have you heard about this guy in Cleveland – he's in for like ninety-nine life sentences and he's still running the drug trade from his cell. Jesus I'm hoping to talk to him.' Academics as armchair gangbangers.

The other two take one car and Mike comes with me to direct me and chat a little. Back on the freeways we angle across the downtown district heading south till an offramp deposits us on Central Avenue. Central is still the main thoroughfare of South Central LA, but forty years ago, when West Coast jazz and blues were riding high, it rivalled 125th Street in Harlem as the main street of black America. Mike points out a few surviving landmarks, notably the Dunbar Hotel, now being restored, one tiny suggestion of resurgence. Just around here, Mike reminds me, is where Chandler set the beginning of *Farewell My Lovely*, this is the street on which Moose Malloy went searching for his Velma, looking, as Chandler put it, 'about as inconspicuous as a tarantula on a slice of angel food'. Compared to most of LA it can't have changed much since Chandler's day, nothing new has been built, the old has just got older.

Moose Malloy went looking for Velma in what Chandler's white characters refer to as 'a dinge joint' and Central used to be full of places where one could go looking for a good time of one variety or another. Now it's windswept and empty, cold enough to keep even the crack heads indoors. As we get down to 52nd Street the road surface is already starting to deteriorate, not to the undercarriage-destroying extent prevalent further south in Watts or Compton but enough to warm up your suspension and provide one more indication as to where the ghettos figure in the priority stakes when it comes to public funding. We pull up on Central, just past 52nd, one of precious few cars parked on this once busy road. As I'm locking the doors the wind carries the sound of a series of loud popping noises. It takes a couple of seconds to register: oh, that's gunfire. It's not the bang-bang of the movies, just an indistinct, muffled exhalation.

It's odd how fear works; had someone said, 'If you go to South Central there will definitely be people shooting in your vicinity' the prospect would have terrified me. However, actually being there, my frame of reference changes – what is significant is that this shooting is at least a block away and not directed at me.

Precisely where I am, there is no shooting, so why should I be scared? Which is not to say I wasn't in a hurry to get inside Babe & Ricky's Inn, our nightspot of choice.

The inside of Babe & Ricky's Inn is a pop video director's wet dream. Instant back to the fifties. First thing you encounter is a giant floor-standing fan, that's on your left, then there's a long bar on the right; further along on the left, opposite the middle of the bar, there's a small stage. Keep walking and the place opens out into a poolroom with a jukebox and doors to the outside toilets. On the wall near the fan there is a 1989 calendar depicting great kings and queens of Africa, a hangover from pre-civil-rights Marcus Garvey-style black nationalism. The only visible impact the last thirty years have made on the clientele is in the styling of the three-piece suits worn by most of the men here; these mostly look to be as recent as the early 1970s superfly era. So here we are in this place where everyone else is black, the average age around fifty, the men in suits and hats, the women in sporty dresses reserved for Sunday-after-church, in the last place to go in a neighbourhood that has gone to hell. And all we receive is friendliness.

Mike has been here before, is greeted effusively by the woman behind the bar who runs the place. He introduces his friends. We are not exactly inconspicuous and soon most of the customers pass by our bar stools, say hello, wonder how a guy from England likes it here. Then the band start up, playing jump blues as if it's still 1952 and Little Richard, Elvis Presley, John Coltrane and Grover Washington and all the rest of them had never happened. After the first set the band stroll over to say hello. They're all veterans of the LA black-music scene, and most of the time they make their living playing to tourists and white college kids at the clubs out along the beach. But Sunday nights they come home to Babe & Ricky's and play for their own. The bandleader is a guy called Ray Brooks. He toured with Chuck Berry for a while in the 1950s and 1960s, and he tells me he was in London once: 'I just stopped over at the airport, man, it was grey and raining and Floyd Patterson was there, he'd just been fighting that Swedish guy I think, yeah. All I remember 'bout London was playing poker in that airport lounge with Floyd and a few of the guys.' So we talk about boxing for a while. Sugar Ray Robinson had just died and Mike reckons he was the all-time greatest. Me and Ray put forward the claims of the Marvelous Marvin Hagler, Ray and Mike run down Rocky Marciano – 'overrated, he only fought kids and old men', and then Mike starts telling us about the time he saw Archie Moore, the man who fought on well into his forties, at which age he was still able to give the young Cassius Clay a fair fight, when we're interrupted by the arrival of the comic.

The comic is a black woman of indeterminate age wearing a little red dress and a glamour wig and she tells jokes that aren't funny about being black and poor in South Central LA and reading the *National Enquirer*. She's trying to model her style on a hip lifestyle comic, finding fun in the little details of your life you have in common with your audience. Unfortunately this is difficult when your audience's major desire is to forget the little details of their lives. So you are left with a comic who would like to be funny but has nothing to laugh about. Finally she takes refuge in sex jokes, but still there is too much real bitterness for humour; hers is a feminism informed by the politics of desperation. It's a relief when the band comes back on, this time with a singer, Eddie Cleanhead Vinson lookalike Delmar Jackson. For this set, the band move into Bobby Bland territory, soul-flecked blues, slow to mid-tempo, and soon the floor is filled with couples slow dancing. And for a moment everything is all right.

Mike's girlfriend has shown up. She's been working as a waitress and she's tired, so the Davis party leaves. I stay for the end of the set, drink one more Corona, say goodbye to one and all – 'Come back soon, y'hear', well I certainly hope so – and walk out to the car. A woman is walking down the street, wearing nothing but a nightgown. Mike has told me this is a common occurrence: 'They call them strawberries,' he says. These are women whose drug habits are hurting sufficiently for them to appear on the street at any time of night, looking to earn the price of a couple more rocks in the back of someone's car.

Which is as stark an example as you like of the effect of drugs on the dignity of a community. Efforts have been made by the likes of Chief Gates to suggest that the degree of the drug problem is to do with some kind of black pathology, a supposed

lack of stable family structures and suchlike. To this end anec-
dotes of doubtful authenticity involving crack welfare mothers
with Uzis and suchlike are quoted. All of which, as Gar Haywood
pointed out to me earlier, is a large ration of shit: 'We're looking
at crimes of economics more than anything else. I mean there's
no doubt – you can't sell crack on every corner and it not have a
negative effect on the community. If you told the LAPD hands
off Westwood, leave it to the crack dealers, you'd have the same
situation in Westwood. But they're not going to allow that,
because those people in Westwood are not expendable, they have
value to the economic wellbeing of the state of California. The
people in Watts, in Compton, are unemployed to begin with so
what are you losing if you make junkies out of them? So crack
has a great deal to do with it. People keep saying, "War on
drugs, war on drugs." We haven't seen a war on drugs; a little
bit here a little bit there maybe. That's not a war; you've got to
bring out the tanks, bring out the guns, go to work on it.'

Ruminating on this last, and on what it points up – that the
majority of writers of crime fiction, too, are more interested in
the denizens of the Westwoods of this world than the Wattses;
that the democracy of the form is still very much a relative
democracy; that a James Ellroy may be some way closer to the
street than a John Updike, but is still scarcely hanging with the
brothers – I get in the car and look for a freeway to take me back
to Hollywood.

5

San Francisco: from the Frozen Yogurt Parlors to the Tenderloin

The movie of Hammett? *I'd give it a B-plus. Francis Coppola bought that from the manuscript and hired Nic Roeg as director. I did two scripts with Nic, the second of which is one of the best scripts I've ever written and then Nic quit because they couldn't cast it. They looked around for other directors; one of the guys they went to was Truffaut, who read the script, said it was the best script by an American he'd ever read, but he couldn't do it. So it ended up that they hired Wim Wenders. Wim didn't want to work with a script done for another director so we went back to square one. I did three scripts for Wim, at which point I said, 'That's it, guys, I've done two versions of this novel and five versions of this script and that's it.'*

Wim was a ... I love Wim, I think he's a very funny guy, a very interesting man. But he's very Germanic and so I'd gone to Las Vegas researching a script on guys who try and beat twenty-one at blackjack, card counters, it was gonna be for Richard Gere, never got made. I was there researching with my wife and I got a phonecall. It was Wim saying, 'Joe, ve haf to do another version of the script.' I said, 'Jeez, I'm sorry, Wim, I'm in Las Vegas ...' 'I vill come down there.' I said, 'Jeez, Wim, I'm just leaving tomorrow for Guadalajara.' Our son was going to summer school there. Wim says, 'And vere vill you be in Guadalajara?' I said, 'Phoenix Hotel.' 'I vill be there.'

So a few days later here comes Wim trundling in. So Dori and Tim, my wife and son, saw all the sights, had all the fun. Me and Wim are locked in this hotel room rewriting the script. I'm writing in longhand on these yellow legal pads, cause we don't have a typewriter. As I finish each sheet Wim grabs it, runs downstairs to the desk and types it; they have an old manual Underwood there. So day and night we're doing this. So along by the second night the desk clerk doesn't show up. So Wim is typing away down there and checking people into the hotel cause there's no one else there to do it. By the third night he's selling tickets to the disco that's up on the roof of the hotel! It was after that that I quit.

Then they brought in a guy named Tom Pope. He did two versions of the script. Next they brought in a guy named Dennis O'Flaherty and they started to shoot. Meanwhile Coppola is in the Philippines doing Apocalypse Now, *Fred Schepisi who is the line producer is in Malta making* The Black Stallion, *so there's nobody watching the store. So there's Wim who's shot all these little movies in Germany with budgets of eighty-seven cents, suddenly here he is on his own in the big city and he's writing scripts in every direction and they're shooting, and O'Flaherty does eighteen scripts. Then Coppola returns, after they'd shot eighty per cent of it, which was the most beautiful footage you ever saw in your life but didn't go anywhere because they kept changing the concept. Wim was hung up on the idea of Hammett the man and he sort of forgot: 'Hey we're doing a suspense movie here, guys,' so Francis came back and he saw the footage and he shut it all down for a year.*

Then Coppola bought Zoetrope Studios, and they built a big elaborate set and they hired Ross Thomas. They showed Ross the footage and said, 'What do we do with it?' He said, 'Junk it.' They said, 'We can't junk it, we've got ten million dollars there.' He said, 'OK, I'll try and jack it up and write a new script and put it underneath. I'll use all of it I can and we'll have to reshoot the rest.' So he did eight versions. That brought the total up to thirty-two scripts and they finally brought it out. And they didn't distribute it or anything. It wasn't as bad as it should have been. It should have been horrible and it wasn't. It was interesting. It just wasn't the film that should have been made from the book.

But in a way that's nobody's fault, that's what happens in Hollywood. I mean I sit here, we start out with a script I write which is one thing, then they take it to Florida and start shooting and come back here and what comes out in the end doesn't have a whole lot to do with what went in. Writers are always fighting for control, control, control. If you have ego problems on that level you shouldn't work in Hollywood, because – TV especially – it's gonna get slaughtered.

Joe Gores talking. Joe Gores is a San Francisco private eye turned novelist. His best-known book is called *Hammett* and is a novel based on the character of another San Francisco private eye turned novelist, Dashiell Hammett.

Running Joe Gores down took a little time. A slew of phone-calls from LA finally revealed that he was not in San Francisco at the moment but in Burbank, just north of LA, at Universal

Studios. So I call him up and he tells me to call by the studios. 'Just ask for me at the Black Tower,' he says and I decide to drive up from LA, stop off at Burbank, and carry on, via Ross MacDonald's Santa Barbara, to San Francisco.

To get to Universal Studios I take the Hollywood freeway north, take the Universal City exit, carry on past the tourist entrance from which they run tours around the back lot, and get bounced from parking lot to parking lot as I try to explain the nature of my mission. Having parked, the Black Tower is fairly self-evident. First though, I stroll around the studios a little, and find that they are a community in themselves with shops and restaurants and full of people with somewhat questionable tans looking purposeful. Ever keen to fit in, I get purposeful myself, enter the Black Tower, ask for Joe Gores and get directed to Bungalow 3H or somesuch. Eventually I find a network of bungalows and, by dint of a judicious amount of standing about looking lost, succeed in entrapping someone into pointing me at 3H.

I knock on the door and hear an indistinct noise which, as I open the door I realize was probably 'Hold on.' Too late, I catch Joe Gores in the act of stashing a voluminous sandwich in his desk drawer. Slightly flustered, he jumps up to say hello. Joe Gores is a short, fat man in an open-necked shirt, white-haired and authentically jolly. Of all the writers I met, he is perhaps the only one who unreservedly comes over as fully contented with his life. Certainly he's the only one I can imagine telling such a story about the making of a movie from one of his books without the account being drenched in rancour.

We leave Joe's office in search of a coffee shop on the back lot. First, however, he leads me into a nearby room. Apparently this was Hitchcock's office. It's plain enough, the kind of size that would barely satisfy a junior vice president of an infotech software outfit. It does have, though, a kitchen and bathroom where Hitchcock could prepare a sandwich or, uh, take a shower. Like all I've seen of the studios, it is surprisingly simple, functional. The glamour is all in the product; the lot is a place conducive to hard work. 'I love being on the lot,' says Gores. 'I often work here alone at night on my other stuff – you can wander around and on the back lots you can find streets you remember from old films.'

As we talk people bustle by with bits of scenery and appear from make-up trailers. Above us a giant Don Johnson billboard beams down as a reminder that the biggest stars in this Hollywood-at-one-remove are those of the small screen. Most of the production here is for TV rather than cinema and my autograph book remains unopened, frustrated by my inability to recognize the leading lights of 'Remington PI' or 'Murder She Wrote'. The back-lot coffee shop is a pleasant outdoor works canteen with an unusually high percentage of regular guys in panstick. We settle down to iced tea and Joe Gores starts talking about his previous job, the one which taught him to enter and drive away a locked car in sixty seconds, the fastest repo man in the west.

'I was living upstairs from a gym and I would go to the gym each morning. It was run by a guy named Floyd Page who died not too many years later. There was a guy used to work out there called Gene Matthews and he was a PI. He used to tell these wonderful stories about all the stuff he was doing every night and I thought, "Jeez, that's exciting." And I thought, "Well, I've got to find something to do that is gonna be fun while I learn how to write," as I'd already realized college wasn't going to teach me. The only way to become a writer is to write and I didn't have anything to write about. I wrote about what you always write about in graduate school: the girl with the pony-tail. So I asked this guy, Matthews, if I could ride around with him at night. He said fine, so I did that for a couple of months, not paid, helping him repossess cars, skip-tracing and stuff. Then I went into San Francisco to his boss, Dave Kichert, and I said I wanted a job as a detective. He said, "You're over-qualified, too much college, college guys don't make good detectives." So I hung around and pleaded and he let me start finding cars. Finally, they hired me. It was $275 a month, a car to drive, and I did that for twelve years, seven years full-time, five part-time.'

Meanwhile, he was always writing. At college that was his ambition. He wrote some short stories and applied to get on the Creative Writing Programme. 'They sent them back and said they wouldn't accept me because: "These stories read as if they were written to be sold!" Which tells you much of what you need to know about Creative Writing Programmes.' After his first couple of years' work as a PI, Gores took some time out to write. 'I went to Tahiti for a year, 1957 I think. I went down on a freighter, went down with another guy; we got a little house, two rooms, $25 a month. Sink was half an oil drum, grass roof. Lived there for a year, wrote and wrote and wrote; finally I sold a story to *Manhunt* magazine. Sixty-five dollars; I was so excited.'

Next up came a spell in the army, two years made a lot easier by a chance meeting with a guy named Willard, making the same journey back from Tahiti. The guy was a member of the Atomic Energy Commission and he told Gores he could probably help him out if he needed it. 'So after I got through basic training I was assigned to Fort Lewis, Washington, up on the coast here. I don't know if you've been there but it rains all the time in Fort Lewis, Washington, 320 days a year it rains. First bar I went into, there was a big sign saying NO DOGGIES ALLOWED. Doggies being dogfaces or soldiers. Then I was assigned to the adjutant general's office, the sort of legal office. When I got there the woman said, "Boy, are we glad to see you. We've got three million file cards to type." And I thought, "Oh my God, two years of typing file cards." So I wrote a postcard to Willard. It just said: "Joe Gores, US 55556748" and the address and I wrote "IIELP" on the bottom, and I forgot about it. Three weeks later the commanding officer calls me into his office, stands me up in front of his desk and says, "I hate guys that suck." And I didn't know what he was talking about. He said, "You guys that pull strings and have influence." I said, "I don't understand." He said, "Here's your orders, soldier" and that was my posting to the Pentagon. Willard had written this letter to the secretary of the army saying: "It has come to my attention that this fine writer is out in Fort Lewis; he could be better used at the Pentagon." What was so funny: as I'm leaving the office, the CO says, "Soldier" – he's a general and I'm a private – "when you're in Washington, remember my name!" I thought, "You sonofabitch, I'll remember your name all right."'

Out of the army, Gores went back to work as a PI. He'd been working under Dave Kichert for a big firm, LA Walker, out of Los Angeles. Walker died and the new management sucked, so Gores and Kichert and three others at the San Francisco office decided to go out on their own, trading as Dave Kichert Associates or simply DKA. Later, when Gores decided to write a series of novels featuring a firm of private detectives, he called them Dan Kearny Associates, thus keeping the same DKA initials. He also kept a decade's worth of great stories locked in his head. 'Yep, I changed Dave Kichert to Dan Kearny and used all the real stories. I saved all my reports, thousands of them, and used bits and pieces for the stories. I'm starting a new one in June called *Thirty-two Cadillacs*, that's based on a real incident where some gypsies ripped off a bank for thirty-two cars. In one day they went to every dealership this bank dealt with and they bought a Cadillac in each. They bought them giving a cheque for a down payment, all the cheques drawn on one bank account that had just enough money in it to cover one cheque, but each time that the agency would call up and say, "Is there enough money to cover a cheque for $800?" or whatever the deposit was they would say yes. So they all gave phony references, and they had a phone room set up, one guy with a whole bank of phones and a whole list of names – each phone would correspond to a particular false name being used at a particular dealership. The phone would ring; he would pick up and say, "Acme Roofing", because that was that phone, and they'd say, "Do you have a Steve Miller?" and he'd say, "Oh yes, he's been with us for twelve years, a very reliable blah, blah." So in one day they drove off with thirty-two cars, no money down, phony names, phony references. The bank came to our agency in a screaming fit and said, "You've got to get these cars back." It was a very intricate case; we dropped everything else for a couple of months and just did that. It was really fun, a lot of exciting stuff. We got twenty of them back, picked one up in Alaska, picked four of them up in Florida, a couple in Hawaii, three or four in Mexico, just all over the place. We had a ball. And that's the story of my new novel.'

The DKA File series are, unsurprisingly, the most realistic series in modern private-detective fiction. The private eye as envisaged by Chandler, 'who walks the mean streets but is not himself mean', is nowhere in sight. Like Hammett's Continental Op, Gores's multi-racial cast are simply doing a job they're paid to do to the best of their abilities. The books are private-eye procedurals, carefully stripping the private eye of the mythic dimension but without losing the excitement and danger that are features of the profession. They are very 1970s books too: grim skewerings of a decade as extended hangover. Gores's San Francisco is not a place to which you would wear flowers in your hair, rather it's a city in which junkie whores in the Tenderloin and fancy lawyers from Nob Hill are tied together in webs of small-city corruption.

Bleaker still is the one book Gores wrote about a lone-wolf private eye, *Interface*. This is a chill book; its protagonist, Neal Fargo, is the private eye as iceman. 'That book came about with the first sentence – "The dead Mexican lay on his back and stared at the ceiling" – that sentence came to me, I wrote it down and I couldn't get rid of it. I was rereading Hammett's *Glass Key* at the time, which is a very cold novel, very abstract, no heat in it at all. Hammett is very careful to do that; he always calls his protagonist Ned Beaumont, never Ned or Beaumont. I thought I'd like to try and create some emotion in a novel where you don't know what anybody's really thinking, you only know what they say and what they do. It is a bleak San Francisco. I did it very deliberately, all of that, and the extended profanity, relentless profanity, it's all done to keep the reader off balance. As a detective you don't usually see the high-class end of town. It's just a matter of the character you're working with. In *Interface* the character is a bleak man. The *File* novels, though, are set in the same areas of San Francisco and those guys are having fun, as I certainly did at the agency. But when you're out alone on the street at three o'clock in the morning and some guy's after you, it's bleak. And there was enough of that over the years.'

Similarly lacking in much faith in the milk of human kindness is Gores's other mid-1970s novel, *Hammett*. *Hammett* is a bleak and playful reconstruction of the corrupt city Gores loves and of a key year in the career of a writer with whom Gores feels a peculiar affinity. 'After I moved into the gym and met the private eye, all of a sudden I was doing the Hammett thing without meaning to. How the novel itself came about: I was driving across the Golden Gate Bridge with my agent, it was a foggy night and I said, "It's a very Hammett kind of night, Henry," and he said, just musing, "Gee, I wonder what the legal implications would be if anyone wrote a novel using Hammett as a character." He was thinking of Lillian Hellman, who was a real tiger with Hammett's memory. But it just stuck in my mind. I wanted to explore that thing of stopping being a detective, starting being a writer; you love them both but with one you're actually doing it and with the other you're making it up. The detective work is more real in a way, but the writing gets to you more, and so there was never any question that once I got good enough to make my living as a writer I quit instantly, apart from working odd days when I needed the money. But I still had a feeling of loss. There's an attitude of mind you have as a detective. It's seldom dangerous but it sometimes is and when it is it's very dangerous. So you have a fearlessness that I certainly don't have today about going down dark alleys, going into places, you know. My partner Dave Kichert, who died in 1984, he never lost that; he would always go in there no matter who he was up against. I was a little more cautious.'

I wondered whether this jolly fat man, whose books feature half-dead whores begging for some pure heroin they can use to overdose on, and retard families torturing kittens to pass a rainy afternoon, sees his work as a little cynical with regard to human nature. 'As a detective I knew that if I wanted to find someone bad enough, I could just corrupt his friends or family by offering them money and they'd turn him up; very often a mother would turn up her son for twenty bucks. Maybe you think it's cynicism; I think it's realism. I look at myself and I see things inside myself that if I was strong enough and bright enough I would certainly change. I don't think I'm particularly susceptible to money corruption or sex corruption because I'm wonderfully happy with my wife and I'm doing what I want with my life, I'm writing, I've had a charmed life in that way: I found out in college that I wanted to do something and, Jesus, I've done it. So in those ways I'm not corruptible but I'm corruptible in other ways. I think we all have ways in which we don't meet the image we'd like to hold of ourselves. Yet you take a novel like *Interface* and it's a romance. It's about a man and woman who love each other. They go about solving their problem in a very odd way, but really it's a love story. So no, I don't think I'm cynical. I think Ross Thomas is a cynic!'

Joe Gores has got to get back to work doctoring scripts for another American cop show about whose merits he seems fairly philosophical. Gores sends his best to most of the writers I'm going to see, laments the fact that James Crumley has never had any of his scripts made ('*Dancing Bear*, that's one of the best scripts I've ever seen') and I head up north towards San Francisco, wondering if it's really going to be the 'rat's nest of junk, alcohol and vice' that the jacket copy for *Interface* promises.

From Universal Studios I drive north on I101, a road that looks appealing enough on the map, but turns out to be busy and boring as hell. The first forty miles or so are the worst; at least once you reach the Ventura exit you're in sight of the ocean. But by the time I reach Santa Barbara, a couple of hours' drive, I'm feeling tired and wound-up.

Santa Barbara was Ross Macdonald's adopted home town. Renamed Santa Teresa, it's the home base for the series of Lew Archer novels that MacDonald wrote between the mid-1950s and early 1970s; books which are easily criticized for consistently reworking the same theme – the past coming back to haunt the present – but which, taken as a series, provide nothing less than a social history of the underside of the southern California you see in the movies. Now another Santa Barbara resident, Sue Grafton, is also using the place (again as 'Santa Teresa') as the setting for an epic series of private-eye novels, this time featuring a female PI, Kinsey Milhone. The first of these was called *A is for Alibi*; the one in the windows of all the Santa Barbara bookstores now is *F is for Fugitive* and, when I meet up with Sue Grafton months later on a train across France, she seems blithely happy at the prospect of continuing on until *Z is for Zero*. She's also one of only two contemporary private-eye writers whom Joe Gores rates as really convincing. Unfortunately, when I call her up on arrival she's busy having her picture taken by *People* magazine, an eventuality she had warned me was on the cards, but is still irritating.

So I take my increasingly ill temper for a stroll around Santa Barbara. And find a place that resembles an unholy cross between what I always expected California to be like, a retirement seaside town on the south coast of England, Hastings maybe, and somewhere snotty on the Côte d'Azur. That's to say boring, wealthy, full of indecently healthy and good-looking blond people and possessed of some quite nice Spanish-ish architecture. The thrift shops are pretty good, though. I pick up a couple of paperbacks, decide against a Levi corduroy jacket and, worn out by the exertion, buy a copy of *Vanity Fair* and sit down in one of Santa Barbara's extensive selection of authentic Italiano-style pavement espresso bars to watch the world go by and read about Ted Bundy.

The world's representatives on the next table are clearly the bad boys of Santa B cafe society. Looking perhaps to feature in *P is for Poseur*, one of them sports a shaved head, goatee beard, tattoos, tanktop and Nautilus muscles; the other looks like Mr Clean-cut American Small-time Coke Dealer in a 'Miami Vice' hat. Both of them try to pick up each girl that passes by, until along comes a big girl who looks like a Sunday-school teacher and turns out to be Goatee's girlfriend. Meanwhile I'm getting fascinated by the pictures of Ted Bundy, a man who would have fitted in perfectly here, in this halfway hippie town: a nice-guy grin, English-teacher-next-door looks. A guy who had no trouble picking up women, and no scruples as to killing them either. Current estimates put Bundy's victims at between twenty and forty. And he went to the chair still asking how people could believe a nice guy like him could have done those dreadful things. This despite being caught red-handed. A psychiatrist is quoted as being upset that Bundy wasn't kept alive, used as a research item for those interested in studying 'the mind of the serial killer'. Clearly the shrink had not read Thomas Harris's novels *Red Dragon* and *Silence of the Lambs* in which the monstrous Hannibal Lecter sits in prison tormenting those who earnestly seek to 'understand him'. Outside of an outbreak of Bundy-style American madness, though, it's hard, sitting on a Santa Barbara pavement, to imagine much activity here that would spark the crime writer; certainly I wouldn't like to try and construct an entire alphabet of such activities.

One conclusion I do come to is that I don't want to drive too much further past yet more of these places called Santa this or that. That and the realization that it'll be the middle of the night before I reach San Francisco propel me to drop off the car at Santa Barbara's airport and catch a plane up to San Francisco.

From the airport I call up a guest house in Chinatown that my guidebook recommends. They've got rooms, so I take a ride in on a minibus which drops me at the door. The guest house turns out to be run by a very stroppy woman with a crop, going under the *nom de guerre* of Bambi, and with a mission to impress upon me the severity of the reprisals were I even to *think* of smoking in my room. I assure her that the odds of my starting up a nicotine habit in a San Francisco hotel room are on the downside of slight, and she eyes me suspiciously. I check into my room, shower, and on the way out ask Bambi for some change for the phone, receiving for my pains the kind of response I might have expected if I'd asked if she had a handgun I could borrow for a little errand.

Out on the quiet mid-evening streets of Chinatown I look for somewhere to eat. Something a little upmarket I think would be nice, and when I see a place with a signed photo of Paul Newman in the entrance-way, that's good enough for me. It's a place called Kan's, and entering the first-floor dining-room is like wandering on set in Polanski's *Chinatown*. It's a dark, ornate room, full of rich men and younger women, occidentals almost all, though midway through the meal a group of Chinese appears from some other, unsuspected room. The atmosphere is sufficiently enveloping as to detract attention from the food, which is little more than so-so.

Later, looking for a drink, I find myself on Broadway in the rain, amid tourist-town sleaze, sex shows for the out-of-towners. A shover-in tries to solicit my interest in naked women, or naked men, or any damned thing my perverted imagination could dream up and he could then persuade me was available inside for a buck or seven and a half. What he didn't offer was a drink, so I pressed on, ending up in North End, the Italian zone where beatniks once roamed. So the streets are now renamed after Corso and Kerouac and if you accost any passer-by and equip them with the first line, 'I have seen the best minds of my generation . . .' they can carry it on for at least fourteen stanzas. Which makes a place pretty unbearable to drink in, so it's a beer then a coffee then bed.

After an indigestible breakfast listening to an Aussie journalist earbash some art-Yanks on the subject of graffiti, followed by the three of them joining together in extolling the virtues of San Francisco as opposed to dirty smoggy tacky LA, I leave the hotel determined to hate the place. First stop is a Chinese bank, where I finally score a roll of quarters for the phone. I want to get hold of one of San Francisco's working PIs; Joe Gores suggested I talk to Dave Fecheimer or Tink Thompson and furnished me with the number of a third eye, Hal Lipsett. Lipsett's assistant holds me on the line while she calls Gores to check me out, and finally divulges Fecheimer's number. I call it and get my call rerouted to a woman who tells me that Dave's in Boston on a case and what's it about? I explain, more or less, and ask for Thompson's number. I explain some more and she gives it to me. Then I call Thompson's number and speak to his machine, say I'd like to meet that afternoon, could he leave a message at the hotel?

The morning gets spent seeing some sights: Chinatown, Fisherman's Wharf, taking a cable car, peering through a telescope at Alcatraz. Which are the kinds of thing you do in San Francisco; like Florence or Bath, it's a preening city which loves tourists to come and admire it. And in its gratitude it provides them with more frozen-yogurt parlours than you can shake a stick at. The whole place seems to be yelling at you: 'Isn't this nice? Isn't this in the best possible taste? Isn't this old-by-American-standards? Isn't this better than Los Angeles?' Then I call the hotel and Thompson has left a message, to meet him at 4 P.M. at his office on Fillmore and Union.

By now I'm over on Market, a downtown shopping street. I walk south a few blocks, till I see the Greyhound station to my left, and suddenly the street's classiness has taken a nosedive, and just as I was wondering whether Joe Gores's San Francisco had been entirely replaced by Frozen Yogurt Heaven, I've found it. This is the Tenderloin, the strip of scuzzbag hotels, peeling porno palaces and semi-derelict topless bars that is the territory upon which Gores's grim *Interface* unfolds. Now, around noon, there's little action around the Greyhound station, just some drug dealers working the graveyard, daytime, shift. There's a few winos stumbling along Mission and a couple of deadbeat bars whose customers have found their level. The impression is, that even as rats' nests of junk, alcohol and vice go, the Tenderloin has seen better days. There's little illicit glamour here, just a quotidian despair.

From Market I catch a bus along Haight Street, heading for Haight-Ashbury, subliminally impelled by watching one too many Summer of Love retrospectives. Along the way the bus passes through the Fillmore, traditional black stronghold, and I remember Joe Gores telling me about one of his scarier experiences as a repo man: 'You come up against a lot of people who say they're going to kill you. That's as bad as it gets for me. I remember two guys once. I was trying to repossess a car; we'd been looking for this car for a couple of months, it was a couple of black guys in the Fillmore. I was just cruising the Fillmore – whenever you had black guys, they'd do a lot of cruising, so you'd cruise around on Saturdays. I spotted this car, a 1955 Dodge in purple and black, and shortly they stopped to pick up their laundry from the cleaners. So I parked, ran over, jumped into their car and I was trying to hot-wire it when both doors open and these two guys jump in.

'There's one on either side, I'm sitting in the middle, and this one guy goes *kershiiiitttt* and he's got a straight razor and he says, "What freeways do you want them to find you under?" I go, "Oh Christ." So what do you do in that situation, you start talking very fast: "Hey guys, there's no problem between you and me, I'm just doing a job. You're just doing your thing. It doesn't mean a thing to me if I get this car or not, no problem between you and me, it's between you and the bank." So they let me go.

'I took their car about a week later. It was really funny; I was cruising around the Fillmore at about three in the morning. The Fillmore was pretty rough in those days. There was a knife fight going on out in front of an after-hours bar on Divisidero St, six or eight guys with knives out there, and I stopped to watch. When I stopped, the car in front of me was the one I wanted. I don't know if they were in the fight or what. I just grabbed the car and took off. Cars were real easy to break into in those days. The average sedan I could open, start and be gone in sixty seconds. I'd use picks and filed-down keys or hot-wire it under the hood, which was real easy. I used a three-prong wire, went from the solenoid to the battery and used a third prong which you just touch to the starter, kick it over.'

* * *

Haight-Ashbury, unsurprisingly enough, is not the boho zone half-visualized from a teenage reading of Tom Wolfe's *Electric Kool-Aid Acid Test*. There are no Merry Pranksters hoving down the street in a psychedelic bus marked Furtha (most likely that's on show in the Haight-Ashbury Museum of Psychedelia, guided tours available from authentic former Moby Grape roadies). It's not even the place depicted in the Mothers of Invention's caustic San Francisco hippie satire *We're Only in It for the Money*, where the neophyte could arrive, kit himself out from a head-shop and sit and play his bongos in the dirt.

What it is is a generic youthzone, like Bleecker Street in Greenwich Village, Camden Lock in London or virtually anywhere in Amsterdam; it's laden down with Vintage Clothing stores, rare-record shops, a branch of the Gap, indifferently stocked and pretentious second-hand bookstores, new-age and occult boutiques, leather-jacket, pointy-shoe and sunglasses vendors, plus a selection of mock-1950s cafes in which to hang out. Walk into any of these stores in any of these cities, not only are the shops interchangeable, so too are the people who work in them and the people who shop in them: hippie punks, punky hippies and Japanese tourists. Maybe because I've spent a lot of time working in precisely this kind of place, I find it fairly comforting. It's like a little piece of home to walk into the Haight-Ashbury branch of Reckless Records and see the same allegedly rare records hanging on the walls as you'd find in their Soho, London branch: the Beatles album with the dead-baby cover, a Thirteenth Floor Elevators original and a selection of early punk singles, items whose value has little or nothing to do with what's on the grooves, existing only to be traded and retraded till one day, the prices having reached the stratosphere, they are all bought up by the rock'n'roll archive of a Tokyo bank.

After this immersion in the familiar it's time for something new: a visit to a real live private eye's office. Josiah 'Tink' Thompson works out of an office on Union St. He doesn't answer his bell, so I sit down on his doorstep to wait. Ten minutes later a stocky man with a weatherbeaten face and a moptop-inspired haircut shows up. I say hello and he, slightly puzzled but assuming I'm some neighbourhood character, says hello and brushes past. I say, 'Excuse me, are you Tink Thompson?' and he looks a little alarmed, doesn't say anything. I say, 'I'm John Williams, come to talk to you,' and he wants to know how come I recognize him. Actually it was easy: he has written a book about his trade and the publishers sent me a press shot. Mollified, he shakes hands and tells me to follow him upstairs to his office.

The office is a two-room flat with big windows giving a great view of the bay, stretching from Alcatraz to the east to the Golden Gate Bridge to the west; as nice a juxtaposition of images as a philosopher turned detective could wish for. Thompson leaves me in the sitting-room while he calls up his answering service. In the sitting-room there's a sofa on which I sit, a couple of easy chairs, a coffee table and some bookcases. The bookcases contain, among other things, a selection of Bay Area detective fiction: novels by Stephen Greenleaf, a lawyer-turned-private-eye chronicler of the 1960s legacy; Joseph Hansen, creator of the first gay PI, Dave Branstetter; and, of course, Hammett – there's a considerable selection of different editions of *The Maltese Falcon*. On the coffee table there's a copy of New York's satirical *haute* trendy *Spy* magazine and in a corner on the floor there's a pile of *Playboys*. The other room, from what I glimpse, has a computer and telephones.

Thompson comes back in clutching a large envelope 'Can you believe this stuff,' he says, tipping out an assortment of diagrams, blown-up photos and a shell casing. It transpires that Thompson is something of a Kennedy-assassination buff. Twenty years ago, he wrote a book called *Sixty Seconds that Changed the World* or somesuch, and now he continues to attract mail from conspiracy theorists. The one responsible for this envelope apparently reckons that he has found the shell casing from 'the shot that really killed Kennedy', which had remarkably lain undiscovered in the centre of Dallas for the past twenty years. The enclosed blow-ups from news photos are meant to demonstrate that what you or I might have taken for a piece of shrubbery or a fault on the negative is in fact the real gunman. What is weird, though, is that, after we've laughed about this, Thompson suddenly brings out his own bafflingly blurry blow-up, points to another indistinct smudge and tells me that that is the real real gunman.

As always seems best in such instances, I smile and nod and speedily ask what he's working on at the moment. 'Present time

I've got several cases on: a death-penalty murder case plus the usual mix, some criminal, some civil. The usual law applies: the most interesting cases pay the least money,' he tells me, talking fast, with a slight edge implying a disdain for the question-and-answer routine. 'The murder case is a triple murder, happened almost two years ago. The defendant was picked off the street the next day. It happened in a Tenderloin hotel, so I'm looking for some people down there, to get some information. One witness last week was staying in an hotel with the unlikely name of the Anxious Arms – couldn't believe that – on Howard and 6th. In this case you first have a hammer attack which is so vicious it removes the victim's left ear, followed by equally vicious knife attacks on two other victims that night, thirty-two puncture wounds. Why? A television set was stolen. Five bucks! The motives are not interesting. That doesn't mean that the case isn't interesting. The case is becoming absolutely fascinating as we begin to unravel the prosecution's case and work out which threads to pull.'

Thompson explains that the bulk of his criminal work is not provided by people coming in off the street asking him to investigate murders, but supplied by the state, which provides funds for the defence to hire investigators to help their case: a low-budget parallel to the prosecution using the police to make their case. 'In this murder case the defendant is indigent and, since it's a capital case, special state funds are available for investigation and experts. I'm contracted; the San Francisco Public Defenders Office contracts its murder cases out to me and I take them at reduced rates. Almost always in criminal cases I'd be employed by the defence; only in certain unusual circumstances are you employed by the prosecution – never by the state, usually by relatives of the victim to get evidence for an indictment. It's a game; the prosecution in a criminal case is charged with coming up with a clear account of what happened and clear proof that the defendant did it. The job of the defence is to undermine that clarity, a job which I find particularly congenial. My job as a defence investigator is to extract ambiguity out of clarity.'

Which provokes the question as to whether he has any standards concerning what kind of person's defence he will work for. Would he see some people as simply too evil to defend? A question which produces considerable disdain from Thompson, a man with Beyond Good and Evil tattooed on his heart: 'Be tough to find one; I've worked for child molesters, rapists, triple murderers. I mean the character of the crime is not of much relevance. What's alleged to be the crime is not something I'm going to consider in deciding whether I'm going to take the case or not. Cases I generally dislike and stay away from are personal-injury cases and the reason for that is they're very sleazy in terms of how the cases are done and the attorneys who do them. So I don't do much of that, even though it's very lucrative. They're sleazebags, those guys. But I wasn't put on this planet to decide who gets put in a cage. I find it exhilarating to be working on the side of the defence in major criminal cases because in those cases you have arrayed against you the full *armamentarium* of the state with unlimited resources and considerable, albeit limited, author-ity; the defence has very few resources and no authority at all. So in that kind of a battle I'm delighted to be on the side of the defence, and the question of whether my client is guilty is not a very interesting question.'

It's becoming rapidly clear that Thompson cannot have a lot of time for Raymond Chandler's notion of the private eye as a moral agent, a notion that has permeated private-eye writing ever since, particularly in the liberal post-1960s school exempli-fied by someone like Greenleaf. And, indeed, when I put this to Thompson, he is classically contemptuous: 'I think the vision of the PI as a moral hero is hogwash; that's Chandler's view, not Hammett's view. Just as a sort of prologue to my answer . . . when Camus described the absurd hero in *The Myth of Sisyphus* as a man who lived a life "without justification or excuse", I think he's describing Spade in *The Maltese Falcon*. I would like to think in my cockier moments that that description would fit me too. I think the detective's life is ultimately that kind of a life, that has to be lived without justification or excuse, because, first of all, if you're dealing with action, excuses don't matter, results do. In terms of justification I don't think you can ever get into a situation in this world where you can choose to do what is justified.

'A good example of that would be the Indian kidnapping (a

case of his in which an estranged father had kidnapped his children and taken them back to India; Thompson eventually succeeding in bringing them back to California). Here, my intervention changed many people's lives. Let's say I had said to myself, "As a moral agent what I have to do is consider the situation under the lens of 'what's best for the child' and I will only do this if I'm convinced . . ." Well, you can't even get to the point where you can ask the question, because it's crystal-clear that all the information you're getting comes from a biased party. You can't look down on human life; all our perspectives are partial. A nice irony – when that Indian case was finished and I got back to the States, a shrink for the woman called me up said, "Congratulations, but you know the mother's a psychotic?" That's the way many cases end up. You want to be a moral agent, go be a social worker.'

At this point Thompson pauses to sneer briefly, before continuing: 'I would reject the notion that there are moral stances in this world and that most people choose to live by them, but detectives live amorally. That's horseshit. I think the real distinction is between lucidity and self-deception. The problem is that once one has that lucidity, that there is no finite justification for anything, then you still have to live. I think the idea of the detective is based in that lucidity, which is why the climax of *The Maltese Falcon* has Spade saying, "I won't play the sap for you."'

In an earlier incarnation Thompson was a philosophy professor, which explains no doubt the unflinching nature of his logic. So, tired of being seen as the agent of moral order, I decide it's time for the obvious question: how did an acerbic philosophy professor like you end up in a job like this? 'Well, it probably has something to do with some psychological peculiarity. It has to do with some sociology too. I came from an upper-middle-class family, had an establishment education, chose one very respectable way to make a living, climbed up that ladder and was rewarded. And, in doing all that . . . I never really believed it, I thought I was cheating. At the end of the *Challenger* report it says, "Nature will not be fooled." I think in some inchoate way I was aware that nature will not be fooled; sure I was a success in that world, but something was missing. What I wanted was difficult to describe . . . otherness . . . some sort of encounter with that which was not wrapped in language. The point of the life of the detective is that it is not cerebral. It is not cerebral even in the way of detective novels, it has to do with sensing the world not in terms of general principles about the world that can then be put together in some sort of theory, but with some much more immediate, intuitive understanding of the way things operate. I think the reason for that is that the world really does not operate within the terms of the theories we lay on it. Theories fail again and again. The detective's job is to go out into the world and effect changes. It has to do with action.'

What it does not have much to do with, Thompson is clearly saying, are the standard fictional representations of the private eye: 'I think TV private eyes are complete caricatures, bear about as much relation to what a PI actually does as Popeye does to a sailor. As for private-eye fiction I think it ends up having the lens of the particular writer. The only commonality is that they are called PIs, that their alleged occupation is that of the private investigator. There seems to be some sort of competition: the next fictional PI's probably going to be a dolphin. Jesus, you can have scientists as PIs, homosexuals, women, priests. Everybody runs the changes; a particular writer knows a lot about oceanography, so his PI is an oceanographer, and his cases will have something to do with oceanography.' The only contemporary PI writer Thompson thinks comes close to the reality is James Crumley.

This seems to be the prevailing sentiment among private eyes. Joe Gores is also unimpressed by most of the fiction: 'There are very few of them that I believe today. I'm trying with the *File* novels to bring it back so that you are writing about what's really happening today. Too many PI novels are written as if we're still in the 1930s or 1940s. It's the guy with the bottle in his drawer. That guy isn't around any more. PIs use computers today, they live in the present. The crimes they solve are the crimes of today. And a lot of people who are writing PI novels, these tough vicious novels, they have obviously never been out in the street and terrified the way you are in the street. They've never had people beat up on them. They've never shot a gun.'

I wondered whether Thompson was tempted to follow the twin examples of Hammett (whom he admires) and Gores (whom he thinks is OK) and write private-eye novels himself. 'If it were possible to do a detective novel from another perspective that would not be just an entertainment but would reach deeper and farther, yeah I would like to do that, but I don't see it clearly yet. I think that takes the form of being captured by a story. I've seen some possibilities in a particular story, but somehow it never works. I went up to the Sierras trying to find a twenty-three-year-old dropout from Princeton, a beautiful young woman who, according to her parents, was a manic depressive who had zonked out on drugs and various things. The particular area in which she was last seen was within a mile of where gold was discovered in California, up in the gold country. I drove up there in a winter storm and started to hunt. I thought this one had real possibilities, the search and what she'd be like when I found her. Well, I got close. I got to forty-five minutes behind her, then twenty-five minutes behind her, and then I lost her and that was the end of the case. I keep thinking that there'll be another one like that. I'm not quickly going to forget how it looked up there. The contact with the woman there was a guy who was running a new-age crystal shop. He presented himself as new-age, mellow, but the more I found out about him . . . He'd only been there a month, been in the music business in Hollywood – and what's going on is a lot of coke dealers are getting out of the business and this looked like the perfect cover. What was funny was that I was conning him, telling him I was a friend of the family, but all the while I was wondering if he was conning me, had her in the back room.

'So that one didn't work out, but I think perhaps there can be a way of telling the surface story so that the background claim is made. One wants a specificity as to precisely the way in which the world is anarchic. If one could get that right, the telling it the way it is, which is what Elmore Leonard does, it would have this kind of resonance to it. That's what I'd like to do. But you don't get there by just talking about it and I don't feel equipped at the moment.'

Now the conversation wanders over the surface of the job, the relation of the private eye to the police (cool unless the eye is an ex-cop; the only friends most real-life PIs have in the police department are ones they buy), the complexity of motivation in rich people's cases and the awful simplicity of motivation in poor people's cases like the Tenderloin murder. Eventually we alight on the question of what his most frightening experiences might be. 'Oh, the standard war stories are not that frightening because they're over quickly. The most seriously frightening adventure I had was in a murder case where I was working for a family member of a woman who was murdered. Her ex-husband was in all probability the killer, but he was enormously powerful. My job for about three weeks was to rattle his cage, to go about on the surface trying to make a case against him, interviewing various people so it would get back to him, bluffing him. That was a very anxious period; he ended up killing our client, four years later, and got away with both murders. So I would shift motels every three days, look under the car, and watch the rear-view mirror. Why? Because it's very very different if you're working a money case, you can assume rationality, but this guy was a psychopath, so I was trying to rattle the case of a madman.'

Next morning I can still taste last night's bad sushi and I decide to take a walk. Up Market, on to Mission, past the Tenderloin, past the thrift shops at the start of the Mission district, to the infamous corner of Mission and 16th where the people stand around waiting for something, anything to go down, and follow 16th to the start of the Castro.

The Castro – a stretch of Castro St heading uphill from here – has long had counter-culture celebrity as the capital of Gay America. It is still clearly the fulcrum of gay San Francisco, and the cafes are full of same-sex couples, but wild it is not. Every counter in every shop or cafe carries an AIDS charity collection box, and too many faces are too thin. The community, of course, is not suffering passively; everywhere there is evidence of activism, of extraordinary communal courage in the face of this horror, but as an outsider it is hard to feel anything but saddened. The cheerily camp California waiter asking me 'Are you English? Bitchin' accent!' raises a smile though, as does encountering, just off the Castro, an emporium called Good Vibrations – new-age feminist sex shop and, uh, vibrator museum. On which definitively San Francisco note I head back to the hotel and onward to the airport.

6

Missoula, Montana: Saturday Night at Charlie's Bar

Sitting at the bar of the Top Hat on Front Street, I make another attempt at calling James Crumley, and for the fifth time I get his answering service, who will once again certainly give him the message as soon as he calls in. It has not been a good day. Most of it has been spent in airports or aeroplanes, including an enchanting stopover in Salt Lake City, where you can't get a drink except with food, which means that the bar does cracking business with a peculiarly repellent line of cookies which apparently conform to the Mormon definition of food. My big mistake was actually eating one of these cookies rather than just piling them up on my plate after the fashion of my fellow drinkers, who had clearly passed this way before.

Arriving in Missoula I was welcomed by a wave of unforced friendliness and the news that my credit card was 'maxed out' and thus rendered me unfit to rent a car. After considerable faffing about, the remarkably helpful car-rental folks manage to fix me up with the local branch of Rent-a-Wreck, who are actually willing to accept cash.

An hour later I've checked into a motel on East Broadway, driven around Missoula's new western suburbs, and inadvertently consumed a Big Mac, in between times attempting to call Crumley. Towards six o'clock I wind up back in the old town centre, walk around a little and decide to rest up a while in the Top Hat, a big dark bar, with a stage at the back and pool tables in the centre. It's quiet and it's dark and after a couple of Dos Equis I've summoned up enough bonhomie to start talking to the laidback longhair barman. I explain I'm here to see James Crumley and he says, 'Oh God, Crumley! He was here just a couple of hours ago. Have you tried him at home?' Well, yes, that's what I've just been doing. 'OK,' says the barman, 'let's try Charlie's.' He picks up the phone and gets what is clearly another bar on the line and asks has Crumley been in? The word comes back that Crumley has indeed been in, has just left and was thought to be heading homewards. Another call to his home is picked up by the answering service. The barman says, 'Tell them you're in the Top Hat.' So I do. And barely has enough time to order another drink elapsed before the phone rings and it's Crumley to say, 'Come on over, Philip'll tell you where I live.' So Philip draws me a map which, while somewhat short on street names and long on directions of the 'turn left by the big tree' variety, still proves serviceable enough.

Crumley is easily cast as the Hemingway of the detective novel. He's a big bearded bearlike man who loves to drink and raise hell and talk about literature. He writes books about troubled macho men, adrift in a world where simple values, a desire for decency, can get you killed; books in which the hero is doomed always to lose the girl in the last chapter, desperately romantic novels of the private eye as the last denizen of the old west; novels in which Missoula, renamed Meriwether, stands as the last simple place left.

Crumley has written only four novels in twenty years, the first, *One to Count Cadence*, came out in 1969 and is rooted in Crumley's time in the army in the early days of the Vietnam War. The three succeeding novels, appearing at intervals of five years or so, *The Wrong Case*, *The Last Good Kiss* and *Dancing Bear*, are all private-eye novels of a sort. All are based around the north-west USA.

This tough-guy romanticism peaked with *The Last Good Kiss*, in which Texan Vietnam vet C. W. Sughrue, part-time PI and part-time bartender, searches the north-west states for a woman named Betty Sue Flowers. The book opens, however, with Sughrue running down an alcoholic middle-aged novelist named Abraham Trahearne, a self-consciously Hemingwayesque bull of a man. Trahearne leads Sughrue through a liver-critical inter-state bar-crawl: 'We covered the west, touring the bars, seeing the sights. The Chugwater Hotel down in Wyoming, the May-flower in Cheyenne, the Stockman's in Rawlins, a barbed-wire collection in the Sacjawea Hotel Bar in Three Forks, Montana, rocks in Fossil, Oregon, drunken Mormons all over northern Utah and southern Idaho – circling, wandering in an aimless drift. Twice I hired private planes to get ahead of the old man, and twice he failed to show up until after I had left. I liked his taste in bars but I was in and out of so many that they began to seem like the same endless bar.'

Chasing Crumley around the bars of Missoula is hardly in the same league, but when I succeed in following Frank's map to Crumley's place there's a distinct sense of relief that attaches to finding him in, drinking a can of Pabst Blue Riband and talking down the phone to someone who would appear to have a) just got married and b) stopped using cocaine, both admissions provoking gales of laughter from Crumley. He puts down the phone and welcomes me in, *mi casa es su casa*-style, fetches some more cans of Pabst from the refrigerator and introduces his kids, two boys, aged around four and six, the product of his now defunct fourth marriage. They're watching cable TV and do their best to look interested in the visitor for at least fifteen seconds. A couple more Pabsts and liquid provisions are looking low, so Crumley calls up a neighbour to come over and watch the kids while we go out for supplies.

The neighbour turns out to be a young man on a motorbike named Steve, a student out at the university. He's brought over a story on which he's working. We leave him to it and head over to Charlie's, where I get introduced to a bunch of people including a man named Denis MacMillan who looks like one of the Flying Burrito Brothers circa *Gilded Palace of Sin* – somewhere between country hippie and riverboat gambler. He turns out to be the publisher Denis MacMillan, the man responsible for one of the most interesting small presses currently extant in the States, specializing in neglected works by crime writers like Charles Willeford and Jim Thompson, and recently responsible for putting out a collection of Crumley's short stories, simply entitled *Whores*. We discuss the possibility of shooting some pool, but by now it's time to leave and put Crumley's kids to bed. On the way out we pick up a crate of beer. 'Just put it on my slate,' says Crumley and the woman behind the bar smiles the resigned smile of someone used to dealing with writers whose income comprises irregular large cheques leavened with long stretches of scuffling.

After all, everyone in Missoula seems to be a writer. The guy in the Top Hat told me his brother had a book out. Crumley's telling me about a great book written by a local cop, James Lee Burke will be moving up here for good soon, there's a major Creative Writing Programme out at the university and then there's the likes of William Kittredge, Jon Jackson, Richard Ford and Thomas McGuane all living within hailing distance.

Back at Crumley's place, he disentangles the kids from the TV, gets into a little horseplay and puts them to bed. Meanwhile I sit around talking to Steve and listening to Jimmy Buffett sing 'Margaritaville' on the tape player. Crumley comes back into the living-room and starts talking about how he finally doesn't care if people call him a crime or mystery writer. 'I used to be ashamed of it,' he says. 'But I look at Elmore Leonard, I look at Ross Thomas, and why should I be ashamed to stand alongside these guys? Great fucking writers!' We're all happy enough to drink to that and the evening starts to blur. Crumley's firing on all cylinders. People from Charlie's start drifting by. Denis MacMillan comes by with a pile of his books for me, for which I'm incoherently grateful. We send out for sandwiches in an effort to moderate the booze, but they take a couple of hours to arrive, by which time it's far too little, too late.

Last thing I remember is digging through Crumley's tape collection and finding a David Allan Coe collection. Coe is one of country music's major mavericks. He certainly did some time in the Ohio State Correctional Facility in the 1960s, and he claims he killed a man while he was there. Others doubt this, but the fact he makes the claim gives you some idea of what you're dealing with. After he got out he built a career as the troubadour of the outlaw biker gang, selling albums of deliberate obscenity through the small-ads columns of *Easy Riders*. Meanwhile he was also writing straight country songs and hawking them around Nashville. One of these, 'Would You Lay with Me in a Field of Stone', was a country number one for Tanya Tucker in 1975, and is as lovely and tender a song as country music has produced. Since then Coe has carved out a career which veers between extremes of braggadocio and self-pity, shot through with moments of something like beauty. His ethos is outlaw country through and through; one of his mid-1980s albums features songs dedicated to no fewer than four ex-wives. I put the tape on and Crumley reacts the way you do when an old friend turned reprobate drunk shows up on your porch and you're half cut yourself. Like 'Oh Jesus, here we go!'

Next morning I'm woken up by some bastard banging on the door at what must be about six o'clock. Wrapping myself in a sheet, I drag myself to the door to encounter a grinning Crumley, looking disgustingly healthy in a sweatshirt and jeans. He tells me it's eleven o'clock, he's taking the kids for breakfast and aren't I coming along? Slowly my eyes start to focus and I notice that the kids are waving at me from the back of the jeep. Half an hour, I plead and go and throw some cold water at my face.

Forty minutes or so later we're in a booth at the Tropicana, a vaguely hippified place near the railroad tracks, the part of Missoula where you turn in any direction and see an Edward Hopper vista. Crumley's jammed on to a bench with his kids, they're both burrowing into him, and he tells me he's taking them back to their mother in a couple of hours. She's looking to find a job out of state, which Crumley is all in favour of, inasmuch as it'll relieve him of a crippling burden of alimony, but which turn of events is also desolating him and the children both. Watching them clambering all over him, in the mood of morbid sentimentality that acute hangovers provoke in me, is almost too much to take, so I speedily order up the giant Tex-Mex-style breakfast, a mammoth plate of chilli, hash browns, sausages, tomatoes and an omelette, which has a sufficiently cathartic effect on my nervous system to put aside sentiment for the moment.

After breakfast we head back to Crumley's for a warm-up beer and to meet Bob Reid. Bob's a detective with the Missoula Police Department and, this being Missoula, he has of course written a book. He's got a copy with him for me; it's a paperback original called *Big Sky Blues* and reading it on the plane to Chicago it turns out that the quote on the back has it about right: 'Perhaps the finest police novel I've ever read . . . wonderful writing, fine characters'. The author of the quote is James Crumley, of course; Missoula writers looking after their own.

Bob Reid is a clean-cut guy in jeans who looks a little like a sporty teacher and, to coin a phrase, not old enough to be the father of teenaged kids. Bob tells me he works violent crime; it's 'more interesting' than the other kind. He just drifted into the police about eight years previously, needing, apart from anything else, the money to support his family during Reagan's first years. He took a while to fit in; he'd been writing before, 'kind of subversive stuff, I guess'. Like Ray Bartell in *Big Sky Blues*, Bob seems like a huntin' fishin' and poetry-readin' kind of guy, so after a while his colleagues figured that two out of three ain't bad. Further suspicion was generated when they found out he'd written a book. But *Big Sky Blues* is no *Serpico*-style tale of one honest cop fighting the bad guys off and on the force with only his trusty magnum to protect him. Rather it is a genuinely sensitive attempt to get to grips with what being a police detective is and, from that, what masculinity is and how decency can operate in an unjust and unfair society. It's not a book in favour of the police or opposed to the police, it's simply a book about the police written by a real writer who is also a policeman. And now his colleagues are coming up to him quietly: 'Bob, let me tell you about the time . . .'

By now it's time for Crumley to get the kids ready to go to their mother's. He suggests I call back around late afternoon; there's something going on at Charlie's. I decide to take my hangover out into the big-sky countryside and, just for reference purposes, ask Crumley if he can recommend a nice drive with perhaps a good bar at the end of it. He tells me that the Lumberjack, out past Lollo on the Idaho road, is the place for me. Bob says, 'Oh yeah, uh, you mean the place where the bikers hang out? Well . . . it should be OK this time of day.' What the hell, I say, enjoying the sensation of invulnerability that goes with having recently and voluntarily destroyed millions of your own brain cells. So it's goodbye to Bob, Crumley stomps off to see to the kids, and I head off in the Chevy.

Out through south-west Missoula, with its shopping mall and McDonalds, past the timber yards on the way to Lollo, through Lollo itself – less a place than two bars and a truckstop – I miss the turnoff, double back and climb for a while up the side of the valley, before turning on to a dirt track for a mile or so. I see a building built entirely from giant logs laid horizontally on top of each other; that's the Lumberjack.

And after a brisk stroll among some very tall trees, a babbling brook and the remnants of the winter's snow, designed to convince myself of my love of nature and devotion to the cult of the body, it's time to venture into the Lumberjack for a little rest and recuperation, I hope non-inclusive of a skull-busting from crazed bikers. Inside there's absolutely no sign of any bikers, crazed or otherwise; instead there's a collection of notably rowdy young people playing pool, drinking beer and singing along to party records on the jukebox, all of which young people, as it happens, or female. I park myself at the bar which, like my seat and the vast majority of the place's furnishings, is constructed out of huge logs.

Nursing a beer, I start to suffer intensely from the strain of listening to Chris Montez's 'Let's Dance' followed by Danny and the Juniors' 'At the Hop', followed by The Contours' 'Do You Love Me', all with whooping accompaniment from the pool crew, so I gingerly make my way to the jukebox and put on my quarter's worth: Rodney Crowell's miserable going on maudlin country ballad 'After All this Time'. The intrusion of this note of beer-sodden gloom doesn't go down too well with the gels, and angry muttering starts up as they try to figure out which killjoy was responsible for putting this on. They're just about to get it right when some other stranger in town walks up to the bar and rings the big old bell hanging there. 'Do you know what you just did?' enquires the woman behind the bar gently, 'because what you just did was announce you're going to buy a round for the whole bar.' And sure enough, there's a faded note next to the bell explaining this quaint local custom. The resultant debate as to whether the sucker should pay up distracts attention from my questionable musical taste and I decide it's time to get back, leaving just as the first strains of my second selection, the Shirelles singing 'Baby It's You', waft from the jukebox. Shame.

Back to Crumley's and he's not there. So, figuring that when in Missoula . . . I head on to Charlie's and sure enough Crumley is holding court at the front of the bar. He's still on a high and falls on me as his nearest and dearest. The place is packed already; turns out this is the occasion of J. Rummel's birthday.

J. Rummel is Missoula's resident artist, and one of his pieces hangs behind the bar at Charlie's, another is on Crumley's wall. He's fifty today and is holding forth at the back of the bar, another big bearded man running to fat in jeans, cowboy boots and a Stetson. The atmosphere in Charlie's suggests a kind of gathering of the clans, following the literal big chill that's gripped Missoula for the past months. The wind-chill factor had brought the temperature down on occasion to minus 100; everyone's been too cold to go out. Denis MacMillan says he's had enough and will move to Hawaii before next winter. Now everyone's jumping at the first chance to get out and party without risking frostbite setting in on the way home. The place is full of authentic 1960s survivors.

History is being rewritten so fast these days that it's easy to believe that the kind of people you see on 'thirtysomething' are 1960s survivors, radicals turned yuppies; in fact, they're 1970s survivors, people who caught the fag-end of the hippie thing, people who maybe saw *Woodstock* when it showed up on TV, but whose formative musical memories are later, of Joni Mitchell and the Eagles. The 1970s generation never sold out, they had nothing to sell. Liking the Eagles and then working in advertising hardly indicates a loss of faith, simply a tendency to go with the flow.

The fortysomethings in Charlie's, celebrating J. Rummel's fiftieth, have signally failed to go with the flow; these are people who used to like the Grateful Dead or Country Joe; now they'll listen to Hank Williams or Patsy Cline. They're people who've mostly been divorced at least once and still come to Charlie's to drink and flirt. It's easier for the men who have, at forty, a range of flattering adjectives available – rugged, lived-in, experienced, worldly – enough to let them try and charm the pants off stray college girls looking for adventure. For the women in Charlie's it looks like murder; at forty you've been married to every damn man you can stand in the place, and so you say what the hell and you try and act like the guys act but you know that sooner than later people are going to tell you you're an embarrassment.

Still at seven o'clock the joint is jumping. As I push my way through the throng, looking for the toilets, Denis MacMillan calls me from the bar, wants to buy me a tequila, so I fall in with him and his drinking buddies for a while. The drinking buddies include an old guy who says he came over here from Ireland to work in the mines, but is too drunk to remember when, and a guy with an unnerving stare, who says his name is Jim and that he's a painter, also he's the short-order cook at the place where we had breakfast. He saw me with Crumley and would like to know what I'm doing here. I tell him I'm a writer and he enquires as to what the fucking hell writers think they know about anything and why they fucking think anyone should pay them for it. I equivocate a little and he debates whether or not to hit me. Fortunately he realizes that in the state of drunkenness he's achieved he is more liable to fall over than connect, so he settles for giving me his life story instead. Turns out he's half-Indian, which maybe explains his remarkable cheekbones, and that he has no money, which maybe explains his antipathy to people who do. By now Denis, wearing a superfine western shirt that turns out to be an early Ralph Lauren, has bought us all further tequilas and beer chasers and my second evening in Missoula starts to blur like the first.

Crumley disappeared at some point to go and have dinner with his new girlfriend. 'A feminist,' he says, 'she keeps me in line.' Denis tells me that Crumley has only two states: 'in love or hurt in love'. A western-swing band starts up and soon the whole place is dancing, apart from those of us welded to the bar. J. Rummel gets up to sing some Hank Williams songs, and there's a commotion when an Angel on a Harley drives right through the bar as a mark of respect to Rummel. By the time I leave, the men are all singing and the women crying into their beer.

Next morning, after another kill-or-cure breakfast and the discovery that even Missoula has a Sunday paper it takes two hands to lift, I decide it's time to try and get some kind of formal interview done with Crumley. So around one o'clock I go and bang on his door. After a minute or so, I hear a grunt and then Crumley staggers up to the door, half-dressed and looking decidedly rough. 'How are you doing?' I say, somewhat unnecessarily. Crumley groans and says, 'You know, you can have too much fun.' He's going back to bed and suggests we meet up in the evening, try and do the interview then. So I decide to go and visit Denis MacMillan. I get around to his house only to find nobody home. As I'm wondering what to do next, a figure with longish fair hair, wearing a white suit and walking a large dog, hoves to. Lo, it's Denis. He invites me in and says he'll make himself something to eat, then we'll go for a ride in the Cadillac he bought from Crumley, maybe drive out down Bitterroot Valley and call in on Jon Jackson, another Montana crime writer.

While Denis is getting busy in the kitchen, he plays me some videotapes of his friend Charles Willeford being interviewed on Miami public-service TV. Willeford is great, looking like a caricature of a gin-soaked old soldier; bald-headed, with a huge, bristling moustache, courteous to interviewers who clearly know next to nothing about him, but possessed of a ferociously dry sense of humour. Denis is clearly much saddened by Willeford's death last year, and tells me with some frustration that Willeford's widow, Betsey, is putting a stop to the exceptionally well-presented series of reissues that he, Denis, was putting out, apparently having acquired a somewhat inflated idea of the commercial potential of her husband's catalogue. By now Denis is ready to go, so after giving me a quick guided tour of his awesome book collection, we head out to the car.

Which is a Cadillac Fleetwood limousine, which may not be as large as a house, but the back seat alone is bigger than certain hotel rooms I've stayed in. It does approximately zero miles to the gallon, but it drives like a dream once we hit the open road, out past Lollo. The Bitterroot Valley is extraordinary, a green I've seen before only in pictures of China. Then we turn on to small country roads heading to Jon Jackson's place. Jackson wrote two books in the late 1970s, *The Diehard* and *The Blind Pig*, both fine urban thrillers featuring a Detroit cop named Mulheisen. Since then it's been hard times for Jackson; his first wife died, he was drinking heavily, couldn't get another novel published. Now maybe things are looking up; he's remarried, quit drinking, Denis reissued *The Blind Pig*, and he's reportedly hard at work in his garden shed. Not today he isn't though; when we arrive at Jackson's place both shed and house are locked up.

Such is life. We head back down the valley, and seeing as it's now late afternoon we stop off at one of Lollo's bars, the Traveler's Rest or somesuch. There's a bunch of bikes outside.

When we go in it turns out that one of them belongs to Steve, Crumley's babysitter of the other night. He's deep in conversation with a moderately serious-looking biker named Mel, who gives us the hard-stare treatment until Denis's Southern charm wins him over. Apparently he and Steve met by the side of the road, where Mel was having something of a bust-up with his old lady, the upshot of which was that Mel and Steve went racing along the road to Idaho, and the old lady got left in the middle of nowhere, trying to thumb a ride home. Which she appeared to have succeeded in doing by the time Mel and Steve came back to see if, as Mel put it, 'she'd learned her lesson'. Mel's clearly enjoying impressing Steve with what a bad motherfucker he is, tells us that he's serving some kind of apprenticeship before joining the local chapter of motorbike desperadoes. Then he tells us about some real bad guys he knows, survivalists living up in the Idaho hills.

Frightening people he says, which is about right. The north west's deserved reputation as the last unspoilt place left has appealed not only to migratory writers but also to that section of American society which combines belief in such things as the literal truth of the Old Testament with a conviction that nuclear war is both inevitable and survivable. Which combination of beliefs leads people to arm themselves to the teeth and head for the hills, there to form post-Manson communities which have a tendency to start killing anyone who comes near them and eventually each other. What is worrying is the prospect of these various communes starting to organize together. This weekend the local papers are full of news about a neo-Nazi skinhead get-together in Idaho. The general consensus seems to have been that it's a hyped-up non-event. But there is certainly some scary shit stirring in the beautiful north west.

Back in Missoula, Crumley is partially revived but obviously down. We head off to Charlie's but conversation is hard work. I make the mistake of asking what's happening with the script Crumley has written for *Judge Dredd, The Movie*. Last time I'd met Crumley, this actually looked like getting made. Crumley had written it, like several previous scripts, with his friend, the director Tim Hunter, and he felt that here at last was a project so copper-bottomed commercial that it had to be made. He should have known better, maybe; he's now been working on and off in Hollywood for twenty years. Each one of his books has been bought for the movies, yet none of his screenplays has been made or his books been filmed, despite Joe Gores telling me that Crumley and Hunter's screenplay for *Dancing Bear* was one of the very best he'd ever read. The trouble this time seems to be that the people with the money had fixated on Schwarzenegger as the man to be Judge Dredd, a part in which you would never see the actor's face anyway, and it turns out that Arnie is booked up to somewhere round the year 2000 and much as he might like to can't do it . . . Talking about the screenwriting now, Crumley is distinctly wearied: 'It's too much work for too little return. When you finish a screenplay, you've put a year's hard work into it and more often than not all you've got is the cheque. It's a survivable experience but not a very pleasant one.'

We adjourn to a nearby Italian restaurant to see if food will liven the conversation up. It doesn't – even the Chianti fails to help – and shortly we abandon the attempt at an interview till first thing the following morning. At which Crumley suddenly brightens and tells me about the time a German film crew came to interview him, but were never able to pin him down at all. On this ominous note he goes back home to get some sleep. Showing rather less good sense, I head back to Charlie's, meet up with Denis, and in the course of the next several hours play some pool, adjourn to a place called the 8 Ball where we can play snooker till it closes, return to Charlie's for several nightcaps and round the evening off back at Denis's, tearing the passenger-side door off the Chevy somewhere along the way.

So at nine the next morning it's a rested, if still subdued, Crumley who has distinctly the advantage as I attempt to conduct an interview.

James Crumley is not an easy man to interview. The turning-on of a tape recorder has a tendency to send him into instant English-professor mode; the simplest query will receive an answer of considerable abstraction, both formal and rambling. This stems in particular from the entirely reasonable desire that his work should be seen as work and not as autobiography. It's a fear particularly well-grounded for Crumley. More perhaps than with any other crime writer outside of Hammett, Crumley's readers want to believe that this is a man who walks it like he talks it. Crumley's heroes are so much the dream apotheoses of every 1960s survivor, so simply romantic. Sughrue in *The Last Good Kiss* is the perfect hard-boiled hero for the fortysomething Vietnam generation.

'Home? Home is my apartment on the east side of Hell-Roaring Creek, three rooms where I have to open the closets and drawers to be sure I'm in the right place. Home? Try a motel bar at eleven o'clock on a Sunday night, my silence shared by a pretty barmaid who thinks I'm a creep and some asshole in a plastic jacket who thinks I'm his buddy.' (*The Last Good Kiss*).

And, of course, what makes Crumley so keen to distance himself from his characters is precisely a sense that perhaps he isn't that far away from them. It's undeniably tempting, the Hemingway idea of the man behind the books being his ultimate creation. In Charlie's a couple of nights before, Crumley was revelling in it. Now he's weary, wrung out from the effort of being the public James Crumley: 'I guess I'm the last writer in Missoula still to spend some time hanging out, to have a home bar. But even I feel like drifting away from that now.'

After talking for a while about writing in fairly general terms, Crumley suddenly shifts up, or perhaps down, a gear, snaps out of literary-interview mode and starts talking about the vicissitudes of a writer's life: 'I've been broke almost all the time. Everybody thinks I'm this successful Hollywood screenwriter now, but that's not even true. Most of it goes on the enormous expense I have for alimony and child support – $2,000 a month is a tremendous sum for me. It's one of life's little ironies that as soon as I get into a position where I'm going to be financially secure for the first time in my life, that doesn't even last a moment . . . that marriage broke up two weeks before I had to go and work on the script for *Dancing Bear* . . .

'. . . I'm a much different person now. I've lived alone for four years and I'm much more careful about, you know, who I fall in love with, and what living arrangements I have. I have more energy and have survived more things than most people, and because of that I've done too many things without thinking of the consequences. I've now learnt the consequences, to say the least. So I'm no longer engaged in domestic disasters. It might make me a better writer, it might make me a worse writer, it might make it impossible for me to write, but, whatever, I'm fairly content with my life, I've lived in this house longer than any house since I got out of high school. This is the longest I've gotten to live in Missoula at one stretch. I always come back here, but always before I've gotten broke and had to go away.'

Not that being broke has simply been part of Crumley's adult life. Given his background, his career is practically the American Dream in action. Like those of C. W. Sughrue, Crumley's origins are in Texas-dirt poverty of a kind few contemporary American writers have experienced. 'Oh, yeah,' says Crumley, only half-joking, 'the only writer in America who is as down-home as me is Harry Crews. I grew up out in the country in South Texas. My only sibling was ten years younger than me. My father worked in the oilfields, my mother was a waitress. I was lucky, during the war, to live in New Mexico so I grew up with Mexican Americans and I didn't have that Texas prejudice when I moved back there. I grew up wearing chickenfeed shirts to school and the only reason I had shoes was because my mother always insisted I wear shoes. I'd hide them under the cattleguard before I'd catch the bus and I'd go to school barefoot. We were country people. My mother wouldn't go to church, she sort of insisted I belong to a church and she would take me to Sunday school, and then she would come and pick me up, but she wouldn't go into the church because she felt that people might make fun of her. This was in a town where the richest people who belonged to the Baptist church made $3,000 maybe! Her father was in prison, my father never finished high school . . .'

It would be a mistake, too, to see this poverty as in some way romantic. As Crumley observes: 'South Texas has certainly lots of charm, but it was never a place I was very happy. It's a place I was always uncomfortable about going back to. Over the last few years I've felt somewhat more comfortable. The part of south Texas I grew up in is different from Texas and different from Mexico. When I was growing up there my home town was sixty-five per cent Chicano yet it was ruled by the Anglos. I found it to be a really repressive and uncomfortable place; also the wind blows all the time and it's unbearably hot in the summertime . . .

It took me coming to terms with south Texas, finding things that I honestly like, to write about it.'

Crumley got out of south Texas by the classic route: working hard and going to college. 'I got a scholarship to Georgia Tech when I got out of high school. At the time, in the 1950s, engineering was going to be the big thing, and I did well in physics. Plus south Texas is tremendously anti-intellectual, nobody reads much, so reading gets to be a secret habit like masturbation. Nobody ever told me what to read, I taught myself, so I had a very odd education. I didn't read the books that influenced me until I was in my mid-twenties. So I went off to be an engineer, but I didn't like Georgia much and I clearly didn't want to be an engineer, and after a year I hitch-hiked back to Texas and joined the army.

'I had a good time in the army but I didn't do well. I was always in trouble. I had the chance to spend a year and a half in the Philippines, ten days in Hong Kong, saw some parts of the country I wouldn't have seen otherwise. I also got busted twice, spent some time in the stockade. I hit a cook one night – he was being snotty to me, army cooks are traditionally snots – I knocked the snot out of this guy. Then I got busted again when I was playing baseball with the base team and we were smuggling cigarettes and Dewar's White Label scotch and stuff like that to sell on the black market. The major who sat at my court martial had moved his entire household full of new appliances from the States, had the army move them for him, had showed a month early to be sure he couldn't have a house on base, got a house off base. One night when he was conveniently drunk at the officers' club, the entire contents of the house and a new Cadillac were stolen. He made about $30,000 on that deal; the most I ever made was about $300. I didn't feel that the black market was a major crime as long as you weren't dealing with medical supplies or weapons. There was a basic problem in the Philippines: we had things they wanted and they were figuring out ways to get them.'

It was only after coming out of the army that Crumley started to make some moves towards becoming a writer: 'I didn't know what was going to happen to me till I was twenty-two or twenty-three and I started writing a story. In the real, autobiographical story my father put a sledgehammer through the top of a mudpump in the oilfield, but as I was writing, and I remember the moment exactly, in the story the father picks up the sledge-hammer and instead of hitting the mudpump he hit the son in the head and didn't kill him but made him into the kind of son his mother actually wanted. Now, my father had only spanked me twice, he'd never hit me or anything, this was nothing out of my past, but it was then I realized, "Jeez, you can write about stuff that didn't happen." It was then that I realized I was a writer and not some kid looking for . . . dust.'

After leaving college Crumley worked for a while before, aged twenty-five, sending a story to the University of Iowa and being accepted on to the justly celebrated writers' workshop there. Among the writers teaching there were Kurt Vonnegut and the great Chicago novelist Nelson Algren. 'He never taught me but I played poker with him a time or two,' says Crumley. More directly influential on his writing, though, was the presence of R. V. Cassill, a prolific writer of pulp novels for the likes of Gold Medal Books and a seminal critic, one of the very few American critics to realize at the time the value of 1950s pulp writers like Jim Thompson and David Goodis. It was Cassill who introduced Crumley to the greats of American crime writing and to the idea that they might be taken seriously.

At Iowa Crumley began writing his first novel, *One to Count Cadence*, a book which drew on Crumley's army experience, and which stands up now as a remarkably mature and considered novel about the realities of war. However, it alienated critics at the time by refusing to propagandize for either left or right. It did well enough, though, for a first novel; it sold to paperback and was bought for the movies, suddenly and temporarily shifting Crumley into an unsuspected tax bracket. But its aftermath left Crumley with enough problems of one kind or another for it to take six and a half years for the next book to appear. Crumley chuckles sardonically going on bitterly when I ask him what took so long.

'That might have had something to do with three different teaching jobs, two divorces, the adoption of my three older children and, back of the row, 800 pages of a novel called *The Muddy Fork*, which I later destroyed. A lot of it was education, I wrote that first novel without really knowing what I was doing. You never get to do that again. Once I knew what I was doing then it became more difficult. I think some of it, too, had to do with the reaction I had from reviewers. As with most first novels, it was soundly ignored; those who did take time to review it, with a few notable exceptions, took sides – it came out while the war was still going on – it wasn't anti-war enough to suit the left and it wasn't pro-war enough to suit the right. It was ambiguous, which was maybe necessary. I'm not sure what it would be like if I wrote it now; it might be somewhat more anti-war, anti-military; more compassionate of the Vietnamese people and also less forgiving of them. A lot of people hated that book when it came out. I had put everything I had into that book and it looked like it might sell some copies, it sold to the movies . . . then all of that fell apart. The producer ended up not paying me a third of the money. That caused me a great deal of trouble, cost me a house, a couple of cars, and sent me back to teaching.'

The key problem in Crumley's career, though, seems to have been the pressure of literature, the desire to do something truly epic and great, a desire strong enough to lead him to burn far more work than he has ever published, and a desire that must have made him hell to live with. The complexity of Crumley's domestic arrangements at this time make it amazing that he ever wrote anything at all: 'My first marriage broke up two days after I finished the first book. I married again a year or so after that. It broke up four years later, and then I was living with a woman in Colorado when I was writing *The Wrong Case* and then that broke up. By the time *The Wrong Case* came out I was married a third time. As happens when you're young, you don't understand the emotional energy that goes into things like that. It seems like it might be civilized but it takes more time than you realize. It made it difficult to write. I finished *Cadence* here, moved to Arkansas, moved back here, moved to Colorado, moved to Seattle, moved back to Colorado and moved to Texas before *The Wrong Case* came out.'

The Wrong Case was Crumley's first detective novel. It was intended as a one-off, a way to cure his writer's block and make some money at the same time. 'It was something I started when I realized I was going to quit teaching at Colorado. It seemed quite quick and easy to do.' It introduced into Crumley's fiction both the town of Missoula, disguised as Meriwether, and the character of broken-down private eye Milo Milodragovitch, the alcoholic scion of one of the town's founding families. Milo will be rich when he reaches the age of fifty-two, when he comes into his father's legacy. Meanwhile, he's been scraping a living doing divorce work and destroying his self-respect. But, as *The Wrong Case* opens, the divorce laws have been liberalized and he's contemplating ruin from the vantage point of the bottom of a bottle. Milo is a man much taken advantage of; in both books he appears in, *The Wrong Case* and *Dancing Bear*, he is set up to be the patsy, never sees the big picture till the end. But his progress is an effective illustration of the maxim that you can't con an honest man, even if he is behind the game by enough coke and booze to stop a regiment.

Milo is also the character closest to Crumley's heart: 'He comes from the good side of my unconscious; at the worst moments of my life I think, "I can't be a horrible person because I invented Milo." He takes care of things, he takes care of all the drunks in the town, he's kind of a saint. None of Milo's background is mine, but I'm sure it's somehow connected metaphorically, in the search for the lost father. When we came back from the war my father was off working all the time in the oilfield and I never saw much of him. He was a very quiet, gentle man and my mother was a very forceful, violent woman so I got an atypical American upbringing. I'm sure the things I write about Milo and his father, or Sughrue and his father, come out of my feeling when my father died thirteen years ago. But,' he hastens to add, 'none of the experiences are mine; I'm a writer not an autobiographer.'

I comment on the disparity between Milo's social origins and Crumley's, to which he replies, 'The rich and the poor have more in common than the middle class. That's one of the funny things in the *Kinsey Report*. About the only people who were engaging in oral sex, or at least admitting it, were the highest-income groups and the lowest. My friends say that Milo's the character that reminds them most of me. Whether in his good-heartedness or his self-destruction I don't ask!'

The Wrong Case wasn't a one-off; both the novels Crumley has written since have been crime novels, more or less, but it has only been lately that he has stopped regarding them as a waste of his potential. The book he's currently working on is another version of *The Muddy Fork*, one that will have some kind of crime format. 'I'm trying to do a new book, an even less traditional detective novel than anything else I've done. It's more of a family novel, in the Faulkner sense rather than the domestic sense, narrated by the Sughrue character.'

This latest version of the south Texas novel Crumley has been trying to write since the early 1970s stems from his discovery of an attempt he made at writing it in thriller form in the late 1970s, right after *The Last Good Kiss*: 'I discovered the opening fifty-odd pages by accident, didn't even know I had it, because I had burnt or thrown away most things. On rereading it I discovered I couldn't see why I stopped, so I went back to it. I suppose, at the time, because of a certain feeling that you get sometimes in academic circles that detective novels are a lesser form, I felt like I was giving this novel short shrift by using it as a detective novel. I no longer feel that way. I no longer not only do not have the notion that the serious novel is more important than the detective novel, I can't remember why I ever had that notion. Must have been crazed, ignorant or stupid to have fallen prey to the cheapest kind of intellectual snobbery.'

Now Crumley has come round to the view that the detective novel has a particular usefulness in dissecting modern-day America: 'You can do what you want in a detective novel as long as it's entertaining and interesting. I've never been much interested in traditional crime, solving a mystery. It's a nice literary conceit, but most crimes are solved because somebody rolls over, somebody grasses. It's like the courtroom novel; most things never reach the courtroom, way less than a third of crimes are ever solved and, of those that are, more than half are plea-bargained.

'The real criminal thing that happens in *The Wrong Case* is simply a personal failure. In *The Last Good Kiss* I think the real crime is a sort of literary arrogance on the part of the Trahearne character. Then there are other kinds of crimes in *Dancing Bear*: the dispersal of toxic waste across an entire countryside, for instance. There are other things: international arms-dealer cartels, the sort of casualness with which greed seems to rule things out there, but I've been out of politics too long to feel qualified . . .'

Qualified or not, Crumley is always keen to talk politics and his books, while scarcely overt revolutionary texts, have politics as a continual subtext. Crumley, like his characters and like the people he hangs out with, is a man who was changed for ever by the political upheavals of the 1960s and, while he may be disillusioned, he is certainly no born-again Republican. Crumley's 1960s did not begin with the hippie period either, but came out of the militancy of the civil-rights period and the attraction of the proto-hippie beat lifestyle centred around San Francisco in the late 1950s, which Crumley came into contact with while waiting to be shipped out to the Philippines. 'I was in San Francisco waiting to go overseas in 1958. Had I had a little more control over my life I would have stayed there when I came back from the Philippines. But I had to go back to Texas for six months. Then I got engaged to a woman there, went to college there, played football for the college as a linebacker . . . Also there was a kind of prejudice against California, full of kooks and nuts and freaks. So while the 1960s were going on I had long hair and I did a lot of drugs, but I didn't identify with the movement in any great way. In my most political days when I was in the SDS (Students for a Democratic Society), what I liked best about it was that middle-class kids discovered how the police had been treating blacks and Chicanos and poor people all the time. Suddenly middle-class white kids from Evanston Illinois were getting their heads busted. I think it changed the way America looks at itself. It was a good time, it was a revolution that failed but made some significant changes.'

As the 1960s wore on, though, the pitch of Crumley's political involvement slackened: 'I was ready for revolution at the point of a gun, then I realized I didn't want to kill anybody. It took the edge off my politics and I backed away somewhere in the early 1970s. I stayed active in the Vietnam veterans against the war. I donate money for environmental things, I try to save what's left of the west. Mostly it's money and time, whereas in the 1960s it was passion. I'm not sure which is better. Once you discover that you're not going to blow shit up . . .'

And a degree of scepticism as to the usefulness of much of the

1960s idealism crept in, a suspicion that much of it boiled down to rhetoric and posturing, summed up today by the way in which Kennedy's memory is revered as a secular saint, while Lyndon Johnson is firmly consigned to the dustbin of history by both left and right. 'I never much admired public figures. By the time Kennedy was president I knew enough about history to know he came from the most corrupt political machine anywhere in the world and I knew what kind of guy he was. He thought he was untouchable, he could fuck any woman he wanted to, nobody would say anything about it. I don't think he had any ideals at all. Lyndon Johnson was someone who grew up in the same town my parents did. I liked Lyndon's programmes and ideas, but he was the kind of guy who would sell you a pair of socks and there'd only be one sock in the package. But every now and then I try and remind myself that we got Lyndon Johnson not to run again and what we really did was to elect Nixon. Being right is not always the best thing there is; being thoughtful and kind is more important than being right.'

The interview is winding up now, and as ever it degenerates into both of us coming out with political commonplaces and the kind of literary conversation that tends to run along the lines of 'Have you read so-and-so?', 'No', 'Oh, well, they're good'. Then Crumley tells me that he's recently read a thriller – *Ladies' Night* by Elizabeth Bowers – put out by a feminist publishing house and he's looking to pick up an option on it and, together with his girlfriend, work it up into a script, to see if he has better luck getting someone else's book made. By now he's cheered up somewhat, and feels like summing things up: 'It's nice now I'm forty-nine, to feel it's OK to be an outsider; all through my youth I always wanted to belong. I was a juvenile delinquent, a football player, I was on the student council, I was on the yearbook staff, I was in the army, I went to a good college on a scholarship. I went back to college on a football scholarship, I played everything but quarterback, mostly I was a linebacker. I grew up learning to run into people at high speeds.'

On which note we walk outside to inspect the damage I'd done to the rental car the night before. Which provokes, one more time, the James Crumley laugh.

7
Chicago: 'That's About As Cold As It Gets'

Sara Paretsky is a woman who wears aviator shades and has discovered, at forty-two, the appeal of American football as a sexual spectacle for women. She is also a shy woman who combines diffidence and elegance in more or less equal measures and who worked for some years for an insurance monolith before making her name as the prototypical author of detective fiction with an avowedly feminist slant with a series of novels featuring PI V(ictoria) I. Warshawski. 'I wrote the first one in 1979. That really came out of several different impulses. I had wanted for years to see if I could actually write a novel and you get to be thirty or thirty-one and you realize that a lot of the things you thought you might do simply aren't possible any more. In your twenties you think you're immortal and will always be at a high level of physical ability so you can defer making choices – and then you come to the realization that you are going to die. It seemed to me that the time had come to see what I could actually do, to stop living a fantasy life.

'I decided to write a detective novel because that's what I mostly had read, so I knew them better than any other kind of writing. And I very much wanted a book with a female protagonist because, particularly in American crime, it's hard to find a woman character you can really identify with. I tried a couple of things that didn't work and then one day I was in a management meeting – you know when you're in middle management you're really the baloney in the sandwich, you have to execute the really dorky ideas of your seniors and get people who don't have any desire to be at work to do them. So there I was, sitting listening to this real conehead that I worked for, pretending that I thought he was a genius while the balloon over my head said, "This is so stupid I can't believe it." Then suddenly I just had the idea that

I would have a detective who was not a parody of Spade or Marlowe but just a woman doing a job that had traditionally been done by men. So she would be facing the typical difficulties but she would have the advantage of being able to say what was in the balloon over her head because she doesn't have to worry about being fired. I wanted her to be very Chicagoan, which means very ethnic, so I gave her a Polish father. I'm not good with ethnic last names so I thought, "OK, Warsaw's in Poland, so Warshawski is bound to be Polish," though people tell me it's not. Anyway it's Polish to me.'

Sara Paretsky scared the hell out of me when I met her outside my hotel on my first morning in Chicago. Missoula had left me a physical wreck, and a night spent in a fleabag motel in a nowhere suburb of Chicago listening to glass breaking, deals going down in the parking lot and screaming children had done little for my mental equilibrium. I had too many clothes on and the sun was out; still it was probably the residual alcohol in my blood which was causing me to sweat like a pig. I arrived at my new hotel in the city centre late, just at the time I had arranged to meet Paretsky, having intended to leave time to shower and change. Instead I'm stood in the office, checking in and dripping sweat when this purposeful woman in huge shades and a mass of frizzy hair gets out of a car and approaches, holding what gradually reveals itself to be the new Margaret Atwood novel.

Oh shit, she's here already, I think and, completely discomfited, do what I generally do in such situations: behave with staggering rudeness, grunting rather than speaking. Without realizing or intending it, both of us have succeeded in thoroughly intimidating the other and the first half-hour or so we spend driving around Chicago is distinctly sticky.

Sara Paretsky has now written six novels, all of them featuring V. I. Warshawski, a character who, as ever with the fictional private eye, has elements of the alter ego. V.I. has a background working for an insurance monolith, she's an anglophile, a dog-lover, has similar political views to her creator and started out at around the same age though, again in the private-eye tradition, she seems to be ageing at about half normal speed.

The fact that the novels are centred around the character of V.I. is both their abiding strength and potential weakness. A strength inasmuch as V.I. is emerging book by book as a tremendously convincing heroine, a woman holding her own in a man's job in a man's world. But a weakness because if, as the likes of James Ellroy or Tink Thompson suggest, the male PI hero is fundamentally unbelievable, then that goes double for a female character. And at first V.I.'s credibility as a working PI was somewhat lacking; Joe Gores proposes the descriptions of firearms as an acid test of whether the author knows what he or she is talking about, and one of the acknowledgements at the start of Paretsky's third novel, *Killing Orders*, runs as follows: 'Kimball Wright, enraged by repeated errors regarding the Smith & Wesson in V.I.'s previous adventures, provided me with better information about the weapon.'

Paretsky, though, in a way that is pretty much analogous to the likely experience for a woman in real life becoming a PI, is learning as she goes along. However, she is well aware that the convention of the private eye is not strictly realist: 'In some ways my books are very unrealistic, in the things that V.I. does. I sort of think that a significant thing for women is being at home in their own bodies, and the idea that – of course it's becoming increasingly difficult for anyone of any sex to walk on any street in America – the idea that you don't have to worry about what street you walk on would mean that the goals of feminism have been achieved. In a way V.I. acts out of what I idealize; she's someone who doesn't have those fears, which is really not true of any woman I know. My ground rule is that she will not be sexually assaulted at any time, and of course that's not realistic with the kind of risks she takes, but it's something that's important to me.'

The hotel I'd found was just north of the loop, Chicago's business district and, after dark, muggers' heaven. The hotel itself was blandly similar to every other down-at-heel motel I'd stayed in, just three times as expensive, reflecting the incredible lack of halfway bearable, low-budget hotel accommodation in the city. V.I.'s office is down in the loop, but first we're heading north towards the area she lives in, the gentrifying near north side. It's a pleasant neighbourhood with a lot of trees, big houses, mixed population. Its major north–south artery is Clark Street, which has its share of the trendy restaurants, second-hand record shops and comic stores which signify a neighbourhood in transition from multi-ethnic to yuppie via bohemian; but for now it's a relaxed area well served with good diners and containing, at its northern end, Wrigley Field baseball stadium, home of the Chicago Cubs and something of a shrine to Paretsky, who is a major baseball fan: 'I think that the high point of my life so far was when I was selected to play third base for our baseball team when I was twelve. I was a great fielder but a terrible batter. Great on defence, that's my story!'

From there we swing west; Paretsky wants to call by an abortion clinic that she's been helping out at. As we speak the Supreme Court is engaged in deciding whether or not to uphold a challenge to the legality of abortion. That abortion should be freely available is a cause she believes in passionately, and she's worried. Her feeling, which turns out to be correct, is that the Supreme Court will hand back to the individual states the right to make abortion illegal, potentially meaning that abortion would be unavailable outside a couple of liberal states like New York and California. So she's been demonstrating and organizing in favour of a woman's right to choose. The day before she'd been down at the clinic to help combat an anti-abortion picket. Today she wants to see if there's any more trouble expected. As we drive she expresses her concern for the men involved in demonstrating for abortion. She's worried that if they're arrested, they'll be thrown into Cook County Jail, a place where the weak or naïve scarcely prosper. Rape, she points out, is not something that happens only to women.

All turns out to be quiet at the clinic and our conversation moves on to the question of how politics, in this case specifically feminist politics, should influence the writing of a mystery novel. 'I think I wanted to write a novel, that was my first goal,' she says. 'I have very strong political beliefs on a lot of subjects other than feminism. Actually I was thinking about this last week, that even though I'm opposed in general to all these -isms, feminism is sort of a religion for me, I suppose, a kind of organizing principle. But still my first goal is to tell a story that is interesting and has characters the reader can believe in. I find that when I take my characters seriously, they have points of view that I wouldn't accept if I was working with them. In *Killing Orders*, which is partly set in a Dominican monastery, I found that I was being empathic with these Dominican friars in a way that I wouldn't . . . I mean my older brother converted to Catholicism and became a Dominican, which is why I picked that denomination, but they really get on my nerves when I go and visit them at his monastery. But when I'm writing about them I have to see their point of view. So my books are more political than a lot of people like but they're not as political as I am. I mean I'm not interested in writing political tracts and I'm certainly not interested in reading them – I can write essays and I do do that – but for me telling a story is in a way more valuable than writing an essay. I don't think you ever understand exactly what's happening in your life – or anybody else's – but telling a story about it makes it clearer than any description can, at least for me.

'So that's why I like to write stories and having them be political is not a very great goal of mine. Actually I've been wrestling with this, I've been approached to write a short story for an anthology, and I have a short story that I kind of like about this man who lives with these two horrible women, his wife and his mother, and what happens to him. I was feeling a little bit chicken about sending this in because the feminists, who are my major supporters, might be offended by it. I was thinking, do I have the guts!'

Now we're heading towards the near west side. The south side may be Chicago's largest and best-known ghetto area but the near west side takes some beating for concentrated grimness. Along the way we pass a high school where Paretsky has been involved in setting up a birth-control clinic, hoping to bring down the unbelievably high pregnancy rate, an initiative that is now in severe jeopardy. Next we encounter some local landmarks: the Cook County Courthouse, the Cook County Jail and the Cook County Hospital. Each of these is bleaker than the one before. The hospital looks grimmest of all; it's one of Chicago's few public-health resources and an icy reminder that in America you get the healthcare you pay for. Sara Paretsky tells me about her stepson, a machinist who lives and works in a Hispanic neighbourhood, in which he has something of a reputation, there not being a whole heap of other 6' 4" blonds in the locality. He's her main source of information as to what's happening, as they say, on the street – with the gangs and all. He's also self-employed and without healthcare, because it would cost him $5,000 a year. So if he gets sick or hurt he is, bluntly, fucked. Paretsky is less than impressed with this state of affairs. Her fourth novel, *Bitter Medicine*, vividly illustrates the extent to which running medicine as a profit-based industry is in the long-term interests of virtually nobody.

Bitter Medicine also features an absolute rainbow coalition of women, blacks, Jews and old people fighting back against the inhuman manipulations of the WASP doctors. Unfortunately the effect is ultimately more hopeful than realistic. I wondered whether the multi-hued array of good guys'n'gals was influenced by the politics of Jesse Jackson – perhaps Chicago's most famous resident. 'I think the idea of the rainbow coalition seemed possible when Harold Washington (Chicago's first black mayor) was alive; I think it's largely disintegrated since his death. I found him a very hopeful figure; he brought out the most hopeful side of people. I don't think there's anybody on the political scene right now, white or black, who can generate that kind of feeling. Jesse Jackson is not a very popular figure in Chicago; we see him too closely. I don't know . . . he's the ultimate opportunist, I guess. I was writing *Bitter Medicine* early in Washington's administration, maybe that influenced me.'

Washington's (black) successor, Mayor Sawyer, signally failed to capture the hearts and minds of anybody at all, and in the lead-up to the upcoming mayoral elections the Democratic nomination, traditionally a shoe-in, had been wrested back for the Chicago establishment by Richard Daley, son of the infamous Mayor 'Boss' Daley. From out of the south side, however, a challenge had emerged from Alderman Tim Evans, running as an independent with the full weight of Jesse Jackson behind him. The election is imminent as we speak but Paretsky is hard pushed to work up much enthusiasm one way or the other. Daley, she reckons, is basically stupid, a man whose Spanish-language election posters are so badly translated as to be meaningless. Evans, on the other hand, she sees as a charlatan, happy enough to radicalize the black proletariat, but preferring rhetoric to practical help that might lift them out of his automatic electorate.

Heading back in towards the centre we pull up in an old Italian enclave, a few spacious red-brick blocks surrounded by factories and the elevated railroad tracks ('the el') that are the defining feature of inner-city Chicago. This is where we're having lunch, in a dark, airy and half-empty-at-this-time-of-day Italian restaurant that firmly subscribes to the Italian-American habit of ladelling an insanely large quantity of sauce on to your pasta. Having battled my way through as much of this as my ongoing hangover would stand for, and resolved to impersonate a decent human being by joining Paretsky in drinking mineral water, we're both starting to relax a little and begin to figure out that both of us are nervous, not trying to be cool. Up to now I've been having trouble producing anything much more coherent than a grunt and Paretsky has a diffident way of talking. She's halfway into a sentence before it's actually out of her mouth, hurrying as if she's afraid of boring you. Still, things are flowing a little better now and after I mention that Denis MacMillan in Montana had told me that he had been taught by her father in Kansas, she starts talking about her background.

'I was born in Iowa in 1947. I grew up in eastern Kansas. My father is Jewish and was the first Jew to get tenure at the University of Kansas. In those days there were zoning laws that were very restrictive as to where blacks and Jews could live in the town, so my parents bought a house in the country, which was wonderful for my brothers – four brothers, three younger, one older. It was great, uh, I don't think I'd want to live there as an adult, but as a child it was really wonderful. I went to a two-room country school and all that . . .'

Kansas in those days, however, was scarcely a hot bed of radicalism of any kind, certainly not feminism: 'My father grew up in New York and he never really adjusted to the Mid-West – he certainly never adjusted to not having a building superintendent to call in when things went wrong – but my mother's a good ole Mid-Western girl and in the Mid-West in those days girls grew up to be mommies. And if they were going to work they were secretaries or school teachers. My father insisted when I was sixteen that I get a secretarial training, so if I didn't marry I could support myself. Well, I won some scholarships and went to the University of Kansas, which had always had a tradition of education for women. And there I fell under the influence of a rather radical Dean of Women. I think a lot of parents, like my parents, their sons they would send away to expensive eastern schools but their daughters they'd keep close to home to see they didn't come under evil influences. Ironically enough, we couldn't have had a more radicalizing influence than this woman, who had made it her life's work to electrify Kansas women.

'That was my first introduction to feminism, at the University of Kansas from 1964 to 1967. Under her leadership I chaired the first university commission on the status of women and got involved in a lot of research on wage and salary issues. It was in 1964 that the Civil Rights Act was passed, banning discrimination on grounds of race or sex, and later, first under Johnson and then under Nixon, surprisingly enough, there were several executive orders that really put some meat into it. I came to Chicago first in 1966 to work on an inner-city summer project and then moved back permanently in 1968. I worked for a small firm that did conferences on affirmative action and how to implement it in universities and corporations, that kind of stuff.'

So she arrived in Chicago just in time to catch the city at the most turbulent point of its recent history, when the civil-rights movement exposed the degree to which segregation in Chicago, bastion of the Democratic north, dream destination for millions of Southern blacks, made the Southern variety look half-assed. In particular the western suburb of Cicero earned itself a reputation as the most racist township in the whole USA, a place that Chicago blacks had learned to avoid at all costs. 'I was here in the summer of 1966,' Paretsky remembers, 'when Martin Luther King came to Chicago, marching for open housing, I was working in a white community on the south-east side, a blue-collar Lithuanian community, which happened to be where the King march went, and I think it was my active involvement in that community which made me want to move to Chicago. I didn't have any sympathy with the racism, but I also felt that . . . these blue-collar workers who had put their life savings into one thing, their little bungalow, voted for Mayor Daley routinely; nobody cared if they lived or died, certainly Daley didn't – he never *did* anything for them, it wasn't like his home ward where people got patronage jobs and that kind of thing – these people were left to rot, for all anybody cared, so I could sort of see both sides of the issue. On the other hand, it was a predominantly Catholic neighbourhood; the local Catholic church could get 4,000 people to mass on Sunday. The Sunday before the march the pastor preached in favour of open housing and the Sunday of the march they had 200 people instead of 4,000.'

This neighbourhood, known as Hegewisch, is where Paretsky chose to set V. I. Warshawski's roots. And in the fifth Warshawski novel, *Blood Shot* (published as *Toxic Shock* in the UK) she returns to those roots to discover, among other things, something of what she loved in the place and more of why she left it. In Paretsky's Hegewisch men range from the violent to the broken, women from the strong to the stubborn.

This is where we're headed after lunch. We take the inevitable expressway that carves through the middle of the huge south-side ghetto. Off to our left are endless housing projects, high-rise blocks where the youth get their kicks by sniping from the upper blocks at anything foolish enough to move around without a tank for protection. There was no need for the projects to be built, Paretsky tells me, but there was profit in it, and Chicago runs on graft. Daley proclaimed it the housing of the future (God help us all if he was right) and Daley's friends got richer. Business as usual in a city where corruption is merely routine. 'This is Chicago; last year the chairman of the Cook County Board, who has a tremendous amount of importance and patronage, a man in his seventies, appeared in a news story. It wasn't even a scandal, just a news story, about how he was having sex with women in exchange for them getting jobs on the Cook County payroll. So at the next meeting of the County Board he got a standing ovation. People thought it was wonderful that old George could still get it up in his seventies, and that was the limit of the political fallout. This is a city where it really doesn't matter what you do. The Mayor of Milwaukee practically had to resign his job because he had attended a $100-a-plate lunch when he was a council member, given by somebody who was a lobbyist for the city. People in Chicago were just rolling in the streets. I'm not going to pretend it's any different to that in the resolutions of my books. V.I. is not capable of changing that, she's only capable of doing some very small things for individuals.'

Turning off the expressway on to Stony Island, we head south into a jungle of heavy industry and its side-effects. The road degenerates into a heavily potholed track, and we bump around, dodging flying trucks as we head through an area of landfill, grey grass covering God knows what kind of chemical waste, towards Dead Stick Pond. Dead Stick Pond is a key location in *Blood Shot*. V.I. is left for dead there while investigating a local chemical company. It's a bleak enough place, looking like a location for a film set in the immediate aftermath of nuclear war. What amazes Paretsky is that despite its devastating man-made forbiddingness rare birds still come here to feed.

So too do people hang on in Hegewisch, just a little way north and east of here, the place that provided the labour when all around here was the hub of American industry. Now that the States has given up on manufacturing – American capital preferring the Pacific rim where no one hears of union organizing – Hegewisch remains as a dormitory community bereft of a place to go in the daytime. The potholed streets are lined with little wooden-frame bungalows, bargain-basement American dream homes. Paretsky points out one of these; on Houston St and painted yellow, she tells me it's the one she imagines as V.I.'s childhood home.

Heading back northwards on I41 along the lakeshore fringe of the south side we're on our way to Paretsky's home in Hyde Park. Along the way we pass the South Shore Country Club, a Gothic tribute to Boss Daley's ego, a symbol of exclusivity in happier days for the area. Now it's semi-derelict, given back to the people; today it's deserted, bar a few black kids playing crazy golf. As we're driving I ask Paretsky what she reads. 'Books about people surviving in extremity,' she says, 'I want to be prepared for being taken off to a camp.' And suddenly she is talking about her father, who is Jewish, and was a hard man to his family. His hardness she feels was born out of the sense of futility brought by the knowledge of the Holocaust. 'This probably sounds really pathetic, but I think that the guilt of those who were never in the camps is something people should be aware of.'

This is the kind of heavyweight territory that she would like to explore in her writing. Whether such ambitions are compatible with writing detective fiction is something that is starting to bother her. Particularly as she has recently signed a contract with Dell that is considerably lucrative but commits her to writing several more V. I. Warshawski novels. 'I've been writing nearly my whole life. I learned to read when I was four and I've sort of been writing since. It took a long time for me to think about writing for publication, and it's still kind of an awkward issue for me. I'm going through a fair amount of personal conflict right now because writing for me was always something private. It was a way for me . . .' she pauses here, suddenly looking almost stricken, 'I hardly know how to say it and I don't even know if you care, but writing for me was a way I could develop some personal space for me inside, a way of buffering me against the world around me. Now my books are getting popular and I write under contract. And I've found that writing under contract has destroyed the personal aspect of my work and I don't really know how to fix that problem. I worked for many years for this large insurance company and I wasn't economically dependent on my work and in a way it was much better. It's nice now, not to have to work downtown, but on the other hand I'm not independently wealthy, so to pay the bills I sign these contracts . . .'

Ironically, too – and maybe here is something of the truth about writing – she has also got far far better as a writer even as the thrill has gone. *Burn Marks*, the latest in the Warshawski series, is a modern thriller that neither begs nor needs special pleading. It's as good a Chicago novel as has recently been written; certainly it compares favourably with anything lately produced by the man who lives opposite her but never says hello: a professional pessimist by the name of Saul Bellow, a man who neatly symbolizes for Paretsky the smug American literary establishment.

Home for Paretsky is in Hyde Park. Hyde Park is a strange enclave in the south-side poverty. Its *raison d'être* is that the University of Chicago is set squarely in the midst of the south side around 57th Street; and Hyde Park is essentially the area between the University and the lakeshore. For a long time it was a lone beacon of integrated housing in Chicago. It is still integrated today in a toney kind of way; not only Saul Bellow but also Jesse Jackson live here. And it's more than pleasant; it's leafy, it has second-hand bookstores, it has students on bicycles, it has little Victorian-style carriages that ferry tourists around, and it has some quite remarkably pretty buildings. One of the prettiest of these is lived in by Sara Paretsky, her husband Courtney Wright, a physicist at the university, and their dog Cardhu. Inside, the house has been painstakingly restored to its original American Gothic glory. Courtney, who has lived here for years and is responsible for most of this restoration, offers me a glass of sherry while Paretsky goes to run off a copy of an autobiographical piece she has just written for an anthology.

The piece is a straightforward and moving account of the difficulties of becoming a writer when your childhood, spent on a farm in Kansas and occupied almost entirely by schoolwork and looking after two younger brothers, has left you with two distinct impressions: one that as a woman you don't measure up – hair too frizzy, body too ungainly, ergo you're a tomboy; and two that as a woman your creativity should be confined to the making of cakes and babies:

Male writers such as Sartre and Bellow have recorded knowing early in life that their destiny lay in literature. Bellow knew he was 'born to be a performing and interpretive creature', Sartre that he was born for words. I call myself a writer, but feebly, without conviction. Where did they get this sense, I wonder? Were their childhoods spent like mine? . . . Was Jean-Paul or Saul's first responsibility to look after the little children – to spend summer vacation and evenings after school taking them for walks, changing their diapers, feeding them, reading them their stories?

Now Paretsky has a talk to give on women crime writers, so she arranges for Courtney to give me a ride back to the hotel. Driving north along the lakefront we pass the various Chicago museums and the art gallery with all the Impressionist stuff in it, which is, as they say, a must for every visitor. I express my eagerness to go and visit all these places while suffering the sinking feeling that comes from knowing you're the kind of person who, given the choice between whiling away an hour in a sports bar or a major art gallery, will take the sports bar every time. Courtney is charming, some way older than his wife, and keen to talk about England, his parents' birthplace. He drops me off at the hotel; I thank him for the ride and he's gone before I realize I'm still clutching Sara Paretsky's map of Chicago in my hand, an accidental souvenir.

In the hotel I make a couple of decisions. One: I want to change hotel; two: I'd better hire a car. Tomorrow for all that, though. By the time I've had a bath and made some phonecalls, it's time to go out and take a look at Chicago after dark. Clark Street, says my guidebook, is the place to go for chic young things so, hell, I'm on my way, see how it looks by night.

On arrival, however, there is less than a good deal happening: a couple of discos outside which congregate brattish sixteen-year-olds trying to look twenty-one, no bars, and several restaurants which look better prospects for posing in than eating. Still, I reckon that a man has to eat, so I decide it's time to treat myself and head into a plant-bedecked, *nouvelle cuisine*-ish kind of place, where I have a perfectly pleasant meal, interrupted only by the attentions of Craig. Craig being the name, assuming he was telling me the truth, of the guy serving me my food, a chap with a hairstyle ruffled just so. Craig made a succession of fine contributions to my index of sycophantic waiting practices with such gems as, when taking away my first course, informing me that the chef was even now working on my next course. Yes well, I should fucking hope he is; if he *wasn't* working on my second course then maybe that would be news. Then, after the obligatory ceremony of the admiration of the English accent, comes Craig's big scene: the moment at which I bring out my credit card to pay and he spots that we have, gasp, the same surname. That's Williams incidentally, not Cholmondley or Krzywycki, but Williams. There's no holding Craig back now; clearly we are soulmates and Craig is ready to reveal all. Actually he's not really a waiter but . . . an actor. Well, goodness, gracious me.

One whiskey sour in a bar down the street, populated by business-student types who have discovered that with a CD jukebox it is possible to put on a whole side of the Doors' first album as often as you like, and I realize I'm dead on my feet.

In the morning I once more consult my guide to getting by in the USA with not much of the green, and discover that Chicago suburbs are recommended for cheap motels, provided you have transport. Which is how, having rented another car – some kind of Toyota – I happen to be headed for the western township of Brookfield, Illinois. How come I then found myself driving due north up Broadway is harder to explain. The result of my sense of direction being around ninety degrees out was that on a Broadway corner, up towards Uptown, I ran into the aftermath of an outburst of gang warfare: blood all over the street, cops wandering around and people standing around looking grim. It turns out that the blood belonged to a black sixteen-year-old called Marlon Wade. He was leaving a party with a group of friends when a Hispanic gang showed up to continue some kind of feud with some black guys at the party. Marlon was no part of it, but he was the one who ended up dead when one of the Hispanic gang decided that these guys leaving the party would do, and opened fire on them. A couple of days later there's a memorial service at Marlon's school. His grandmother says, 'If I could have two things, that is to let Marlon come and be here for five minutes. The other I'd want is the one who killed Marlon . . . I'd hug him and tell him just what I told Marlon, "Son, I love you."'

Whether this level of Christian forgiveness will be practised on the street is another matter. Marlon's friend Timothy Dodero is quoted in the *Chicago Tribune* as saying of the Puerto Rican students at another high school, who were believed responsible for the attack, that 'they will just as surely feel the pain'. Already Hispanic students are staying away from Marlon's high school, afraid of retribution. And so it goes on in a country where high-school students can take advantage of the inalienable right of each and every American to arm him- or herself to the teeth.

Having mentally and physically reoriented, I take the expressway out due west to the Brookfield Zoo slip. Out here it looks like semi-countryside, prime suburbia, but it turns out that the hotel I'm looking for is a little further on. A little further on and I'm out of Brookfield and into Lyons, which is some way less salubrious. What Lyons is mostly is a bunch of gas stations, truckstops and flea-bitten motels strung along Ogden Avenue, a not-what-it-used-to-be type of thoroughfare. One of these motels, the Pioneer, has its name in my book. So blind faith tells me that it can't be as bad as it looks (i.e. mean, peeling and grim as all get out). It looks deserted and semi-derelict, ready to cater to transient truckers from hell; the note on the office door says RING AND WAIT. So I do and, after a while, a Shelley Winters type emerges from the recesses. I ask if she's got a room for me. She looks at me for a while and says, 'Sorry, son, but we're all booked up, got a convention coming through tonight.' Which is, I guess, a polite enough way of saying, 'Son, believe me, you do not *want* to stay here. It is cheap but there are *reasons* for that.'

Then she tells me that there's a nice place a little way down the road, and with the relief that comes from not being allowed to do something you were dreading, I head on down. The nice place turns out to be the Chalet Motel, a little piece of Chicago that is forever Switzerland. That is it Swiss motels habitually offer you a room called the Warm-up Hutch, complete with a hot tub (nudge), king-size (nudge, nudge) waterbed (nudge, nudge, nudge), 'your own VCR for relaxing pleasure' (elbow in your ribs) and two TVs (two TVs? Why?). The brochure on the check-in desk suggests you consider taking a 'leisure retreat' in the hot tub. Presumably 'leisure retreat' is salesman-speak for 'piece on the side whom your wife will never find out about because you've taken her to a motel in Lyons, for God's sake'.

I decline the once-in-a-lifetime opportunity to stay in a Warm-up Hutch and persuade the man with the booze-stricken face on the desk to check me into a regular room. After a few lengths in the tackiest, not to say smallest, swimming pool I've ever seen it's time to get back into Chicago central, eat some original Chicago pizza at Pizzeria Uno and go shopping. Shopping takes me back to Clark to the first of a string of bookstores that leads me northwards back on to Broadway, where the blood is still on the road but the police have left. Further into Uptown I park under the sign of the big old Uptown cinema, a classic piece of cine deco. Everyone around here looks lost; this is where the Appalachians and Native Americans tend to wind up in Chicago, the country people who've found themselves in the wrong place at the wrong time. Take a picture of the Uptown cinema and the folks lying on the pavement beneath and you could call it the Home of the Blues. Probably someone already has, urban deprivation still being a favourite magazine topic; providing it's sufficiently photogenic, of course.

Hard by the cinema is a used-book-and-record store called Shake Rattle and Roll. Inside I run into a couple of blokes who work in a record shop in London. They're here to buy up the jazz and soul records that America has discarded but attract the attention of collectors in London. So the rest of the day gets spent with Mark and Alan taking in some record stores and ending up in Delmark Records, just north of the loop, where I buy a Chet Baker LP and Alan spots veteran jazzman Eddie Harris hanging out, gets him to autograph an album. Then it's on to Chicago landmark foodstop Ann Sather's for a very pleasant hamburger, to a sports bar near Wrigley Field to watch a ballgame and drink Leinenkugel, a moderately unpleasant beer from Minnesota, and back out to the Chalet Motel, fighting sleep all along the Dan Ryan expressway.

Back at the Chalet Motel the previously empty parking lot is now full of motors of the kind bought by people who believe a car should say something about you: 'I'm a dangerous bastard' in most of these instances. Morning comes around and none of the cars is there any more. Strange, huh?

Eugene Izzi has the kind of logical explanation I was afraid of ... 'Jesus, how come you're staying out here?' he asks. 'Lyons, Jesus, this used to be a hell of a place around here.' Turns out that Lyons was for years the wide-open town that every major city likes to have adjacent, the place just outside of the city limits where all the bad stuff can happen – the gambling and the whoring and the and so on – and the city fathers can tut tut, shrug in despair, and leave well alone. So Lyons was an all-night kind of a place where all-night kind of activities could be indulged in. By day, too, it was none too far from the Sportsman's Racetrack. And of course, what with one thing or another, this made Lyons a popular hot spot with businessmen of an I-talian persuasion.

All this Eugene Izzi, the hottest new name in American crime writing, tells me as we walk out of the hotel lobby to the spot across the road where he's parked the first fruit of his sudden and dramatic literary success: a brand-new Lincoln. Big as a tank and quiet as a mouse, this is the state-of-the-art vehicle for the man who has come up the hard way, and is sure as hell going to get the car he dreamed of when he was a kid, not some candy-ass environmentally sensitive Euro-pean-type car.

Izzi is somewhere in his thirties. He's wearing an old army jacket and his characteristic pose is hunched up, hands in pockets, 1950s-hoodlum style. The effect is to make him appear slighter than he is. In fact he's a solidly-built six-footish type with workout muscles; man likes to box. He has the confidence that comes with six books in three years, two of them currently under production as movies, but he's some way off flash. He may drive a Lincoln but he's still in his army jacket and says, 'You see this shirt, John, pretty good huh? Cost me seven dollars.'

We decide to head towards Downtown Chicago, driving all the way along Ogden, the scenic route. A mile or so down the road we cross the Des Plaines river. Izzi tells me about a paedophile named John Gacey who dumped a bunch of bodies there, as an overflow after dumping thirty-three in the basement crossways from his home. This being a guy who was known as the life and soul of the party: a contractor, a clown, a Democratic precinct leader, got his picture in the papers with Rosalyn Carter. 'You never know,' says Izzi. 'I've got a book coming out called *Invasions*, in which I really go into what creates a monster. We create them. American society creates them. We turn our backs, pretend it doesn't happen. After the deal came out with Gacey suddenly all the neighbours knew there was something wrong; the same people who were going to his parties and drinking his booze and eating his food. Henry Lee Lucas is another one; this is something that could have been stopped at the source. Before this guy was a teenager he was killing animals and having sex with their corpses. It's hard for me to believe that nobody noticed and even harder to believe that nobody did anything. He begged, "Don't let me out of prison," but they let him out ... now he's copped to about 300 murders. [Recent evidence suggests Lucas may have invented his career of mayhem.] The bad guys in *King of the Hustlers* started out as kids who used to hang up in trees and put little nooses around birds' necks. I caught some bum raps on that but, you know what, I knew guys who used to do that.'

It's not only guys who go out and murder children that Izzi sees as psychopaths: 'I think most organized criminals have psychopathic tendencies. There was a major mob boss in Chicago named Sam Giancarna. He was rejected from army service during World War Two. They said he was a raging psychopath – and in World War Two they were taking people with one eye!'

Unsurprisingly, this attitude, coupled with his belief, clearly expressed in a book like *Bad Guys*, that while the law may be corrupt, there are still good guys and bad guys, and that bad guys, specifically Mafia bad guys, are scum who need to be wiped out, has failed to endear him to the Honoured Society. 'I made my opinions on the mob clear in the first four books. Now it's time to move on. I paid the price for it; I get phonecalls, I have to change my number every few months. I just moved house; this car's registered to a PO box, my driver's licence relates to a different address . . . I cover my tracks. There's a difference between paranoia and caution.'

Driving down Ogden, we pass some spectacularly dubious nightspots including a steak'n'cabaret joint done up as a castle, with crenellations and all, before passing through Cicero, blue-collar Italian, a faded industrial suburb, once a byword for racism and still probably not a good place for a black man to buy a used car after dark.

After Cicero we're inside the Chicago city limits and we've gone from blue-collar white to black and Hispanic ghetto. The near west side around Douglas Park is simply despairing. In Paretsky's latest, *Burn Marks*, V. I. Warshawski is scared half to death to visit a witness around here and it's easy to see why. Buildings are burnt or boarded up, fortified or derelict. Storefront churches and liquor stores are about all that hang on. As we drive, Izzi starts talking about the legacy of the Reagan years on racial politics in America: 'When Reagan was elected I worked in a steel factory. I was working with this black guy, seemed intelligent enough to me, and one day he says to me about Reagan, "You know why a man that age has got a full head of hair? It's so you can't see the 666 on his forehead!" There's a culture there believes Reagan was the Beast, the Devil, keeping black people down. The last mayor, Gene Sawyer, had an aide who was putting out tapes for Farrakhan's church, making the statement that Jews were injecting the AIDS virus into black children as a form of genocide. On the other hand I can show you neighbourhoods where you say "black guy" everyone says "nigger, rapist, thief". Nobody individualizes.'

I mention the killing in Uptown the day before and he talks about the way black-on-black killings are seen as barely newsworthy while black-on-white killings are horrorshow headlines. Then he tells me that he has been up all night writing some stuff set in Uptown. 'Did you know Andrew Vachss lived in Uptown?' he asks. Vachss is a New York child-abuse lawyer who writes thrillers featuring a survivalist PI involved mostly in child-linked cases. I'd already mentioned to Izzi that I'd interviewed Vachss before and was scheduled to meet him again when I got to New York. It turns out that Izzi and Vachss are very close; Vachss had in turn mentioned me to Izzi, and was, I now realized, the man who had first mentioned Izzi's name to me. I say I didn't realize he'd lived in Chicago. 'Yeah,' says Izzi, 'he was organizing there with Saul Alinsky years ago.' Which is fairly serious popular radical credibility, and further evidence of Vachss's uniqueness among thriller writers. Of which more later.

I ask Izzi what other writers influenced him. 'The biggest influence on me was Elmore Leonard. I was writing this serious art shit until I read *City Primeval*, which I think is probably the best crime book ever. I realized then that if a book is good the art comes. The Gigi Parnell character in *Bad Guys* is a homage to Clement Mansell from *City Primeval*.' Then, without the tell-tale pause that too often accompanies this kind of statement, he adds, 'Naturally not as well done.' When Leonard was in Chicago for a book signing Izzi wanted to get one of his signed. Too embarrassed to go along himself, he got a friend to go. Now he's really pleased because Leonard had heard of him, sent his best. 'When you reach that level, people either become stone assholes or very supportive,' he observes.

Izzi is genuinely modest about his writing, is amazed that anyone should put him up with the big names, the Leonards and Higginses. Partly this is because he hasn't been at this game long enough to slip into any kind of arrogance, but also it is an attitude that seems to be common to those writers whose backgrounds determined that, as Paretsky put it, they never saw themselves as being writers, certainly not professional writers. Certainly, of the writers I've met so far, it is Izzi and Haywood and Paretsky who have the least sense of themselves as 'writers'. Izzi goes on to tell me that while he hit with his first published novel, *The Take*, it had been no easy road: 'I was broke until 1986. For the last three years I've supported myself writing, the first ten I did it for free. I started writing seriously in 1977 when I got married. I had won an award in the third grade for writing, I came from poverty and that was the only good thing that I can remember from school, the one time the teachers tried to encourage me. Now I'm scared if I stop writing I'll lose it.'

Now Izzi is starting to realize that having come up the hard way has its benefits. In contrast to the Tom Wolfes of the literary world, Izzi's research needs to be done only at the top end of the social scale; the lower end is just as clear as can be in his memory. 'I know my people. They aren't cartoon characters, everybody's a composite of people I've met. Panther Payne (sadistic, slobbish rent-a-sidekick from *King of the Hustlers*) is an example of a guy – who's still living so I don't want him suing me – he pulled up in this car one time when I was a kid, I was standing on the street outside the poolhall. So this maniac's looking at me, he smiles, throws what I assume is a cigarette out of the window. It was one of those cherrybomb deals, and it lands right by me in the alcove. I thought I was deaf. The guy that was driving hit the brake, and there's four guys sitting there waiting to see what I was going to do. I didn't do nothing, looked away. Many years later, I'm about twenty-six or twenty-seven, drinking in a bar; the same guy, who is now a junkie, comes in this bar which is owned by a guy named George. He wants to sell me a hot television set. I say, "No, you got anything real, you think I'm going to do seven years over a TV set?" I took my drink to the john and suddenly here he comes – ba-doom, he hits me. That wound up in the book. Naturally I had him killed off in the end. The real sonofabitch, he's still living.'

By now we're closing on Downtown and suddenly Izzi swings the car north. 'OK John, now I'm going to show you a place.' The place is a housing project named Cabrini-Green. I tell him I've heard of it; the place has its own kind of fame, even had a rap record dedicated to it:

Everything is mean inna Cabrini-Green

If you've been to Chicago, the near north side
Here's a piece of advice, man, just down ride
In a bus or a cab down a street called Division
If you do ride thru you made a very bad decision

You walk across the black top, you prolly get shot
You're bleeding to death but the cops won't stop
Cause you're just another victim of black killed black
And another black death and they like it like that

One of my best friends got shot in the back
While trying to get out of Cabrini-Green shack
Sang lead vocals for Electric Force band
He never gangbanged, just took the mike stand
I never will forget my friend Larry Potts
Or the terrifying night when he got shot
(Sugar Ray Dinke – 'Cabrini-Green')

Cabrini-Green is a housing estate set among a collection of road junctions and rail lines. It consists of several medium-rise blocks, fifteen storeys or so, set in a square. For at least the first couple of storeys of each block the windows are broken or boarded up. In the middle is a bit of scrub grass where we park. Izzi keeps talking: 'Cabrini-Green is supposed to be the baddest of the housing projects in America. The west side is very bad, the south side is a terrible ghetto area, but for concentration this is the worst there is. People live here. They're niggers now because they're raised like this. It's not fair, it's not right, it's not only immoral, it should be illegal. To put people in sardine cans like this and expect them to grow up to become brain surgeons! To these people we're either cops or drug dealers. There are three or four gangs that patrol here. At night I wouldn't bring you here, wouldn't bring the car here, though a couple of bullet holes might give it character.'

This time of the morning the place is yesterday's battleground. On a wall someone has spraypainted the name Arise. That's the name of the white-trash gang in *King of the Hustlers*. Izzi thought he'd made it up. 'Hey,' he says, 'hey.' Meanwhile nothing's happening, which is OK by me as there's nothing I can imagine happening here that could be good news.

So we get back in the car and head eight blocks west along

Division Street. The great Chicago institution Studs Terkel, radio broadcaster, writer and maybe the best interviewer of 'ordinary people' alive, wrote a book called *Division Street USA* which uses the street as a stand-in for America. It's not hard to see why. Eight blocks east of Cabrini-Green and we're on Astor Place, the classiest street in Chicago, lined with Victorian town mansions. Given the right wind you could hang-glide from a Cabrini-Green rooftop to an Astor Place lawn. We walk round the back of Astor Place and the alley is covered in graffiti, the walls topped with razor wire; to keep the wolves out.

Izzi tells me how the Hollywood folks who are making movies out of *The Take* and *Bad Guys* came out to Chicago. 'There were some guys came here scouting locations for one of the movies, and I took them to Cabrini-Green. They'd never seen anything like it. They go: "What are those holes?" I say, "Those are bullet holes, what do you think?" and they go, "Let's get out of here."' Which, in turn, is farther than William '*French Connection*' Friedkin, the director of *Bad Guys*, managed. He wouldn't even venture into the Astor Place alley. 'I tried to get Friedkin out here. I said, "Come out and walk with me, I want to show you the alleys." He said, "Guy, even when I was a kid I saw myself in mansions, not alleyways." I knew right away we were not going to get along.'

From Astor Place we take a walk, wandering through Chicago's Gold Coast, a neighbourhood that Izzi, who's from far south Chicago, down Hegewisch way, says he barely knew existed before he started researching the last couple of novels. He talks constantly about the price of the houses: 'You know they spent four and a half million just on renovating this house, John, four and a half million!' Then we head up towards Lincoln Park, to take a stroll along the lakeshore. Izzi says that walking is the only thing that will keep him awake. He hasn't slept at all, just worked all night. Usually he sleeps in the day.

Up to now Izzi has been cagey about talking about his background. Recently a Chicago magazine ran a piece on him as a literary freak, a criminal turned novelist, and he's really unhappy about it. Now he's keen to stress the marginal nature of his criminal career. 'I've been known a time or two in my life to spend a night in gaol, but never any serious time or any major problems. Still, I know what it's like to get beat up by the cops, I know what it's like to be in a place where I'm not supposed to be, where I could definitely lose a piece of my life if I got caught. In the days before I got married nothing mattered.'

But now he seems satisfied that I don't simply want to focus on sensationalizing his life story and the barriers start to come down when I ask him how he got to here from Hegewisch: 'Hegewisch is economically falling apart because the steel mill has closed. I worked in the mills for years. I was considered a part-time guy till I got lucky with the writing. There, when people lose their jobs, they don't lose their pride. People round here lose their jobs, they're jumping out of windows. You know what money does: it takes away your money problems, that's all. I was a very happy man after I quit drinking, being with my family. In 1983, drinking had me so bad, my wife Lisa left me, took the kids, wouldn't let me see them. I lost the apartment we were in, I wound up sleeping on the floor of a barber shop. I would wash his windows, and the guy would let me sleep in the back room, his toilet, I was sleeping in his toilet. I decided that's enough, I quit drinking and we got back together. Up to that point I had done some things, stealing things, stuff like that. I said, "If I'm going to be straight, I'm going to be straight all the way." We rented a house from a friend of mine; behind it there were some woods. I'd go out there with an axe and chop down the little trees for firewood and go down the streets selling the firewood. That supported us, Jesus, for a year till I went back and got a regular job again.'

Now Izzi lives out in the suburbs in a nice detached house with burglar alarms and dogs to keep out the bad guys and woods where he can run when he finishes writing for the night. Hegewisch, meanwhile, is a place he had to get out of. 'I got together with a guy from Hegewisch, hadn't seen him for fifteen years. We put our heads together, came up with thirty people we knew who had died violently or from drugs. That seems a little high.' One of the dead was a guy named Charlie, Izzi's best friend in his teens: 'I got out of the car; ten minutes later he was dead. That's what taught me not to make friends. Fact is, I like my dog more than I like most people.'

Izzi's passionate belief is that your background may be crucial but it need not be decisive. Like Andrew Vachss, though, he believes that a vast amount of criminal behaviour is rooted in the abuse of children. He tells me about a dinner he went to recently with a cop friend of his, where some politician started talking about the gangs as the city's number-one crime problem. 'I'm much more concerned about the guy down the block fucking his kid in the ass than I am about guys with colours on their heads kidnapping people off the streets – which I just don't believe is happening anyway. And I don't believe the big problem is drugs, either; shit, I was twelve years old seeing junkies. But if we could just stop the abuse of children I tell you seventy-five per cent of crime would stop.'

Linked to this is Izzi's big hope for his writing: that maybe the kind of book he writes ('If you want symbolism go see a Bergman movie; I make it as simple as I can') may get read by the kind of people he used to be and will, just maybe, make them make some connections. 'There's even a possibility I could make a difference, not yet but down the road. When I reach my potential . . . the first books were light punches, jabs, but if I get as good as maybe I can get, somebody might read that and say, "Hey, this is the way it really is." Like I was in the fourth grade looking around and thought: "How come nobody else has got a black eye? Nobody else has got a broken fucking leg?" Then it dawned on me: *other people aren't beating their kids!* That was a big revelation to me. Later I was in the army and I got overseas and found out that not everyone's a drunk, not everyone's a vicious fucking . . . my father was in prison a lot and that was a relief to me; when he was out he used to terrorize us.

'I think I was married a year before I told my wife I loved her. Up to that point I thought it was a scam that people who had stuff made up. Now I want to dispel some myths, I want to let people know that you can overcome this shit, you're not stuck. I was twenty-nine, John, I really believed I was too old to change. I thought; "I'm stuck, I'll never see my wife, I'll never see my kids. I may as well go and fucking die."'

Suddenly we realize we've been walking for miles, up past Belmont Harbor, so we turn and head back towards the car. I'm dying for a cup of coffee. So Izzi says, 'OK, I know a place.'

Eventually we wind up on Michigan, Chicago's swankiest shopping street, and we head up into the Bloomingdales shopping mall; the kind of place which has some guy in a lounge suit tinkling away on a Steinway to entertain the shoppers as they take a croissant and a breather in between deciding which set of Louis Vuitton luggage to buy for their cats. It's the kind of place that tends to feature in Izzi's books. Generally being turned over by some Italian hard guys from Hegewisch.

Back in the Lincoln we're driving down Wabash or maybe Ohio. We pass a hostel and Izzi tells me about a black guy, no legs, lives there, gets about on a cart, guy with a lot of spirit. Other week a bunch of so-called gangbangers decide to have some fun: they flip him off his cart, rob him, rape him, beat the shit out of him. 'That's about as cold as it gets,' says Izzi.

By now he's visibly exhausted. And we quietly retrace our route back to Lyons. He leaves me with the inevitable Hollywood story, Eugene Izzi style: 'Staying in Hollywood, I was going up to my room and this fella says, "Shall I send up a girl?" and I say "No." He says, "How about two?" He's being tough, impressing me. I say, "No thank you, I'm not into that." He says, "Oh, oh, a boy." I say, "No, I just want to be alone." They think I should be grateful, they think they're giving me something by offering me flesh that I never met before. It's enough to turn your stomach. Thank God it's taken so long before I got to this stage or I'd be into that, that's the kind of man I was. Miserable, oh God was I miserable, always thinking about suicide. Staying in that barber shop, at night I'd be spinning round in a chair eyeing those razors – if I get drunk enough it won't even hurt. Thank God I didn't. Look what I would have missed. My God, I've got a woman who loves me, I've got kids who actually want to grow up and be like me. At night when I finish working I go out, run a couple of miles, then I come back, see the trees, see the house, see the Lincoln . . .'

And that's it. Izzi heads home to get some sleep. I pick up my stuff from the hotel and head on out to the airport. On the way I listen to Studs Terkel's radio show. At the end of the show he signs off like this: 'Take it easy, but take it.'

8

Detroit: Where the Weak are Killed and Eaten

At the Motor City airport I picked up the best and the cheapest car yet, a maroon Buick with a mock-mahogany dash, and swing on to the Edsel Ford expressway, heading for downtown. I have not been looking forward to this leg of the trip. You tell people you're going to Detroit and the first thing most of them say is 'Why?' Driving in, I'm envisaging something like the nightmare New York that John Carpenter created for his film *Escape from New York*: a place of decay and violence.

On my left there's a sign to Inkster: the town that Ford built outside the city limits when he bowed to the economic necessity to hire black people to work on his production lines. However, he wasn't having no nigras living in the nice model housing developments he was building for his white workforce, so he built a shanty-town version for the blacks and called it, with redneck humour, Inkster. Now it's subsumed into the Detroit sprawl, but it lives in my heart as the place that gave the world the girl group with the best name of all: the Marvelettes. Tuning my radio, at five in the afternoon, I encounter the usual selection of smarmy drive-time jocks playing the Top Forty, when suddenly I'm struck by the sound of the blues shout of Johnny Taylor. The record finishes and I find out I'm listening to the AM-radio sound of Inkster, Michigan, and it's deep soul and down-home blues all the way; Johnny Taylor gives way to Bobby 'Blue' Bland gives way to Miss Lynn White from Memphis and there is not a trace of anything even remotely urban contemporary. The strange thing is that up here, about as far north as I've been, is the first time I've heard a station like this.

Mark and Alan in Chicago called up a friend of theirs in Detroit, a woman named Marcia. So I've got a place to stay which, I suspect, is a blessing. My guidebook more or less gives up when it comes to places to stay in Detroit, confining itself to the menacing observation that 'accommodations are usually either cheap or safe; if you choose cheap be sure to arrive in daylight and be willing to forgo nightlife'. Which didn't sound like a whole lot of fun, even allowing for the guidebook habit of painting everything about fifty per cent worse than real life.

Marcia's address is on Atkinson Street, which looks on the map to be a little way north of downtown Detroit. So I get off the expressway at the Woodward Avenue exit, head up north and get my first view of Detroit streetlife. Woodward looks like the main street of a ghost city. To the left there are the great deco hulks of the industrial palaces; the General Motors Building and the Fisher Building. Everywhere there are churches, there's a Woolworths on the corner of Grand with a few harassed black and Hispanic folks waiting for a bus alongside, but there is simply not enough life on the street to justify its scale.

Atkinson is off to the left a mile or so up the road and once again as soon as you get off the main road you are instantly in a totally residential neighbourhood. The houses look great, large detached places with big gardens front and back, but looking a little down-at-heel, and the cars parked outside are mostly big old gas-guzzling American motors. I find Marcia's house, park, and bang on the door, which is opened by a tall young woman dressed in black who looks to be both in a hurry and surprised to see me. The situation is resolved by the appearance of third party who says, 'Hi, I'm Marcia, you must be John; this is Heidi, my daughter. I'm afraid she's got to run.'

Marcia, Detroit Italian and possessed of a startling enthusiasm for life and art, sits me down in her kitchen, produces some fine local-brewery beer and starts telling me about the neighbourhood. This was the prime real estate in Detroit in the old days, the housing built by or for car-company executives. Then came the white flight to the suburbs and by the mid-1970s the area was almost entirely black. Which meant – this of course being God's own country where man is equal under the sun – that the cost of housing shot through the floor and kept on falling. Which is how Marcia, a single mother with virtually no money, managed to buy herself what they call round here a mansion: a detached inner-city house with a grand central staircase, servants' quarters and quite as many bedrooms as you would want to shake a stick at.

The place is a bohemian dream home of the sort that is virtually extinct in every other major Western city, taken over by the gentrifiers years ago. The moral presumably being that Yuppies don't mind living in a converted abattoir but they're a bit sniffy about the next-door neighbours. Marcia, on the other hand, has no alarm system, has lived here for fifteen years and never been burgled. So there you go, living proof that it's not the colour of the people in it that makes a neighbourhood safe or unsafe. An all-black neighbourhood like this one is likely to be peaceful enough because it's surroundings are green and pleasant, the scale is human and people know each other. Put people in some conglomeration of twenty-storey rat-traps and it's hardly surprising it's dangerous.

Later in the evening Marcia decides to take me for a drive around downtown Detroit. We head back south down Woodward, more deserted than ever at ten o'clock. Past the expressway, on the left there's a burst of activity; limo-lock surrounds the Art Institute for some black-tie opening. On the other side of the road there's the derelict-looking bulk of the Gaiety Burlesque Theater, a landmark familiar from Elmore Leonard's Detroit thrillers. Detroit not having a whole heap of cultural icons at the moment, a certain degree of civic pride seems to have attached itself to Leonard; his books are well-displayed everywhere and Marcia tells me how well she thinks his latest paperback, *Freaky Deaky*, fixes a time and a place in the city.

A little further down the road is the Fox Theatre, a reminder of Detroit's cultural heyday. This is where the great Motown revues would take place, where once a week you had the chance of seeing the likes of the Supremes, the Miracles, Martha and the Vandellas and Little Stevie Wonder all on the one bill and all for seventy-five cents. Recently the Fox Theatre has been restored to its original deco opulence. It's attracting crowds in from the suburbs and is being touted as a sign that Detroit is coming back from the brink: i.e. becoming a suitable place for middle-class whites to stroll about of an evening.

For the moment though, Detroit central after dark is left to the blacks and the bohemians. We swing east towards the warehouse district over near the big meat market, to visit some friends of Marcia's. As we're looking for a place to park, we see Detroit's current black-music stars Inner City loading their gear into a van. Then we go and visit the chaotic art-strewn warehouse of Marcia's friend, who's a painter, but scrapes a living doing portrait photography, weddings and bar mitzvahs not excluded. Being there is like stepping a little way back in time, to an era of bohemianism of a sort that has simply become financially non-viable in most major cities, a bohemian culture in which lack of commercial success does not make you a non-person.

On our way back we stop off at the Union Street bar, an oasis of life on Woodward not far from the Wayne State University campus. It's a pleasant old-fashioned saloon and, sitting at the bar, we discover Marcia's lodger, an English guy called Malcolm who is part of an avant-garde theatre company, based in Detroit because the living is cheap enough for non-commercial artists to survive, and tough enough to prevent complacency. Malcolm is shattered from driving the company's van back from a performance in Minnesota and soon enough we all head back to sleep.

Next day it's time for some serious sightseeing. First up is the Motown Museum. Down Woodward, take a right at the Woolworths on Grand, and head west for a mile or so to a neighbourhood of ordinary two-storey wood-frame houses. Number 2648 still has the big window with the Hitsville USA sign that it's had since 1960 when it read like a piece of wild bravado, along the lines of proclaiming that you serve the best pizza in America. Now, sadly, it seems rather more like a lament. Motown is at present wholly owned by MCA and has for years, anyway, been indistinguishable in its output from the black-music divisions of any major record label, maybe a little less innovative than most. Inside a couple of oldish women in old-style wigs are deep in debate and don't notice me for a while. When my presence is finally registered they ask me to wait a moment and employ the intercom in an attempt to find someone to show me round. A couple of minutes later a spectacularly pomaded individual who gives the appearance of having been raised from birth in the fabled Motown charm school (which he reveals operated out of a nondescript red-brick building over the road), welcomes me to the Motown Museum and proceeds to deliver a spiel on the greatness of Motown which, considering that his audience consisted of one person paying $3.50 for the pleasure, was a model of professionalism.

It is also some way out of keeping with the tackiness which otherwise characterizes the Motown Museum. After the introductory spiel a junior member of the Gordy clan, possessed of an unfortunate speech impediment, ushers me into a room to watch a video, badly recorded from the TV, of Detroit's mayor, the high-profile Coleman Young, unveiling a Motown plaque in the rain. Then Mr Pomade returns to usher me through the original Motown studio, which has an appealing *Marie Celeste* quality, and upstairs into the historical display section – which consists almost entirely of a bunch of album covers tacked more or less randomly on to the walls. He continues the spiel until his girlfriend appears at which event he breaks off in mid-flow, suggests I might like to explore a little by myself, and retreats into another room to canoodle a little. I stare at the album covers a while and then spot a glass case in the corner containing Michael Jackson's glove. Next to this is a clipping relating that when Michael was last in Detroit he came to the museum and then donated the proceeds of his concert that night – $120,000 or so – towards extending the collection. Presumably Michael knows tacky when he sees tacky. However where the money has gone is hard to divine. Certainly not on a bunch of old album covers and a newspaper cutting in which 'Punk rock group the Clash tour the Motown Museum' which is unaccountably set under glass on top of Berry Gordy's old desk. As memorials go, the Motown Museum doesn't fit too well, but still I acquire Motown frisbees, T-shirts, mugs, caps and drinks coasters to delight the folks back home.

Next stop is some way north, in a down-at-heel black neighbourhood, off McNichols Rd. Here, in a nondescript white-painted warehouse, is the headquarters of a rather less publicized black business empire: Skippy's. Skippy's is a retail, wholesale and mail-order operation specializing in all the little necessities for the practice of Voodoo or Santeria – a for-real magic store. Inside it's white-painted and brightly lit, the products are laid out supermarket-style. Not that there are a lot of supermarkets

with a rack of rabbits' eyes on sale, or selections of ingredients
for a mojo, or bats' hearts. Slightly less menacing is an array of
bottles full of viscous liquid in a selection of spectacularly
artificial hues, including the loudest orange I've encountered. On
closer examination the labels proclaim the bottles to be efficacious in sorting out your problems, whether of money, health or
love. A typical label proclaims: 'Skippy's Indian Spirit House
Blessing – Triple Fast Action Spiritual – Bath & Floor Wash'.
Small print suggests a 'Bath Ritual: Fill bath with warm water,
pour in half bottle. Read 23rd Psalm. Concentrate on your
desires.' What it doesn't mention is whether you should actually
get into the bath, which, having smelt the lethal liquid in the
bottles, would appear to be a piece of tactful ambivalence
perhaps suggested by Skippy's lawyers. The facing shelves
contain the same bottles but with the labels this time in Spanish.
Then, as my attention is caught by the display of bottles of pimp
oil (to perfume your pimpmobile y'unnerstand), someone
emerges from a back room and leaves the door half open. Peering
through I can see into the Skippy factory. Big vats of the alarming
liquids are being tapped into bottles; identical bottles stand
waiting to discover whether they are going to be used to drive
away evil, promote romance, or bring financial reward.

Financial benefit is the attraction of much of the merchandise.
Sticks of Sweet Smell of Success incense nestle alongside a
selection of dream books: pamphlets which explain that certain
kinds of dream correspond to certain numbers which you should
therefore select when gambling on the numbers. The numbers
racket is clearly alive and well in Detroit; as I purchase my
selection of dubious potions the orange-haired black woman on
the till slips a piece of paper into my bag. On it is Skippy's lucky
number for today. Back in the car listening to the Inkster blues
station it strikes me that Detroit is really the last great Southern
town. Here amid the industrial decay of the city which first
offered well-paid work for blacks, back around the time of the
First World War, is where Voodoo and deep soul persist, not in
the shopping malls of the New South.

From here I just drive around a while looking for a place to
eat. I head out to east Detroit, taking the expressway as far as
Cadieux, and find myself in a suburban industrial zone. I head

back towards downtown along Warren Avenue. As you get closer
to the centre the area gets seedier, the road surface deteriorates
and the faces are gradually all black. There are a few record
shops and barber shops straight out of 1972 *Superfly* times, with
names like Soul to Soul, but little life on a grey midweek
lunchtime. Turn on to Gratiot and soon enough I'm downtown,
left on to Beaubien where the police HQ is and left again on to
Monroe, and park. A couple of blocks of Monroe are known as
Greektown, for the unsurprising reason that they've got a lot of
Greek restaurants on them. I pick up a sandwich and wander
into Trapper's Alley, a cutesy shopping mall which is much the
same as any other apart from a nice line in T-shirts emblazoned
with the slogan 'Detroit – where the weak are killed and eaten'.

Next stop is a few blocks away on East Adams, the offices of
the city-funded *City Arts* magazine. I want to pick up a back
number with a piece on Donald Goines. *City Arts* is edited by
John Sinclair, sometime manager of the legendary Detroit rock
band the MC5. The MC5 had one great song, which is fondly
remembered by Skip the ageing counter-culture bomber in
Elmore Leonard's *Freaky Deaky*. Skip requests the tune from a
smarmy guitarist playing romantic tunes for the dinner dates in
a downtown restaurant, it's called 'Kick Out the Jams, Mother-
fuckers'. Sinclair was also responsible for founding the White
Panthers, more of an idea than an army perhaps, but still enough
to make Sinclair distinctly *persona non grata* with the FBI, who
were more than satisfied to see him spend much of the 1970s in
gaol after a highly dubious dope bust. Sinclair's not in the office
at the moment, so I pick up the magazine and head off to spend
the afternoon following the thread of Elmore Leonard's Detroit.

Leonard lives out in a suburb called Birmingham, around
fifteen miles north of downtown, straight out along Woodward.
Much of the action in his Detroit-set novels is set along this
Woodward axis, particularly in swank golf-course country along
Bloomfield Hills, in Highland Park seediness, or in the ghetto
bohemian neighbourhood known as the Cass Corridor.

The Cass Corridor starts just north of downtown and runs
parallel to Woodward, a block or so the west, up to Wayne State
University. In *The Switch*, written in the late 1970s, a black
hustler named Ordell Robbie describes it like this: 'A fine

example of neo-ghetto . . . you can see it's not quite your classic ghetto yet, not quite ratty or rotten enough, but it's coming.' Actually, like much of what I've seen of Detroit, it doesn't seem to have deteriorated much from that time but neither has it improved; it just seems kind of stuck. There are still shopfronts being used by hippie sculptors, just as described in Leonard's *Unknown Man Number 89*, still a lot of heavily fortified corner stores where they'll happily let you buy liquor with your welfare food stamps, as specifically forbidden by the Federal Government, and there are still whores wandering in and out of severely lowlife bars. I stroll around a bit and follow a trail of half-dead records and books into what looks like a derelict basement but turns out to be a second-hand bookstore on the point of collapse. When I wander out again I'm three dollars lighter but up a first edition of Nelson Algren's great novel of heroin addiction, *The Man with the Golden Arm*.

Back in the car, I keep going north on Woodward, past Atkinson where I'm staying and, after a desolate mile or so dotted with churches and crack houses, the street population increases as I get to Highland Park, mostly Arab and black and dotted with storefront mosques, porno parlours that look as if they've seen better days, and motels that offer a special deal: $12 all day. All day?? Just over Six Mile Road and to the left is Palmer Park, with its golf course while, on the right-hand side of Woodward, there are a selection of places with names like the Sassy Cat, Lucky Lips or Tender Trap; topless restaurants offering businessmen's lunches. It's in one of these that Harry Mitchell, the tough-guy hero of Leonard's first Detroit thriller, *52 Pick-Up*, meets the wrong girl: 'We stopped at four of them. Nice sunny afternoon we're doing the topless tour. The last place, she's sitting at the bar. Ross sees her, pats her on the ass thinking she's one of the go-goers, and tries to move in.'

After Palmer Park the neighbourhood starts to creep upscale, and by the time I get to Nine Mile Road it's all funeral parlours, used-car lots and an unaccountable number of rare-book dealers. By now Woodward has opened up into a big multi-lane highway. Apparently this used to be a favourite spot for road racing; hot-rods and muscle cars would congregate from miles around.

Birmingham starts at around Fourteen Mile Road and is a

mall-defined kind of place; banks and CD stores line Woodward, while hair-replacement clinics nestle discreetly in the side roads. The record store I walk into is full of the kind of music Elmore's characters tend to listen to, sophisticated 1970s jazz-funk – Grover Washington, Roy Ayers, Joe Farrell – music for slick black hustlers and bored suburban housewives. Away from the main drag Birmingham is a pleasant surburban district, well-off but not flash. Flash is provided a mile or two further down the road in Bloomfield Hills, with its country clubs and lakes and high-status golf clubs, like the one in which Mickey, heroine of *The Switch*, spends her time being bored out of her mind, until the day that Ordell Robbie and his friend Louis kidnap her and take her back to a house off Highland Park, to see how much her husband wants her back (answer, as it happens, not much).

Drinking coffee in a Denny's on my way back down Woodward, it strikes me that the ideal way to interview Elmore Leonard would be in the course of a slow crawl along Woodward. Unfortunately this isn't going to be; Leonard is too busy and, maybe, too dignified, and I'm going to have to make do with a conversation in an anonymous hotel lounge, one of a series promoting his new novel.

Also, too, most of his Detroit writing was done in the 1970s when he was somewhat less successful than today; his marriage was breaking up and he was, not incidentally, an alcoholic. All of which factors no doubt contributed to the novels of that period having a rather more street-level feel to them. Particularly this is the case with *Unknown Man Number 89*, a pivotal novel that came out in 1977, around the time Leonard was giving up drinking, and features a partially reformed alcoholic named Jack Ryan who makes a living by finding people who don't want to be found, mostly people who owe other people money. At one point in the book, Ryan is looking for a guy, and he finds the guy's wife in a lowlife bar on Cass. She's blind drunk on white wine at two o'clock in the afternoon. Ryan says to her:

'You want to get there, what're you fooling around with wine for?'
　　She didn't answer him.
　　'I used to drink mostly bourbon, over crushed ice, fill up a lowball glass. I also drank beer, wine, gin, vodka, Cuba Libres, Diet-Rite and

scotch, and rye with red pop, but I preferred bourbon, Early Times. I knew a guy who drank only Fresca and chartreuse. I took a sip one time, I said to him, "Jesus, this is the worst drink I ever tasted in my life." He said, "I know it is. It's so bad you can't drink very many of them." A real alcoholic, though, can drink anything, right? ... What time you start in the morning?'

Without looking at him the girl said, 'Fuck off.'

All of which is clearly not a million miles from Leonard's own experience at the time, as he records in an essay written for a book called *The Courage to Change*, a collection of essays by alcoholics about their experiences of quitting drinking:

I never reached the point of a couple of fifths a day. Not until the very end did I drink before noon. Noon was always that magic time when it became all right. Sunday morning I used to hold out and then come back from Mass and have a big bowl of chilli and a couple of ice-cold beers. Hangovers never bothered me because all I had to do was drink a few ice-cold beers or a real hot, spicy bloody mary and I was back. I would drink a bottle of red wine and I'd be off. The next day it might be something else. Scotch or anything, though usually the next day I would disguise it. I would put scotch in something that you never put scotch in − Vernors ginger ale or something like that. I was great at trying to disguise the booze from myself. If I'd put that in a story, nobody would believe it. (Elmore Leonard quoted in *The Courage to Change* by Dennis Wholey).

The mid-1970s Elmore Leonard was in deep shit. He was a screenwriter whose films weren't getting made, a novelist who wasn't selling. He was separated from his wife of twenty years and living in a hotel. And drinking. Now Elmore Leonard, successful and sober, is sitting in a hotel lounge, finishing lunch with his second wife, Joan, whom he married in 1979 and whom he credits with getting him off the booze and on to where he is today. Elmore Leonard is a small, neat man, with a trim beard and a careful way of looking at you. He doesn't miss much; if he played poker they'd call him 'doc' and you would be ill-advised to compete.

Joan, a smart friendly blonde, in late middle age like Elmore, and tired of hearing the familiar questions and answers, disappears offstage. I ask Elmore how he started writing. 'I used to tell stories when I was in grade school; we'd go to a movie and later on they would ask me to tell the movie to them. I wrote a play when I was in the fifth grade – a World War One play – this was after reading parts of *All Quiet on the Western Front*. We put the play on in the classroom using rows of desks as the trenches. After that I didn't write anything till college. I was in the services from 1943–6 then I went to the University of Detroit and entered a short-story contest; 1949 I got married and got a job in an ad agency. By 1951 I had started to write westerns, without enough background, without having done enough research, without even having read very many westerns. I liked western movies and there was a very good market for the stories in the 1950s, a lot of pulp magazines with the good ones paying two cents a word. In the 1950s I sold thirty short stories and wrote five books; two of the short stories were sold to Hollywood, *The Tall T* came out with Randolph Scott and *3.10 to Yuma* with Glenn Ford and Van Heflin.'

Elmore Leonard's westerns are not typical. They provide a simple, clear backdrop for his Hemingway-inspired tough tales of decent men pushed too far, of outsiders fighting back. In those McCarthy years the western was as good an area as any in which to uphold human dignity against bigotry and oppression. You can see that kind of opposition in films like *Bad Day at Black Rock* and you can see it in Leonard's *Hombre* or *Lawless River*. These were not simply 'Bonanza'-style stories of good cowboys and bad Indians. 'I wanted to give them a sense of realism. People said my westerns were too grim, didn't have enough blue sky in them, no romance.'

For all the considerable success of his westerns, writing wasn't bringing in enough to support his growing family. So, through the 1950s he stayed at the ad agency, writing ads for Chevrolet. In 1961 he packed that in and went freelance. 'From 1961 to late 1965 I didn't write at all because I was too busy earning a living doing freelance work scriptwriting movies for *Encyclopedia Britannica*. After *Hombre* sold to Fox in 1966 I had enough money for about six months so I got back to writing and I've been doing it ever since.'

The market for westerns, though, had been drying up since the late 1950s with the proliferation of cowboy TV shows. So Leonard made his first book after the break a thriller called *The*

Big Bounce. Rejected by several publishers as too grim, this short sharp saga of migrant workers taking a little direct action in the pursuit of money was eventually put out by Gold Medal, the great pulp crime publishers of the 1950s and 1960s. The next decade is the most confusing part of Elmore Leonard's career. He succeeded in making a good living writing, mostly from Hollywood, and produced some great books, but had yet to settle into a pattern. He wrote some more westerns, *Valdez is Coming*, which made a fine film, and *Forty Lashes Less One*, which broke firmly with tradition by having as its heroes an Indian and a black man. He wrote an historical screwball comedy called *The Moonshine War* which made a terrible film; and he wrote thrillers like *Mr Majestyk*, filmed as a Charles Bronson vehicle, and *The Hunted*, an oddity set in Israel.

In 1974 he wrote *52 Pick-Up*, which was his first thriller to be set in Detroit, his home town. Like his westerns, it's the story of a worm turning, a regular joe taking on the bad guys. It is marred though by a sadistic, faintly misogynist, edge to the plot. In the next novel, *Swag*, he got it right. Fast, tough and funny, this is the story of two guys, Frank and Stick, who, having made a thorough study of the options, decide that the way to better living is via armed robbery. From *Swag* onwards Elmore Leonard has simply written the best villains ever. His particular strength is for the way people talk, the speech rhythms of Detroit's black and white lowlife: 'When I audition my characters at the start of a book they have to be able to talk or they don't get in. I use a lot of black characters because I can hear them and they use patterns of speech that I like.'

The book didn't sell, though, and meanwhile Leonard's home life was falling apart. 'We always drank. Every single night, we would get into arguments with me drunk and her part of the way, with me saying vicious things, which I couldn't believe the next day' (*The Courage to Change*). Which is where we came in.

The arrival of Joan in his life had an immediate effect on his writing. His next novel, *The Switch*, features his first really strong, autonomous female character. 'Joan has helped me tremendously with my women, to let them stand up and become part of the story. What I had to learn was to treat the woman as a person.'

Next came a move to a new publisher, Arbor House, who had

faith in him, and, alongside further Detroit novels, Leonard started writing books set in Miami. 'I'd been going to Miami every year since 1950. I was drawn to writing about it because of the great contrast in the kinds of people that live in Florida, from very rich in Palm Beach to Cubans in Miami.'

Stick, a follow-on from *Swag* set in Florida, was the first of his books to hit really big. It was subsequently filmed (moderately badly) by Burt Reynolds. The next one, *LaBrava*, was bought by Dustin Hoffman, but was never actually filmed. Then came *Glitz*, which was a major bestseller and is soon to be a TV blockbuster mini-series, which bodes less than well. Elmore, however, is sanguine about the quality of the films made of his work: 'It really doesn't bother me that much because I know the problems. I know going in that you'll be dealing with a lot of people who don't know anything about story, nothing about casting apart from "Let's get the guy who was in a successful picture before," their ideas are all about what worked in another picture. They don't have any story sense at all. But for about twenty years this has supported my novel writing and I'm very optimistic about each film. All along the way I'll think, "This could be a good picture, who knows?" and I'll do what the director says even though I think he's wrong. Generally it turns out I was right, but I don't regret it.'

After *Glitz* came *Bandits*, another slight departure; '*Bandits* came about when a film producer said, "How would you like to write the script of a big caper movie: several old pros get together for one last heist," and I said, "Sure, but I want to write it as a book first and I want to set it in New Orleans". Then, planning the book, I had to think of something for these guys to steal, so I read in the paper about money being collected privately for the Contras. And I thought that this money could be sitting in one place and these guys could find out about it so I introduced the ex-nun who enlists them and told them what was going on down in Nicaragua. But I've been asked if I wrote that book to get my political views across. I didn't. It was only something for these guys to steal. Of course you do get politically involved when you have to explain what's going on and you have to show some passion for one side or the other . . . and of course it's going to be for the former nun against the Contras.'

Bandits seems perhaps a little over-researched and occasionally uncertain in tone. For the next book, *Freaky Deaky*, Elmore returned to Detroit and wrote a much funnier book on a much smaller scale. I ask if this was a deliberate reaction to *Bandits*? '*Bandits* may have wandered a little more than I had planned and, because I make it up as I go along, maybe it took a little longer to decide what was going to happen. A lot of surprising things happen while I'm writing. A minor character, Franklin De Dios, just pushed himself into the story. Certainly *Freaky Deaky* is more compressed and *Killshot* is even more so.'

Freaky Deaky is the story of two former 1960s radicals turning to crime. I wonder what Elmore had been up to in the 1960s. 'I remember that time. I didn't participate in any demonstrations. I saw *Woodstock* when it came out and I saw it again a couple more times when I was writing the book. I was beyond the age where I was going to participate. So it was research, *Rolling Stone* magazine, articles on the weather underground, what they were into. I used my researcher, who did go to the George Wallace rally in Detroit where everyone stood up and said, "*Sieg Heil* Y'all!"'

Elmore Leonard's practice of using a researcher on his recent books has provoked a degree of unfavourable comment, so I ask him what his researcher actually does. 'My researcher, Greg Sutter, works for me part-time. He works with computers, mostly, so he can go into a library and pull the material and bring it to me. When he begins I'm never sure what I'm looking for. For *Stick* I asked for material on the investment world, women in business, the boatlift, what is the main prison in Havana and so on. For *LaBrava* I was trying to find out what Harry Truman's living-room looked like, where his wife was living with secret-service men guarding her. So I called up a retired secret-service man and asked him if he knew where I could get this information and he said there's a guy in Little Rock who had been the duty officer. I called the guy and he said I'd have to get clearance from Washington. I said, "I don't want to know about the surveillance; what colour's the carpet?" and he said, "You'll have to go through Washington." So I called a guy named Gerald Petievitch and he said, "Call him back and tell him I'll vouch for you." So the guy says, "I don't know Gerry

Petievitch's phone voice. Could be anybody." So I told my researcher about the situation. Next day he came back with a picture of the room and a description and I said, "How did you find that out?" He said, "I called the house." He's a researcher!'

One constant of Leonard's writing is his attention to the music his characters listen to. The Detroit villains of the earlier books favour the kind of black jazz that now gets marketed as rare groove – Roy Ayers, Herbie Mann and suchlike. Then again, a Southern boy like Ernest 'Stick' Stickley will show a preference for Waylon Jennings or Loretta Lynn. Elmore's own taste leans towards the former: 'I listen mostly to jazz – in the car I set the radio to a black jazz station and whatever comes on is fine: Herbie Hancock, George Benson, though he's getting more into rock. Recently I took all my kids to Joe Cocker. I always liked him, I like the contrast of him and his band; he looks like he's just come home from work. The way I work the music into the novels is that I like to use what's current. I'll turn the TV on, get MTV, very often whatever's on I'll use. I did get to meet Iggy Pop and talk to him, because I referred to him several times in *Freaky Deaky*. I asked him what it was like, what he was trying to do, was he trying to fly over the audience? (referring here to Iggy's legendary Detroit performances with the Stooges). He said: "No, I just wanted to *hover* over them!"'

Time's up and the successful, sober, born-again, though entirely unpreachy Mr Leonard leaves for photographs and a radio interview.

That evening Marcia says let's go to the movies so we head up to a cinemall in Birmingham, meet up with a couple of Marcia's friends – two young artist-type guys, one black, one white – and watch *Sex, Lies and Videotape*, everyone but me seeing it for the second time. Afterwards we discuss where to go for a drink and the consensus arrived at is that the ideal place would be a transvestite bar on Woodward called the Backstage.

The Backstage is way back down Woodward, opposite Palmer Park and just at the end of the strip of topless bars. However it turns out not to be the kind of dive I'm expecting. Instead it's a swish bar and restaurant packed at midnight with a mixture of what used to be known as theatrical types, some of whom are, indeed, of a transvestite persuasion, and a number of middle-aged black couples happy to have a pleasant place to eat in this otherwise borderline dangerous neighbourhood. Talk at our table turns to whether Spike Lee's *Do the Right Thing* is a better movie than *Sex, Lies and Videotape*. On the one hand it is clearly a political argument – a choice between yuppie introspection or a warning from the ghetto of the fire next time – and sure enough the black guy goes for *Do the Right Thing*, the white guy for *Sex, Lies*, but what, on the other hand, *is* revealing is that there is not much in it. In a city as racially riven as Detroit it is still possible for black and white folks to go and see both movies and here in the Backstage, in a bad neighbourhood in America's most deprived city, the clientele is the most mixed I will find anywhere on my travels.

9

Boston: the Friends of George V. Higgins

'If his view of life would scare the bejesus out of you, nevertheless, he had, literally, the courage of his convictions, and that's more than many of the rest of them had.'

George V. Higgins on Gordon Liddy, the Watergate plotter.

Flying into Boston in a plane small enough to disconcert the life out of me by sporting a propeller, I've got the two Boston songs I know vying for airtime in my head. On the mean and moody front there's the Standells' 'Dirty Water' – 'Love that dirty water, ooooohhh Boston you're my home' (some trivia-obsessed brain cell pops up to tell me that the Standells were actually from Cambridge, the university town that sits cater-corner to Boston across that dirty water). In the hippie sentimentalism corner, meanwhile, there is Kenny Loggins's 'Please Come to Boston' as performed by Tammy Wynette ('You say please come to Boston for the springtime/ you're staying there with friends and they've got lots of room/ I can sell my paintings on the sidewalk/ by a cafe where you hope to be working soon').

From the airport I take the subway through the city centre and out the far side to Brookline, where I've booked a room in a guest house. Boston, like San Francisco, being a toney kind of place that eschews motels in favour of 'European-style' guest houses. The guest house is set in a tree-lined street, there are bicycles parked outside and worldwide student types chattering in the corridors. The room is pleasant and homey, with an absurd quantity of subsidiary light sources. And the place depresses me more than the tackiest motel.

There's little time for contemplation, though; I have half an hour to get back into central Boston and meet George V. Higgins for lunch. Higgins having been a lawyer, I figure I'd better smarten up, so I fish out a pair of navy wool trousers and a tastefully embroidered, if somewhat crumpled, dark-blue shirt, and hie myself to the Locke-Ober Cafe in Winter Place.

Winter Place turns out to be an exclusive little cul-de-sac, adjacent to Boston's main shopping district. As I approach the Locke-Ober Cafe I suddenly have a presentiment that I should have remembered that Higgins was not just a lawyer, but a Boston lawyer. The presentiment, for once, turns out to be bang on. The Locke-Ober Cafe is a cafe only in the old-money understated way that allows 'a little place in the country' to mean Blenheim Palace. In fact it's a Bostonian approximation of a London gentleman's club dining-room. As I enter, the guy in the tux on the door just looks me up and down for a minute. To jolly proceedings along a bit I say that I'm here for lunch with Mr Higgins. He sighs and says, 'Yes . . . sir. You will need a jacket and tie first. Over there.' He points to the cloakroom. I walk over and explain my predicament to a motherly type who is already rooting through her assortment of the kind of jackets and ties people leave in restaurants. In these cases I would presume deliberately. 'Don't look at it, just put it on, honey,' she says, handing me a tie. I should have taken her advice. Instead I peeked. Polyester. Maroon. Cream stripes. A kipper without the courage of its convictions. The jacket that follows is at least plain black. Which is about as much as can be said in its favour. It's made out of some synthetic of peculiar unpleasantness to the touch. Its shoulders are too narrow and its sleeves too long, thus allowing me the unusual sensation of being constricted in a jacket that's too big for me.

Now George V. Higgins must be one of three things: remarkably polite, possessed of appalling dress sense, or accustomed to being interviewed by repulsively attired journalists. Whatever, he shows no surprise at being approached by this apparition. I tell him what's happened and he chortles a little before expressing his dismay that he could have forgotten to tell me – and that I should not have known – that the Locke-Ober is of course a jacket-and-tie kind of place; my God, the Kennedys used to lunch here. It's a formal, oak-panelled kind of place which is still a mecca for Massachusetts powerbrokers; table tittle-tattle tends to run to ongoing trials and Mike Dukakis in-jokes. Higgins, himself, is a big grey-bearded man in an eminently clubbable suit, with a judicial stare and a disconcerting growth on his forehead.

He's an imposing man, partly naturally, partly through tricks he's learned in the courtroom. His attitude immediately is 'come on, impress me, ask me something I haven't been asked a hundred times before'. Choosing the Locke-Ober Cafe to meet is all part of this stacking the odds in his favour. It's a place saturated in tradition, in which you need to know, without reference to the menu, what to eat and what to drink. That the right move is to have the lamb chop becomes apparent seconds after I've ordered a steak sandwich. Similarly whiskey is clearly the right aperitif; not having had breakfast the best I can do is ask for a glass of white wine, clearly a cissified choice. Meanwhile Higgins just watches; inviting me here is an apparent statement that he assumes any journalist will be a man of the world like himself. Its subtext is clearly a statement of who's boss. As is Higgins's smart sabotage of the classic journalist warm-up biographical questions. Before I can ask him anything he produces two sheets of paper that he tells me will answer any biographical queries. The sheets of paper contain a basic cv and a bibliography and are headed 'standard press biographical sketch'. Like hey pal, the standard sketch will be just fine for you. The real function is not to tell you about his personal biography, but to stop you asking questions about it.

Still it would be naïve to expect lunch with George V. Higgins to be easy. In his books, after all, lunch tends to be an urbane battleground. An example: in *The Patriot Game* a City Hall fixer, Seats Lobianco, is called up by a representative from an Irish neighbourhood, Ticker Greenan. Greenan wants a favour. Before Seats will even start listening he tells Greenan that he'll have to buy him lunch, then maybe he'll have an ear free. They meet at the restaurant; Lobianco's there already, drinking a Bloody Mary. Lobianco, then, using a waiter as straight man, proceeds ritually to humiliate Greenan, while stiffing him for a huge meal. Then he gets down to business:

'And you listen to me,' Seats said to Greenan. He pointed his left index finger at him. 'I know you. I've known you a long time. You've got a short memory and it doesn't help you none. You call about seeing me, you've got something on your mind but it's temporary, Ticker, it's temporary. I helped you before, and I did what you wanted, and it was temporary. Many times, I did it many times when you asked me, and many times you forgot that I did it. *All* of the times. Now we are going to play with a little harder ball. This time you are going to remember. And this time you are going to do the right thing.'

So conversing with Mist-ah Higgins requires some concentration. You say something hack or stupid or controversial and he's not going to let it past. He feigns astonishment when I suggest that *Vanity Fair* carries some pretty good articles, and seems genuinely horrified when I suggest that America is more interested in literature than England. After all the old country has a powerful pull to Boston snobbism. They may have thrown the British out of Boston Harbor, but they kept their value system. Higgins is very proud of his reputation in England; his handout is at pains to tell me that all his novels have been published in England. His short-story collection, *Sins of the Fathers*, has only been published there. He is also at pains to tell the world that the British Book Marketing Council, whoever they may be, selected *The Friends of Eddie Coyle* as one of the twenty best novels by an American published in Britain since World War Two.

We've been talking long enough to be about halfway through our first drinks when we're joined by a lawyer called Bob, a clean-cut and cynical Kennedy type, who used to work with Higgins some while back when he was in private practice. After the pleasantries have been exchanged and Bob has charmingly misidentified my accent as Australian, Higgins says, 'Well, let's get on with it.' And it's time for me to attempt to pry loose the background to the bare facts on the info sheets he's given me.

Higgins has made his mark writing about the people that the general public are perhaps most likely to perceive as dishonest: criminals, of course, but also lawyers, politicians and journalists. These are also the people Higgins knows best. He has worked as a journalist and as a lawyer; politicians and criminals are the people he habitually dealt with (often incarnated in the same flesh). Higgins became a journalist after a spell at the ultra-prestigious Stanford University which, like Joe Gores, he abominated sufficiently to be on the point of leaving even though that would have led to him being drafted to fight in Vietnam.

'I was callow. I had signed up to join NavCad – Naval Aviation Cadets – and the reason I had done that was that I was at Stanford University. I loathed Stanford and Stanford loathed me, but in those days if you didn't have 2S then you were 1A and that meant you went to Vietnam, as Bob did. I didn't want to go to Vietnam on foot' ('Neither did Bob,' says Bob). 'I was afraid I'd get my feet wet, and so I decided that I had an advantage which was, and is now, extreme peripheral vision – while I look at you I can see him spilling soup on his tie – and the navy just loved that. So I signed up for that in preference to getting my feet wet. What I wanted was about 20,000 pounds of jetfighter under me with rockets and machine guns and everything else. If they were going to make me go – and they were going to make me go – I was going to have one big damn thing with a lot of firepower.

'Then I developed a bleeding ulcer, *because I really liked Stanford*. And the morning I finally came to at the Stanford Palo Alto Hospital the doctor said to me, "We've figured out what's the matter with you; you've got a bleeding ulcer." And I said, "Oh hell, this is not good news," and he said, "Well, the good news is you're young" – I was twenty-two – "and you'll heal, there's no need to operate." And I said, ". . . and I'll be . . . 4F?" He says, "Oh, I would think so." And I was! And that's the day my recovery began!' he says, breaking up in laughter.

So, instead of heading to South East Asia, Higgins found himself back in New England. He got a job working for Associated Press in Providence, Rhode Island, a hard town by the sea with a heavy Mafia presence. His next posting was to Springfield, where a series of Mafia trials were under way. Attending these provoked a change in career: 'Those trial lawyers were having more fun than I was. I decided to go to law school. Then I started as a prosecutor for the Attorney General's office in 1967.

'It's the only blood sport that's officially sanctioned. Ask him. This man makes more money in an hour than a trial lawyer can make in a week.'

Bob demurs. 'Four days?' says Higgins. 'Maybe,' says Bob.

'These days I make more money teaching, per hour. And teaching is easier. I don't have these confounded judges interfering with me all the time.'

'Let alone somebody on the other side standing up and attacking you!'

'I don't like that either!' says Higgins, laughing some more.

This was a remarkable time for US lawmaking. Robert Kennedy was the Attorney General and was trying to use the courts as a progressive force, pushing through civil-rights legislation and so forth. Higgins, then a Democrat of no deep conviction, had doubts about the political use of the law: 'This was the age of Bobby Kennedy's target prosecutions; it was called active law enforcement as opposed to reactive law enforcement. That meant we didn't wait for a call to come in from the police, we identified the people who were evil and went after them and we would catch them for cruelty to animals if that was the best we could do, and . . . it was a bad idea.' It was a bad idea, Higgins elaborates, 'because it assumes that you or I are running the government and that we won't go after the good guys, but if someone else is running the government, who may turn out to be a bad guy, then they can use this policy to put us in gaol. It's a bad idea, it stinks. And during this time I brought a case that I'm not proud of. I'm not going to go into specifics, but the man is now doing well over twenty years and yes, I was right, he was a bad man. But I didn't have the evidence, didn't have him.'

Meanwhile, he was always writing. His first novel appeared in 1971. It was called *The Friends of Eddie Coyle* and from the first sentence ('Jackie Brown at twenty-six, with no expression on his face, said that he could get some guns') it was a debut of staggering assurance. Its class and its author's day job provoked Norman Mailer to comment, 'What I can't get over is that so good a first novel was written by the fuzz.' Of course, as with many good first novels, it was a first only for the public, not the writer: 'I wrote fourteen novels before *Eddie Coyle*, most of them rejected by most of the reputable publishers on both sides of the Atlantic and I'm damn glad of it today.'

Still he kept writing and kept sending work out. 'I had a friend in California that I acquired at Stanford and he fell victim to drugs, which made me a passionate opponent of drugs, because they ruined him. I have seen some writers who have been improved by this stuff,' he says, hoisting his glass. 'I have never seen anyone improved by drugs. I used to send him everything I wrote. I used to lend him money too, and he paid it back. Not a bad man, a good man. I sent him a story that appeared in the *North American Review* called "Dillin Explained that He was Frightened". And since my friend knew I was working on a novel, he wrote back and said, "Is this part of the novel?" Until that night it wasn't. That night I went into my study and put paper in my typewriter and started . . . "Jackie Brown at twenty-six . . ." That's it. I wanted to know how it came out, and "Dillon Explained" became the sixth chapter.' He waves his hand in the direction of the Locke-Ober Cafe's window. 'It was up here on Tremont Street that Jackie Brown said he could buy those guns.'

Further novels followed quickly, books like *The Digger's Game* and *Cogan's Trade* that did not so much rework *Eddie Coyle* as simply fit alongside it as part of a continuing epic novel of New England lowlife and public life, a project owing as much to Balzac's Paris as Chandler's Los Angeles. Meanwhile, Higgins was looking to combine writing with setting up a private legal business. 'It was time to leave the US Attorney's office. I'd been there seven years. I completed a couple of appeals for the federal government and left to cover the Watergate affair, a job which gave me the money to start my own law firm.'

The time in Washington also produced Higgins's least readable books. The Watergate book, cutely entitled *The Friends of Richard Nixon*, is heavy going, especially at this remove; so too are the novels *A City on a Hill*, in which self-impressed types talk endlessly in a vacuum, and *Dreamland* in which Higgins puts aside his characteristic dialogue-based style in favour of the interior monologue. Both suffer, perhaps, from the dislocation from home territory and also from a degree of rhetorical pomposity creeping into the style; these are the only books of his which read as if they're written by a lawyer. Higgins comments: '*A City on a Hill* is not a good novel, which is mostly my own fault. In fact it's entirely my own fault and I'd like it back. I did *Dreamland* because I wanted to see if I could do a book where the narrator was a liar. And he was and as I got into the book he turned out to be crazy as well . . . It's a favourite of college professors today because it's so damn difficult and inaccessible. Would I do it again? No, but only because I've done it once.'

At which point lunch arrives: lamb chops for Bob and George, steak sandwich for me, hash browns and red wine all round. The conversation turns to Higgins's years as a practising lawyer, and in particular the extent to which Higgins draws from real-life characters for his fiction. Higgins himself denies any such thing, which has a slight ring of the 'he would say that, wouldn't he' about it. Bob, however, decides it's time to wind Higgins up a little.

'What was the name of that judge in *Outlaws?*' he asks, innocently enough.

Higgins laughs and says, 'Hanging Black Buck.'

Bob laughs too, and slips in the sucker punch: 'But he was fair. Frank Keating was always fair.'

'It was not Frank Keating,' says Higgins, stern as can be.

'All right,' says Bob with bland insincerity, and they both start laughing. But Bob's not going to leave it there. 'I remember some of the dialogue being reminiscent of a cross between Frank Keating and our friend the Federal Judge . . .'

'I've met him!' roars Higgins.

'. . . now passed away. Does his name escape me?'

'Yes!'

'. . . Ski . . . Charles Wassanski?'

'Who offered to put me in gaol on several occasions when I was an Assistant US Attorney.'

'Mr Higgins,' Bob does his judge impersonation, 'I find your brief very, very, very, compelling. Extremely well-briefed, right on the law in all points, but not persuasive. Motion denied.'

Before another round of hysterics can break out, a figure hoves towards our table. 'Hi, George,' says Bob to the figure, who has a certain air of gormlessness about him, a little reminiscent of Tony Curtis's yacht-owner impersonation in *Some Like It Hot.*

'Hi, Bob, how you doing?'

'Fine George, just fine. George this is George. George this is John.'

The formalities completed, this other George moves off. Having given him just about enough time to get out of earshot, Higgins turns to Bob and says, 'Does he have money?' (As in why the hell else would you be polite to such a geek?)

Bob leans back and exhales: 'The guy must have around thirty-two million unencumbered dollars. I said *unencumbered*.'

'Ah,' says Higgins, the world living down to his expectations.

So we talk some more about writing. I mention that Higgins's big novel of Boston politics, *A Choice of Enemies*, is my favourite of his books. He says it's his too, and as far as he's concerned, he should have damn well won a Pulitzer for it. In fact Anne Tyler got the Pulitzer that year, and Higgins is less than charitable, not to say printable, in his views on that state of affairs. Suddenly there is a sense that, for all his résumés of literary triumphs to date, Higgins is some way from happy with what he perceives as his status in the world of letters.

I asked him whether he still practised law, and his reply again betokens a certain disenchantment with the way things pan out: 'I stopped in 1983. It wasn't a decision made by me, it was made for me. In Boston, when they say you've quit practising law to write full time, then you have. Took me several years to figure this out! My writing enabled my competitors – of whom there are a good many and some of whom are almost as good as I am – to say that I'd quit practising law to write full time. So eventually I couldn't afford to keep the office running; I had set it up initially to deal with the vicissitudes of a writer's income and now it was eating up all of that writer's income. So I finally faced up to reality: it was costing me $65,000 to run the law office each year with a minimal library, very good secretarial help and a cheap office space. In the ten years I was in private practice I made money one year and broke even two.' Ironically enough, the success of his writing did not even bring him more clients. 'The Mafia was not interested in having me around. I think they believed that I would use what they told me in my capacity as a lawyer as the grist of a story.'

'So did you?' I ask, curious.

'I never did that,' he replies, outraged. 'I never have done. It would be a breach of confidentiality and ethics.'

The Mafia, however, seem to place little faith in confidentiality and ethics, as Higgins discovered. 'Well I got a call one Friday afternoon from a gentleman who is a guest of the government over at Massachusetts Correctional Institution – Walpole as it was then called (it's now called Cedar Junction as people living in Walpole objected to it being called Walpole). He was to be tried for stabbing another guest to death. And he allowed as to how he might need legal assistance, and I said that I would come over on the following Tuesday, his next visiting day. On Monday I got a call from him saying, "Don't come," because he had gotten a call saying, "Not Higgins." Now I suspect that this gentleman was connected to the Honoured Society. I suspect . . . I mean I know damn well he was!'

At this point Bob smartly executes a classic Higgins manoeuvre: the early exit from the restaurant table at which everyone had you figured to pick up the tab. Higgins barely puts up token resistance. As Bob leaves, he sits back in his chair, and suddenly starts talking in a different voice to that used before. He seems taken over by a tremendous weariness. I have the unnerving sense that he doesn't give a damn who I am or why I'm there, he just has something he feels like telling somebody.

What happens next is that George V. Higgins, at forty-nine, tells me he's had it with writing novels. The lukewarm reception for his latest novel *Trust* has been the final straw. 'I think I've overstayed my welcome. I think it's time for me to go. I don't like it particularly, but I think it's . . . necessary. *Eddie Coyle* appeared in 1972. *Trust* appeared in 1989. *George V. Higgins on Writing* appears in 1990 and so does *Victories*. The tone of the early reviews of *Trust* is that I've overstayed my welcome. I'm going to be bleeding from the head and ears before these things are over.

'So I'm tired of it and I don't want to do it any more. And I don't need to. One kid comes out of college this May, one kid the following May and I've got the tuition money in the goddamned bank. I don't like the battering I've taken.

'I've tried and tried and tried . . . I have had more success in your country than in my own. People want to be told stories and I have tried to explain, at what I'm sure is tedious length, that in my novels *the characters are telling you the story*. They do not understand. I am sick and tired of reviews that go, "Of course there's no plot as usual but the dialogue is great." It's as a friend of mine said when George Brett was still in his heyday with the Kansas City Chiefs, "Ah well, George Brett hit 350 again this year and George Higgins still writes good dialogue. You guys should start a club." I'm sick of it. *Victories*, which will be out next fall, is the last George V. Higgins novel.'

Having met a man once for lunch it is difficult to know how much store to put by this kind of talk. Certainly, after the way he had talked earlier about how he became a writer, it is hard to imagine him simply stopping: 'I was an only child, I was a special child, I was the little prince. I assumed from an early age that I should command a room, I always have. I started writing when I was fifteen and a half years old. I wrote a novel; it was awful. That's something I've realized since I've been teaching writing: most of us started young. And writing is great fun, it really is. The most fun there is, if you can make a living at this racket! Man, it's great!'

If he really does quit, and certainly the extent to which he has been patronized by serious literary critics over so many books would be enough to try anyone's patience, then it will be something like a tragedy. Higgins's trouble is that his work is not suited to a world that tries to split literature into the serious and the trashy. Serious writers write long, difficult and occasional books – the new Eco or Rushdie arrives with all the bombast of a 1970s supergroup triple album – while trashy writers write fast and, gasp, for money; so what to make of Higgins, who maintains a rate of at least a book a year, writes in his version of the vernacular, uses no references to medieval lore, describes the lives of lowlifes, liars and thieves but neither patronizes them nor puts them through rent-a-plot thriller contortions culminating in a shootout. So he's stranded: serious types think he writes crime fiction – with great dialogue, of course – and thriller fans bemoan his lack of shoot-'em-up plots.

All Higgins has done is to write a whole slew of great books at around one a year for the last twenty. He's written funny, profane and violent novels like *The Rat on Fire*, *Outlaws* or the new book, *Trust*; downbeat books with quiet resonance like *A Year or So with Edgar* and *Wonderful Years, Wonderful Years*; a couple of novels featuring a Boston maverick criminal lawyer called Jerry Kennedy ('Maybe he's me if I'd never learned to write,' says Higgins) which are the nearest he's come to simple entertainments; and also something like a masterpiece, a novel called *A Choice of Enemies*. *A Choice of Enemies* is by some distance the most acute modern political novel I've read. Its central character is a Boston pol called Benny Morgan who is a monster of corruption, the epitome of the fat-cat politico in a one-party democracy. The novel's triumph is to make you understand, even like, Benny Morgan; finally you are left with the awkward realization that a man like him, a venal man of the people, has more life, and finally even more decency, than the self-righteous ideologues on either flank who engineer his downfall. Listen to what they say, watch what they do, then make your own mind up: this is the method which makes Higgins the most genuinely democratic of writers.

By now the coffee's getting cold and Higgins is indulging in a certain amount of timepiece gazing. So I figure, what the hell, and ask him about whether he's happy to be seen as a writer of crime fiction. With a kind of weary fury he replies: 'I received a letter from a publisher calling me America's best crime novelist. I was going to say I bristled, I didn't. I ate up three yards of the living-room rug. *I am not a crime novelist*; a crime novelist writes novels about crime. I have never done that.'

Well, I demur faintly, your books do, as often as not, have crimes in them. 'I write novels with crimes in them, who didn't? Madame Bovary committed the crime of adultery. I don't write crime novels. I would like the money. I just can't do it. I start to giggle.'

So does he respect any writers of crime fiction? Not really, though he cites fellow Bostonian Robert B. Parker as being a rare beacon of literary merit. Which, as far as I'm concerned, can be made sense of as a critical assessment only by friendship overriding judgement. Still, I wonder what he makes of Elmore Leonard, with whom he's endlessly bracketed. Higgins remains stuck in maximum-snootiness mode and simply comments, 'Leonard has told a number of reporters that he got it all from me. I regard that as extremely flattering.'

As we're leaving I ask him about Hollywood, which made a remarkably good job – artistically if not commercially – of filming *The Friends of Eddie Coyle*, but has never returned to his work since. 'I thought *Eddie Coyle* was a darned good film. I thought Robert Mitchum would have gotten the Oscar he deserved, had he not been such an unpleasant person. I could have no quarrel with anyone who voted against him because he was such an unpleasant person, because he was. He was a pain in the ass.

After that a second film was commissioned and I was asked to write the screenplay. I thought, "Of course I can write a screenplay. I've written all these novels!" And I wrote it and it stunk.' And that was that.

Back in the alley outside the Locke-Ober Cafe, free at last of the dread jacket and tie, Higgins says goodbye and heads south-west and I head north-east into the thick of historic Boston. Which is oldish and profoundly fails to engage my interest at all. Instead I head off to Boston Common to take advantage of the unseasonably good weather, doze off the effects of lunchtime drinking, and see if anybody wants to sell me any guns. Boston Common, if Higgins's books and the warnings in my Boston guidebook are to be believed, having something of a reputation in that direction.

Nothing happened. As neither did it in the coffee shops of Harvard, the derelict bars of the Combat Zone, the hoodlum bars of the Italian North End, the Irish Bars of South Boston, the original Cheers Bar downtown or the regular bars on the way out to Brookline. Maybe it was happening in the black bars of Roxbury, most likely something was happening in the smoke-filled rooms preferred by the guys in the Locke-Ober Cafe. But for me nothing happened in the half-assed, half-European city of Boston. And when I left I was glad to be leaving.

10

New York: Dead End

Standing at the end of the Coney Island pier, staring out at the Atlantic Ocean, Joseph Koenig points out a stretch of beach over to our left across the water – the eastern tip of Rockway Park I think – and tells me that there used to be a ferry going over there, but when you got there there were signs saying: NO COLOURED, NO JEWS. So that's where he and his friends always wanted to go; one time they took the ferry over but they were thrown off straight away. That was the early 1960s. Now, he adds, everyone can go there, and hardly anyone does.

These days another place hardly anyone goes is Coney Island itself. The image I have is taken from Weegee's photographs of the beach in the 1940s; photos in which it is so packed that not a grain of sand can be seen. Now, on a sunny late-spring Sunday, the beach, still only a subway token and a half-hour ride from Manhattan, is near deserted. The once legendary funfair is now a barely functioning shell and few people are going to opt to bathe in sea as polluted as this. The people who are here are mostly Latins and Caribbeans, the new wave of New Yorkers. They're scattered along the pier fishing for crabs, an act of some desperation given the water they swim in.

Joseph Koenig, the man standing next to me on the pier, is a wiry six-footish guy with shortish black hair and a moustache, wearing Levi's, a black leather jacket and a T-shirt. His biography puts him somewhere in early-to-mid-forties but he, as they say, genuinely looks younger. At the moment he's living with his mother on the east side of Manhattan, and he hates everything. He hates his publishers Viking for putting such an ugly jacket on his new book and not pushing him enough; he hates crime fiction; he hates New York; he hates the subway we came here on, and he really hates Brighton Beach where I suggested we should go today. 'What do you want to go there for? I never go there.' He was driven to distraction by the slowness of the subway train and threw himself around the carriage, led me up to the front of the train so we could see where we're going, as if it would help us to get there quicker. The homeboys fooling about in the front carriage made way for him instantly; this man is too manic to mess with.

The only thing Koenig seems to be happy about is the amount of money he's been making from his second novel, *Little Odessa*. He tells me the rights sold to Hollywood for half a million; apparently Demi Moore, Bruce Willis's actress girlfriend, is just dying to play the lead. Koenig, in contrast to virtually everyone else I've met, reckons making money from writing is a cinch. He tells me that James Ellroy had called him, mentioned that I'd be interviewing him soon. I ask Koenig how he gets along with Ellroy, and he says, 'Oh, we just sit round and laugh about how much money we're making.' The implication is that if you can write, and have a reasonably pragmatic attitude towards the matter of giving the people what they want, then your financial worries are at an end. After this reverie, however, Koenig is rapidly back to remembering how much he hates everything: 'Goddamn Ellroy,' he says, 'he's always calling me up. He wants to be *friends*; I don't need friends.'

Little Odessa is the nickname for the Brighton Beach area of Brooklyn, just along the way from Coney Island, a neighbourhood dominated by Russian Jews. The novel's heroine Kate Piro lives in Little Odessa and much of the action takes place round here, including a classically Hollywood-friendly climactic scene on the Cyclone, Coney Island's great roller-coaster, still just about in service. So that's why I've dragged Koenig out here today.

Back along the pier and we're on the boardwalk, the identical boardwalk that the Drifters serenaded, as essential a part of mythical America as you could wish for. As a child I used, on special occasions, to go to Coney Beach, Porthcawl, Wales's approximation of the great American funfair, and I loved it but would speculate as to how much greater Coney Island, New York must be. So it's strange to see the place at last, and find it no bigger than the Coney Beach I remember. It is beautiful, though. I'm struck once again by how much better places look when left to age rather than artificially resuscitated and filled with retro burger bars. Koenig, however, is at pains to tell me how much better it used to be, and how dreadful it is now.

Big attraction on the boardwalk in Koenig's youth was the parachute jump, a two-hundred-foot-high construction built for the 1939 World's Fair, the idea of which is to climb up to the top and – again as Koenig tells it – attach yourself to a kind of giant elastic band and throw yourself off, hoping that the elastic band will pull you up before you spatter your brains on the boardwalk. Unsurprisingly this was a popular activity with teenage boys intent on impressing teenage girls. It's still here, standing apart from the rest of Coney Island like a giant, derelict pylon, lengths of elastic still hanging down from the top. I look up at it and feel sincerely grateful that I was not a teenager in love on the boardwalk twenty years ago, as wild winged horses would not have dragged me up this thing.

Walking along the boardwalk, past the main body of the funfair, Koenig tells me a little about the summer he spent here in the mid-1960s, after being kicked out of college: 'After I was kicked out, well, I wasn't the nicest person of all time. I wanted to go out west, but I didn't have any money, and I didn't want to work, get some menial job, and I had this buddy . . . so I hung out here. I wasn't in Brighton Beach for the whole year, but certainly for the winter. A lot of nights we'd just come out here and hang out. It was real dismal and dank, but there was still a little bit left of Coney Island then. Even on a cold January night there would still be a few thousand people playing Fascination and going on the rides. It was good. I spent most of the winter here, then in the summer I started hitch-hiking around the east coast, and then they let me back into college . . .'

On the boardwalk itself are the usual amusement arcades and stalls selling the requisite candy floss, hot dogs, french fries and all. Behind the stalls is the funfair, with the Cyclone looming largest. Then, as we walk further along, the backdrop changes to the apartment buildings which signal the beginnings of Brighton Beach. Here we turn off the boardwalk to walk along Brighton Beach Avenue alongside the el train tracks. As we're turning the corner Koenig points out an anonymous-looking apartment block. That's where Trump started out, he tells me. Apparently this was Trump senior's legacy to his son, Donald of that ilk; the entry-level stake that Trump parlayed into one of the world's more spectacularly tacky empires. Tacky above all, as Garry Trudeau has long been pointing out in *Doonesbury*, in its relentless pursuit of the kind of 'quality' that has its apotheosis in an Andrew Lloyd Webber musical.

Walking along Brighton Beach Avenue is a flashback to Manhattan's recent past. It's a distinctly ethnic neighbourhood, in this case Russian, of the kind that used to flourish all over Manhattan, from Little Italy to German Yorktown to Irish Washington Heights. Trump-led property-price hikes have made such places all but extinct in Manhattan, but here there are restaurants with the menus in Russian, shops with Russian signs, and the faces on the street are of people transplanted from a Europe which also barely exists any more. Koenig confines his conversation to commenting on how ugly and/or ill-dressed everybody is.

After a while we stop under the el for me to buy a knish from a place that specializes. It's pretty good in the kind of ultra-starch way that may explain why everyone I see tends to be on the thickset side. Koenig eats nothing.

Next it's back on to the boardwalk and a stop in a Russian cafeteria where we sit down to do some questions and answers. I order a cappuccino and Koenig tells the waitress that nothing would be just fine for him. And so we start talking, Koenig so fast as to be scarcely intelligible. 'Don't worry, even my mother can't understand me,' he says, before launching into a potted summary of his career to date: 'I was born in Brooklyn, school in New York. When I was twenty-one and finally graduated college, I immediately went up north and started working as a reporter/ photographer in Providence, Rhode Island. Providence is the headquarters of the Mafia in New England, so I was immediately thrown into the world of violent crime and I liked it. Not that it was my hobby, but I wasn't put off by it. I'd see guys shot to death and . . .' He breaks off into a little merry hum before continuing.

'In 1967 I left that job and went to Haight-Ashbury to do . . . that. Came back to New York very late 1960s and got a job

editing *Front Page* and *Inside Detective* magazines. After four years
of doing that I quit to be their east-coast correspondent, which
really meant that I drove up and down the east coast harvesting
homicides. I had a whole network of stringers, guys who'd call
me up and say, "Hey Joe, I've got a good one here in Coke
Island North Carolina." Then I'd drive down and I'd talk to the
cops and I'd talk to the DA, maybe I'd sit in on the trial and I
would come back to New York and file copy. And then I decided
I didn't want to live anywhere, I just wanted to live on the road.
So I did that for years and years and years, just went around the
country harvesting murders until I started writing fiction. I
continued writing for the *True Detective* magazines for a while
then my price went up to the point at which I couldn't afford my
own time any more, so I gradually phased it out. Now all I do is
write novels.'

Finally a shaft of idealism appears in the Koenig diatribe when
I ask him why he moved to writing fiction: 'It seems to me that
if you write anything, and you take any kind of pride in your
work, then ultimately you're going to want to write novels. It's
the hardest kind of writing to do, it's the ultimate test of a
writer's craft. In my case it's not as if I got out of college and
thought, "One day I'm going to write novels," but I had to test
myself. Writing is a miserable life. It's a life of incredible
loneliness and pain and misery – though you make a lot of dough
if you're any good at it – but it's the kind of intellectual challenge
of doing it.'

As to why he should turn to crime fiction, it was something of
a foregone conclusion: 'Because you've got to write what you
know best in this world, unless you're so self-absorbed that
you're going to write another coming-of-age novel that the world
doesn't need. What I know better than anything else, and better
than most people, is crime. Also it seemed a handy genre to slip
into; there's a market for crime novels, but if I was to write a
"straight" mainstream novel it would be very hard to sell.'

The main legacy of Koenig's epic stint in true crime reporting
seems to be an entire lack of respect for the, uh, professional
practitioners. This applies to both sides of the law, though the
encounters with the bad guys tended to be the more personally
alarming. 'I used to meet them in the worst kind of way. We'd

write cases up pre-trial and very often guys who'd got off would come up to the office and start threatening us and screaming and yelling; that was always a delight. I've been associated with those magazines for twenty years, so in the last three or four years a lot of the guys I wrote about in 1969 have come out on parole. You get twenty to life, you could be out in some states in thirteen, fourteen years. They show up now wanting to talk to me. Well fuck 'em, bunch of geeks. They all blame me for being put in gaol, especially the ones whose cases were written pre-trial. And they're all psychos. Murderers might be portrayed on TV as slightly troubled people who acted oddly in a moment of passion, but most of the criminals I meet are guys who, if they hadn't murdered the person they did, would have murdered somebody else. Despicable human beings . . .'

Not that he's got any great sympathy for the police, either: 'I'm not a cop-lover, in fact I don't much like cops. The ones I've met are dull, racist, narrow-minded, extremely right-wing people. I don't enjoy the company of those kind of people and it seems very dishonest to me to make my life's work portraying those people as heroic. That's crazy, so when I write a book about a cop he's usually a very flawed character. That's quite the opposite of the genre where the cops are these incredible, chivalrous honest people and the PI is a slightly drunken white knight and so on. That hasn't been my experience of the police I've had to deal with, on any level. When I was a newspaper reporter I found them to be extremely cowardly, guys who were afraid to talk in case they said a word out of place and lost their job. I don't like them. So my cops are always that way, and yet . . . There's an expression, "what's your hero's franchise?" – what right does your hero have to carry a gun? – so rather than write about PIs, which is even more dishonest than writing about heroic cops, or inventing some ridiculous excuse for a guy to have a gun, I use cops. But they're jerks because I find cops to be jerks.'

Koenig's first novel was called *Floater* and has the bones of a classic *True Detective* story – a serial killer meets a female con-artist and they cut loose across the Florida Everglades. Unsurprisingly, it was started while Koenig was still in the true-crime business: 'I knew I wanted to write a novel, so I tried to write a thousand words every day and after a year I had 100,000 words, and I thought I had a novel. But I didn't and I couldn't even get an agent for the longest time. Then I got my agent who is a saint [he is in fact the massively influential Knox Burger, one of the major editors at Gold Medal in the 1950s and 1960s], and he helped me a lot. I rewrote a lot and immediately got four offers for the book, got nominated for three awards . . . Originally most of it took place in Canada, as I used to live in Montreal. When I sent it to my agent it was the part that took place in Florida he liked best, so I realized that no one in the US gives a shit about Canada, and the Canada stuff fell off.'

As for choosing the Everglades setting: 'I lived in Miami for a while; it seems I've lived in every inch of the US. I know the Everglades real well. When I was in Miami I had this jerky girlfriend who I didn't get along with, so I would spend one night at her house and six nights out in the Glades by myself.'

Floater features about the most sympathetic cop Koenig has come up with, who is, incidentally, a black man. I ask Koenig how he came up with the character. 'Whenever I'm in the South all the cops I see seem to be black, except those awful blow-dry guys in Fort Lauderdale named Ricky and Bobby, and they were just too boring to write about. But the book is very dishonest. There really are no black people in the Everglades; there are a lot of Indians, and a lot of rednecks, but no black people. I don't think they would have survived. But it made for dramatic tension so I . . . stuck it in.'

Floater also features a particularly anti-social bad guy, a man named Francis Narodny who crashed out of a New England bourgeois upbringing in favour of an itinerant lifestyle spent in the pursuit of sociopathy, particularly the drowning of women. A trifle unnervingly, he is also the one character with a hint of a autobiography, sharing with Koenig his age and Russian name, even approximate physical description. Narodny is a man whom one of his conquests likes because of 'the nervous energy he seemed incapable of harnessing, so that it was asking too much of him to sit still for more than a few minutes', which doesn't seem too far away from the speedy, fidgeting guy I'm talking to.

With his next book, *Little Odessa*, however, Koenig was concerned to do something about his image: 'I began writing *Little*

Odessa a year before I sold *Floater*, while I was acquiring all these rejection letters. And the rejection letters for *Floater* were extremely harsh. I got one from a woman suggesting I was a serial killer. The book seemed unremittingly grim to the people who rejected it, they said there's not enough of the good guy, Koenig must be crazy, blah, blah. I wasn't going to write another one, but my agent said, "Don't worry. I know I can sell this. Write another one." I said, "Yeah??" I was a little bit embarrassed that I had written such a grim book. I mean I'm a pretty funny guy, though you might not believe it from the way I am today, and I thought I'd write a funny book. And instead of writing about someone who can't stay in one place, I'd write about people who are trapped in their environment. And I was aware that this scene in Little Odessa was taking place, so I wrote the book.'

Not, of course, that he will admit to any fondness for the area: 'I'm not interested in Little Odessa, I never come here. As you've seen for yourself it's such a boring place, with very little colour to focus on, so I had to make it all up. But I like *Little Odessa* best of the three books because I was really on solid footing. I could really write New York dialogue because I know that cold; it's the way I speak myself.'

With his latest novel, *Smuggler's Notch*, the restless Koenig has changed tack once more. 'It's a real morbid book, it takes place in northern Vermont and the characters are all WASPS. After I wrote *Little Odessa* and got the big movie sale I didn't have to prove I could write a funny book, I had the cancelled cheque to prove it. And I'd just as soon write morbid books. I mean crime is morbid. After 1,000 true-crime stories I wasn't going to write a cosy vicarage-tea-party murder story. Murder is morbid. Chandler got it right in *The Simple Art of Murder*. When that woman wrote back saying I was a serial killer my agent said, "That's good, she was real moved by your book, just too stoopid to realize how moved she had been."'

At the moment he's working furiously, frightened like Eugene Izzi that maybe one day he'll just dry up: 'Right now I'm writing a book set on an island off the coast of Maine. It's not something I'm particularly proud of. It's a very honest book, but the crime is too small. Sometimes I get hung up on that honesty. My cop's life is too drab; a lot of cops I know are very drab and unexciting. So I wrote a book about a very drab cop with a very drab wife, involved with a very drab crime, and I wrote a very drab book. And now I've got to undrab it somehow. The book is in place and it makes sense but it's not exciting enough and so I'm sticking in some random sex and violence to liven it up. And I've written another book, that no one's seen, which takes place in Chinatown and I think is my funniest book. But I'm saving that in a trunk for my old age. Next up will be a longer book. After *Little Odessa* I started to think people would like anything I wrote as long as every third line was funny, and it has started to show. So I'm going to try to plot a very complicated book, and have the concern of the main character as something more than catching the bad guy.'

My coffee finished, this seems like a good time to start heading back. A little way along the boardwalk we come across some of the more unusual buskers I've encountered: a trio of old men, one playing accordion, one a pre-war drum kit and the other singing, in what I take to be Yiddish, into a microphone hooked to the tiniest of speakers. It's a somewhat atonal but endearing racket, and what with that and the extraordinary pleasantness of the weather Koenig seems to be lightening up a little. While earlier in the afternoon he had seemed to me to be coming over as an Ellroy-style maverick right-winger, now his liberal roots start to show through as we talk about the political implications of crime writing: 'You say you believe in law and order, you're implying you're some sort of right-wing nut. I don't believe in the death penalty or anything like that. I just think that guys who murder people should be put away for, like, ever. People who commit sex crimes should be put away for doubly ever because they can't be rehabilitated. But I'm not a law-and-order person. I believe in gun control. I don't have that usual crime writer's right-wing bias.'

In fact crime writers in general Koenig has little time for: 'I read Chandler, Hammett, but I'm not a fan at all. It's my job, not my hobby; I don't take great pleasure from it.' (This sentiment, funnily enough, is almost precisely the same as one Koenig puts into Narodny's mouth in *Floater*, except in that instance he's talking about fraud and murder.) He makes an exception, however, for the work of George V. Higgins.

By now we're back at the Coney Island subway station. Once again Koenig spends much of the journey careening from side to side of the subway car. There's still no way he's actually going to sit down, but either the edge has gone from his mood or I'm just getting used to it. We talk for a while about the cruelly underrated prison novelist Malcolm Braly. Koenig tells me that he committed suicide a few years ago; apparently he could never really handle the outside world. Then the conversation moves to music and he expresses a fondness for 1920s and 1930s jazz piano, particularly the work of Jelly Roll Morton, and little else. Then he confesses that much of his mood is due to splitting up with this woman in Maryland; he had really thought that maybe he was going to settle down and now he's bouncing round again, living out of his car, not so much rootless as uprooted. A state that he attributes to the seminal period of his life: 1967/68 in Haight-Ashbury: 'It colours my life to this day. Those days were so ecstatic, so pleasurable, that they kind of raised expectations for myself and friends of mine to the point at which . . . I'm not married . . . everybody I know is just floating around. I used to go to Berkeley every summer. I've got friends who've been trying to live that life for the past twenty-one years. Now, in their early forties, they are getting their first jobs, they are called re-entry cases because these are guys who have been living outside the economy. Now they're getting entry-level jobs. Those years in San Francisco made everyone think that life would be this orgiastic experience and nobody wanted to go back to the mundane business of having a family, children . . . So now they're dealing with the things that other people dealt with in their twenties.'

As we emerge from the subway, back in Manhattan, the East Village, I ask how come he shifted from the Haight to *Front Page Detective* in the space of a couple of years. 'I don't want to answer that question,' he says, quickly and finally. And shortly he walks off fast, without, extraordinarily for an American, shaking hands. He disappears up Second Avenue, and I'm left with the 'who was that masked man' kind of feeling, and the suspicion that Joseph Koenig's dreams are not dreams I would want.

* * *

A fifteen-block walk north on Third Avenue and I'm back at my hotel, the Carlton Arms on 25th and 3rd, an old welfare hotel that's now a refuge for bohemian tourists and East Village artists who can't afford to live in the East Village any more. The presence of the latter means that the rooms tend to be decked out in murals; the one I'm in has been tricked out with a sign proclaiming to be 'The Lust Museum', which means that most of it is painted black apart from a series of extremely sub-Munch panels in luminous pinks and oranges. The effect unfortunately is to make a depressingly seedy welfare-type hotel room into a depressingly dark bad-art experience. Still the Carlton is friendly and about half the price of any other hotel accommodation in New York, cheaper even than the grossly depressing YMCAs. And it still provides a home for a number of welfare cases who mix amiably enough with the newer arrivals (first time I stayed here, around five years previous, about half the residents were hookers, but that seems to have all changed now that the Carlton's room decor is being written up in the art mags).

Being in New York is like being part-way home. It's the one place I've been before, a couple of times, and there are people I can call, places I can revisit. After the continual adjustment to new environments over the past weeks this place – which on my previous visits had seemed overwhelming and at least a little dangerous – now seems sweetly familiar. Humming Oddyssey's 'Native New Yorker' to myself I'm able to walk down to the payphone in the Carlton's lobby and start calling people up. Early evening I head up to the Upper East Side to meet my wife's aunt and cousins for dinner. After that I call up an old schoolfriend who's working for a New York law firm, but he says he'll be working through till about 1 A.M., and I end up drinking in a quiet bar on York Avenue with a woman named Stephanie Lee who writes stories for porno magazines.

Next morning I wake up late and still tired. Even breakfast in the very fine diner across the street fails to make me more than lethargic. It's an unlovely day and my mood permeates what I see of the city. Just along from the hotel, in the middle of a perfectly ordinary pavement in an average, bustling neighbourhood, I spot a strange pile of cardboard boxes. As I get closer it becomes clear that what this is is not a pile of boxes but a New

York Camouflage dream home. The boxes are actually a make-shift tent. Inside I glimpse a double mattress and a couple of human shapes. No one passing by bats an eyelid at this. In New York, after all, you do what you gotta do to get by, and every man and woman has the god-given right to live in a cardboard box in the middle of a pavement (except of course when the city decides a cosmetic clean-up is in order).

None too cheered by all this I head on south and west to Nick Tosches's apartment just off Seventh Avenue in the West Village, the relatively quiet and traditional part of Greenwich Village. Nick Tosches has just written his first novel, a book about the end of an era of Italian American crime, called *Cut Numbers* and mostly set around Little Italy.

The Nick Tosches who opens the door to me doesn't look like the Nick Tosches pictured on the back cover of *Cut Numbers*. That Nick Tosches is a serious-looking fortyish fella with slicked-back hair and a big moustache, wearing a chalk-stripe hustler/banker suit. This guy looks about ten years younger, wearing jeans and no moustache, and looks like the kind of guy who would have written the books that made Tosches's name, a series of books about country and rock-'n'-roll, the best and best-known being his classic biography of Jerry Lee Lewis, *Hellfire*.

After a quick glass of juice in Tosches's Manhattan-sized (i.e. nothing the average ant would have to worry about getting lost in) apartment, we decide to take a walk over to Little Italy. On our way Tosches points out the Italian American traces left in the quiet streets around the lower reaches of Seventh Avenue; the Italo-American Friendship Society and suchlike that operate behind blacked-out windows or appear to consist only of a room with a couple of tables and a few broken chairs. These, he tells me, are the places from which the numbers racket and much else used to operate. But now the only places with much evidence of prosperity are the funeral parlours, apart, of course, from the yuppie encroachments. Tosches comments: 'There are people that live within two doors of these places that don't know what's going on. That never used to be the case. New York is changing so fast. A lot of my next novel will have to do with the disparity of having a so-called yuppie boutique next door to a crumbling

Mafia storefront – one world basically not understanding the other and yet converging.'

We cross Sixth Avenue and Houston St and head south down Thompson Street, a typical SoHo street of stratospherically priced lofts and art galleries which sell the paintings of people who used to live round here, before the ad executives moved in, thus pushing up housing prices to the extent that the SoHo artists now live in the East Village, if they're lucky, which has in turn put up prices there, which is why the East Village artists seem to be living in my hotel – those who aren't dead or advertising Absolut Vodka anyway. We emerge on Canal Street which, at this end, is full of the kind of shops which somehow specialize in selling practically everything that is cheap and that nobody needs. Passing through the northern tip of Chinatown – thankfully less of a tourist phenomenon than that in San Francisco – we head left on Mulbery Street into the heart of Little Italy.

Which is all cafes and restaurants and cake shops and people talking demonstratively in the streets, and generally just how you'd imagine it. We settle into a cafe on the corner of Mulbery and Grand Streets to drink cappuccinos and eat dangerously sweet cannoli and talk about how a man's writing career would move from country music to the numbers racket: 'I was brought up in Jersey City. My mother was Irish, my father was from an Italian family, he was from the first generation to be born in America. He ran a bar in Jersey and I worked there from the age of fourteen; nepotism for you! My grandmother took the numbers. She had a dreambook and she couldn't read English so before I went to school she'd say, "Look up the dead baby in the dreambook." I'd look up "dead baby" and she'd bet for a nickel and I'd be in for a penny. So I knew what that was all about. Then I discovered country music by hearing a record by Hank Thompson on a jukebox in Jersey City, and I just followed that up.'

In 1969, aged twenty, Nick Tosches moved to New York and got a job doing paste-up for the Lovable Underwear Company. At the same time he started writing for *Fusion* magazine, a remarkable Boston rock mag that also included Lou Reed and Jonathan Richman among its contributors. He started writing

pieces for *Rolling Stone* and 'one day in January 1972 I just went
out to lunch and decided to be a writer full-time. And that's
what I've been doing ever since.'

His career has moved from journalism to non-fiction books to,
at last, a novel. *Cut Numbers*, published nearly twenty years after
The Godfather, deals with the end of Italian America as a closed
community, the end of the Mafia years maybe. Little Italy is no
longer what it was, the numbers racket has been taken over by
the government and called Lotto, new waves of immigrants are
leaner and meaner, and for Louie Brunellesches, at the age of
thirty-five, getting ahead means Wall St and an uptown girl
named Donna Lou. I asked Nick Tosches whether he intended
the story to have a general resonance for Italian Americans. 'I
hope it does. A lot of people have misconstrued it as simply a
thriller, but to me it's the slow parts that are important. The
background to the story – the whole thing about the numbers
racket and all – I'd never read anything that sort of handled that
well. What things I did read seemed to be on the fantasy level,
say *The Godfather*, rather than the way I'd known it to operate all
my life, which is basically on a street level with characters who
were not necessarily the smartest people in the world. Or the
most romantic or the best-dressed.'

Cut Numbers has now been bought for the movies and, just as
the book provides a contrast to *The Godfather* image of the Mafia,
so should the film. The director is set to be the maverick horror
auteur George Romero, who Tosches thinks could be the right
man to keep intact the combination of downbeat mood with a
hard edge. Though Tosches accepts that realism may not be the
way to blockbuster success: 'One interesting thing about *Cut
Numbers*, translating it to the screen everybody says the amounts
of money aren't large enough. People who go to the movies want
to hear about things in the millions, even though it's not their
money. I had actual amounts, 50,000 dollars, 100,000, but people
like to dream big. So I guess to a certain extent the fantasy will
always be more popular than the fact of things.'

Meanwhile he's busy on a couple of other projects. One has
been in the pipeline for years and should mark Tosches's last
foray into non-fiction: a biography of Dean Martin, Italian
American icon and enigma. 'The question at the heart of it will

be who is this guy and why am I interested in him? It will also deal with the nature of showbiz, the recording industry, the movie industry and connections between organized crime and those industries. Also American culture in general. He's one of the few entertainers who's had an interesting life. Jerry Lee Lewis and Dean Martin were the only two entertainers I ever really wanted to write about.'

Also on the go is a second novel: 'It's called *Scratch* and it's the story of a rather dull, rather unsympathetic, mediocre accountant who somehow becomes interesting in the course of his own downfall and demise. The background of the book is counterfeiting and pornography; everything takes place against those two worlds. This mild inconsequential accountant gets involved in things far greater than he is. No one knows what's at the centre till the final hand is dealt, no one knows what's real or what isn't, so the counterfeiting thing goes right through it. The pornography is just a sideline because that's the counterfeiter's legitimate activity. And, uh, a little sex never hurt a book. And that's that one. It has either the promise or the danger of being far darker than *Cut Numbers* but we'll see . . .'

We get to talking about other writers a little, and it emerges that Tosches has a somewhat unusual set of influences for a man with a lowlife fascination: 'Most of what I have read and continue to read predates this century. I'm pretty much back in antiquity, I read the classics and ancient history, medieval history, and dabble in modern things. Most of the contemporary fiction I read doesn't grab me enough to want to consume very much. In terms of influence, most of them are back in antiquity. I don't know if that makes any sense considering the way I write. I like Thucydides, Homer, Pindar, Herodotus, Hesiod . . . I've always enjoyed seeing who said what first, and if the same thing has been said in 400 B.C. and in 1964, why bother with 1964? Very rarely does a contemporary writer strike me as doing something new; that's what struck me years ago about George V. Higgins – to me that seemed so new and so good. I still don't think his importance as a writer is acknowledged.'

So, turning it back round on him, I wonder why such a classical kind of guy should write about such a bunch of low-rent hoodlums: 'It's like Faulkner said, you write about what you know best in settings you know best. That's pretty much the only way to go about it. You can call it crime fiction but basically, no matter if they are a priest or whatever, everybody has the same criminal elements in them. It doesn't interest people to read something they don't intuit to be part of themselves, that's why people don't really read the lives of the saints.'

Nick Tosches suggests a third round of cappuccinos at this point and, fearing a total caffeine overload, I wonder if it would be possible to get a beer somewhere instead. He pauses briefly and says sure, there's a place we could go. We head back over towards his apartment. On the way Tosches dives into a newsstand to put some money on a Lotto number. Lotto is the scheme New York State came up with finally to kill the numbers racket; basically just a legalized version. 'Even though gambling is illegal, New York State is now New York's biggest bookmaker, if you can figure that out,' comments Tosches.

The bar is tucked out of the way, dark, quiet and old-fashioned in a serene, steady-drinking kind of way. It's not a lot different from the bar called Mona's that *Cut Numbers* hero, penny-ante loan shark Louie Brunellesches, frequents. Tosches says hello to the bar staff and orders a club soda – Louie's drink. Louie's a gambler, an inveterate numbers speculator, and Tosches's talk too is littered with gambling metaphors. Midway through the novel Louie wises up to the fact that Wall Street has essentially the same rules and ethics as the numbers game, but that the odds are better. And suddenly Louie is no longer a lowlife gambler but a high-tone investor. Tosches, himself, is cynically amused by the similarities between the two worlds: 'It's just the same old story; they end up in debt too, just like the people who play the numbers or take the numbers. Except, as I tried to point out in the book, it has a veneer of science to it . . . It's like the middle ages, they think if you use the right graphs and project the right factors into the computer, you can come out knowing what's going to go up or come down. All forms of financial analysis are basically high-class dreambooks.'

So does he have any direct experience of this kind of upmarket gambling himself? 'I had followed it for the last ten, fifteen years, and I got heavily into it when I did a book with Michele Sindona. I had to study a lot for that and, uh, I've done some investing on my own. I've always approached it with the attitude that it was basically a fancily dressed racket.'

Which sounds a little like a euphemism for 'I got shafted', but what the hell. The Sindona book is Tosches's least-known work, but perhaps his most intriguing project; the authorized biography of the man in the middle of the Vatican banking scandal: 'I needed to come up with an idea for another non-fiction book and nothing appealed to me. I had long been aware of Sindona and I caught a flash on the news, saying he was in prison here in America, and I thought, "Boy, that's a guy I'd like to write a book about; he's involved with the Vatican, banking, the Mafia, everything – five hundred million dollars up, then down the drain in prison." But I thought there'd be no way. Then someone said, "Write him a letter," so I did, and then I heard from his lawyer, and that's how it came about.

'In the meantime, by the time I sold the book idea, he had been extradited to Italy to stand trial after he'd been sentenced here in America. The publisher wanted proof Sindona was willing to do it, so I had to go over to Italy, get into this prison. They had him in this women's prison – the only man in what happens to be the highest-security prison in Italy. I had to get all this authorization to get in, then I had to convince him to sign this piece of paper, which is one thing he hated to do. But he did, and then we were in business. Then, not long after I'd finished writing the book, I got a strange letter from him. Actually, first I heard that he was dead, then, two days later, I got the letter – strange to get a letter from someone who is dead. It started off in English and ended up in Italian, and he talked about . . . "If something happens to me don't be alarmed . . . I believe in God and the Final Judgement" . . . all this eerie stuff. That was that book.

'The book was too complicated to have a mass appeal – the average guy would sooner go to the races than put his glasses on and read something like that. It did well in Italy, because he was much more notorious there and the publishers sensationalized it a lot. It was a legal nightmare. I had gone to a lot of trouble to corroborate certain things, but they said no way. And those would have been the most interesting things in the book.

Especially as I knew they were true, had found people who were witnesses, but that's lawyers for ya, I guess.'

And on that rather downbeat note we wind up what has been a rather downbeat interview. It's a grey day, I'm tired through and through, sick of asking people questions. Tosches too had seemed preoccupied, eager to be helpful but slightly abstracted. We walk around the Village a little making desultory conversation with the over-elaborate courtesy of people who've just had a rather indifferent time in bed together. So it goes.

The Lincoln cruised Broadway, hugging the curb. A block-long video-game parlor washed the sidewalk with flashing strobe-lights. Electronic war-sounds poured through its doors, a harsh wave dividing the kids lurking on the sidewalk. Black teenagers were standing to one side in little groups, their pockets emptied of quarters by the machines inside, alert for another penny-ante score so they could go back inside. The white boys on the other side of the doors were younger – they cruised quietly, hawk eyes watching the cars for a customer. The groups never mixed. The black rough-off artists knew better than to move on the little stud-hustlers – a kid peddling his under-age ass and telling himself he's not really homosexual will be happy to stab you to prove it. (Andrew Vachss – *Strega*).

Next morning the alarm yanks me out of slumber at seven o'clock. Half an hour later I'm standing outside the Carlton waiting for Andrew Vachss to show. Right on the minute a sleek white motor draws up and out gets a wiry Italian-looking guy of indeterminate age, wearing an eye-patch. He shakes my hand, says, 'Hey John, how're you doing? Let's get going.' This is Andrew Vachss and he's going to take me on a motor tour round the New York badlands.

I've met Vachss before. He's a lawyer specializing in child-abuse cases who writes novels featuring a survivalist PI named Burke who also specializes in child-abuse cases, books set in a nightmare vision of New York. And, perhaps more than any other writer working in the field of crime, he walks it like he talks it. First time I met him was in his law offices eighteen floors above Broadway at its Wall Street end. 'You're English,' he said. 'I love the English; you like dogs.' He took me over to the wall and showed me pictures of his dogs. First up was a Rottweiler attack hound, pictured leaping, teeth bared, at the camera. I tried to think of something suitably English to say and he pointed at his Neapolitan mastiff. This looked like a panther on steroids. 'Better than a gun,' he commented. 'Dogs don't rust.' Which attitude is no distance from that of the fictional Burke.

Julio loves my dog. Her name is Pansy and she's a Neapolitan mastiff – about 140 pounds of vicious muscle and dumb as a brick. If her entire brain was high-quality cocaine, it wouldn't retail for enough cash to buy a decent meal. But she knows how to do her work, which is more than you can say for a lot of fools who went to Harvard. (*Strega*).

Soon as I've sat myself down in the passenger seat, Vachss asks me to lock my door, being a man who firmly believes that not to be paranoid in New York is a form of insanity, and we're off. Down to 14th Street and then south and west, through the top of the neighbourhood Vachss grew up in, where his grandfather had a half dozen or so different businesses – that being the American way. From there we cut through the meat market on the fringe of the West Village before manoeuvring on to the West Side Highway heading north. Suddenly Vachss swings the car on to a stretch of vacant tarmac and weeds, between the road and the Hudson River. He stops the car and tells me: 'This is a place that's used to meet anybody for anything; you can pull in here at night and you can pay attention to what you're doing, while keeping good control of the situation. There's no place to hide and you're safe behind you, so it's always been a place where people get together to do what they're going to do. You won't see traffic in drugs here much, more likely to see other kinds of contraband, guns for instance. It's also always been a place gay people could operate with some degree of freedom from the fag-bashing idiots in Central Park and this has always been a hustlers' stroll.'

Today's deal is that Vachss will show me some of the places he works in and writes about but not any of the people he works with or for. He is keen to stress that his books are books, his work a matter of life and death. So now we cruise up the West Side Highway for a while, Vachss pointing out the sights as we go along. 'There's some really hardcore bars along here. The Badlands over here is a typical example – not a very inviting-looking place but it has what a certain type of people want, so it thrives,' he says, pointing at a severely mean waterfront bar. Then other landmarks catch his attention. 'This is allegedly a hotel, they work by the hour ... There's a lot of borderline prostitution around here – borderline meaning seventeen- or eighteen-year-olds – nothing the cops are going to pay a lot of attention to, not children which you're going to have to go to Times Square for ... this is essentially the trucker trade ... when you get down by the tunnel, that's the commuter trade.' Soon enough, we're past 30th, approaching the tunnel and the hookers have all disappeared with the dawn, so Vachss contents himself with pointing out 'a nice muggers' roost right on the underpass – you know the guys who come up to clean your windshield? – well the way they work it is, one guy comes to clean your windshield, but there's a post with another guy standing behind it. If you're dumb enough to stop then this guy comes out and helps himself.'

A right turn takes us on to 42nd Street, sex trade centre between 10th and Times Square. On our right is one of the world's seediest public-transportation centres: the Port Authority Bus Station. 'You can scoop kids up there any time you like,' says Vachss, 'mind, you'll have a lot of competition doing it.' For the next few blocks 42nd Street is all porn parlours, cinemas offering martial-arts triple bills, and some remarkably unsavoury eating places – 'See those flamesteak joints – Tads and Embers – they serve food would be outlawed in a POW camp.'

At this hour of the morning the only people out on this particular mean street are the seriously lost. 'See, not a citizen among them. These people are left over from last night, they did not just get up! One of the best spots for little boys is right around the corner in the arcade. You walk down this street with a hundred-dollar bill, by the time you reach the end, you could find five people, do whatever you want. It's supposedly changing, because they're redeveloping, but the notion of this kind of traffic disappearing is ludicrous. You can move it, that's all.'

Someone who looks as if his whole life is a near-death experience staggers out in front of us. 'He's been picked clean,' says Vachss. Past Times Square – seediness tiredly incarnate – and the neighbourhood begins to gain tone. By the eastern end we're at the United Nations, which is about as anodyne as you can get, and we turn left on to the East River Drive, or 'this miserable chunk of battered concrete', as Vachss refers to it.

There's nothing in particular to see for a little while, so I introduce the main topic of New York conversation of the moment: the Central Park rape. This was an incident which happened a couple of days previously: a white woman, twenty-eight-year-old fast-track investment banker, was out jogging in Central Park in the late evening, around ten o'clock. She was towards the northern end of the park, where it borders Harlem rather than high-rent apartment blocks, when she had the misfortune to run into a gang of bored and sociopathic teenagers from the Schomburg Housing Projects in Harlem. She ended up raped, sodomized and beaten so badly that as we speak she's in a coma from which her chances of recovering mentally intact are not rated too highly (although since then, she did come out of the coma, and there doesn't seem to be brain damage). A bunch of boys have been arrested, and the public has been horrified to discover that most of them are thirteen or fourteen years old. Now every pundit in town is having a say-so on the matter. Right-wing whites are going, 'Huh, told you so' or fulminating about the death of the family; liberal whites are hand-wringing about inner-city deprivation; certain blacks, notably the editors of the black New York newspaper the *Amsterdam News*, are blaming the whole business on the brutality of racism; others, while deploring the incident, are pointing out that similar incidents in which the victim too is black go virtually unreported. What has emerged is that New York is a desperately divided city, not that that should be news to anyone.

Suddenly armies of mostly white newspaperpeople are trying to report on the lives of marginal youth, of whom they clearly know nothing. This is neatly illustrated by the 'wilding' business. One of the first reports of the rape quoted one of the boys involved as saying they had been out 'wilding'. Suddenly the New York press is full of articles about 'wilding', the appalling craze that has swept the ghettos. Only trouble is, no ghetto youth has ever heard of such a word. Though, such is the way of things, the term has now had such publicity that it enters the language anyway.

Vachss too has entered the opinion wars; the day before he

wrote a piece for New York *Newsday*, arguing against the focus on one spectacularly appalling event rather than seeing it as a part of a long-running problem: 'What I said was that calling these kids mutants is ridiculous because there have always been such kids. I gave examples through history and I pointed out that with gangs – if they have a sociopathic core – you get this type of behaviour. But to call it the breakdown of the American family . . . it's stupid. The point of my piece was that rhetoric is real cheap and so the politicians are elbowing each other for centre stage to express their so-called outrage, but the real point is that there have been hundreds of gang rapes in this town recently. This is just the one they've reported; giving people a very illusory idea, similar to thinking that Lisa Steinberg was the only child that's ever been beaten to death.'

By now we're up past Central Park and at 125th St we turn right on to the Triboro Bridge which links Manhattan, Queens and the Bronx. But we're going to none of those now. A slip road takes us down on to Randall's Island in the East River, and from there we head on to Wards Island, a desolate spot whose major attractions are a hospital for the criminally insane and a toxic-waste dump. We pull up on a scrap of no-man's-land underneath the bridge. 'At night this is as no-man's-land as you can get. It's used for trading guns or if you're holding somebody and I'm holding somebody, then this is a good place, 'cause we can each see each other. And it's a place where you can fire a gun and no one will hear. I've been here late at night and it's been full of people, like a crazed version of Lovers' Lane. I've had people ask to meet me here, and, of course it's my habit that if they say they want to meet me at eight, I'll be here at four to have a look around. 'Cause the rules are you're supposed to come alone, but nobody does that. That's why the dog is so valuable. If I meet you here and I've got the dog in the car you really can't complain that the dog's an informant. So if your intentions are, if not honourable, at least not homicidal, then you really can't complain about the dog. The other thing I can do is I can put the dog in the trunk, because I've got this switch here, just pops the trunk open a little bit. And the longer you leave him in there the more obnoxious he's going to be when he comes out.'

The place figures in Vachss's latest novel *Hard Candy*, a book that oddly seems to be both the most personal and the most cartoonish of the series. Burke runs through these same routines with his dog, which is of course an identical animal. Another place that figures in the books is where we're headed next, a junkyard out at Hunt's Point. To get there we've got to go through the South Bronx, so it's back up on to the Triboro Bridge and down on to Grand Concourse, the once-elegant main street of the Bronx, now a largely burnt-out Hispanic ghetto. Another grim news story of the previous couple of days records a baby being found dead behind one of these buildings. As far as can be judged, the baby was thrown out of a window shortly after birth and lay there for two days. The neighbours say they thought it was a doll.

A right turn takes us towards Hunt's Point and the neighbourhood gets worse. Now virtually all the buildings are burnt-out. The only amenities are heavily fortified liquor stores and desperate bars. The degree of ruination is shattering; it's not even menacing in the way of, say, near West Side Chicago, it's just destroyed, more like Beirut than a suburb of America's major city.

'It astounds me when people write about what they call the mean streets. The streets they're talking about – they're dirty, they've got a lot of vice on them, but they're not these kind of anarchistic places where there's no law. You can drive around here for weeks and not see a police officer. What it is is exclusively hardcore. Anybody who lives here has got to scrabble.' A young black woman emerges from a burnt-out building; she's smartly dressed, looks to be on her way to work in Manhattan. Which seems like a hell of an achievement, to make anything of your life when you are coming out of this. Vachss concurs, 'This is absolutely the end, you can buy whatever humans have to sell right here.'

Another right turn and the housing stops as we emerge on to what Vachss refers to sardonically as 'the prairie', a maze of junkyards and deadlands surrounding the sprawling Hunt's Point meat-market. On weekdays, when the trucks run through to the market, this road is the centre for the most desperate prostitution the city offers; to be a Hunt's Point whore is the lowest you can go in that particular line of work. The area's only full-time inhabitants are packs of dogs of a strain that even Vachss finds alarming: 'The dog packs come out at night. They are the cutting edge of Darwinism – wild dogs in the city. The dogs are a unique breed because there's the meat-market here and they throw out these huge slabs of fat – so you have seagulls fighting with the dogs for this stuff. The seagulls have wingspans like bald eagles, razor beaks and don't back away from the dogs. The ones that live through this horror are just the toughest of both. People come here to get puppies; you get a puppy out of the pack you've got the toughest thing you can find, it'll swallow a pit-bull.'

We pass the gates of the meat-market, a place that has a level of protection more appropriate to a maximum-security prison or a nuclear-weapons plant than a commercial market: armed guards, interlocking fences and razor wire. Razor wire is everywhere round here, it even protects the junkyards down on the southern tip where we park the car and look out over some deserted badlands at the grey river. 'It's even mean water, if you look at it,' says Vachss, before swivelling and pointing at the sign on a gate. 'See where it says "Dead End"? Truer words were never fucking spoken.' Beneath the sign is an abandoned child's tricycle. God knows how or why.

Driving back around the meat-market there's a dead dog lying in the middle of the road, outsize carrion seagulls circle above it, 'city vultures' in Vachss's lexicon. 'There's one that didn't make it,' he says. 'That about sums it up. She will lie there and rot till you see the bones in the street. Is this too disgusting for you?'

By now I'm feeling too stunned to feel sick and on we go, circling back towards the Triboro Bridge. Suddenly Vachss points towards a stretch of wire with a clump of bushes behind. I can't see anything. He stops so I can take a closer look. After a while I make out the outline of a car. 'You see that, New York Camouflage, that's a pretty new car. Now how did it get there? Who'd go to the trouble of getting it through that fence when you can leave it right here? I'll bet you look in the trunk of that car you'll find something you don't want. You have to ask yourself some questions: here's a fairly new car hidden behind razor wire; right over there is a junkyard buys old cars – how come?'

Gradually the area starts getting residential again. We pass a desolate street named Casanova and Vachss remembers a funny thing that happened when he was working as a cab driver, something he's done on and off for years. 'I still have the licence, it's the ultimate investigator's tool. Nobody sees a cab; you can circle a block twelve times and no one pays attention.'

What happened was like this: 'I was on these streets one night with a complete homicidal maniac, scared me to death. He'd apparently had some kind of horrible tragedy. I was way over on the other side of Queens and his friend said would I take him to the Bronx. The way he told the story his wife was a particularly beautiful woman, much younger than him, and for some reason she lost all her hair. Then she found this lunatic doctor who said he could graft a wig on to her, and she died on the operating table that night. The doctor was from Argentina and this guy kept asking me, "Are you Spanish? Do you know anyone from Argentina?" And he kept saying, "Oh my poor girl, my poor girl," and he'd beat the dashboard into pulp. When we came to a tollbooth he said to the guy, "Watch my face because tomorrow you'll see it on the cover of the *Daily News*. Tonight I kill." And he kept asking if I could find someone from Argentina so he could kill them. And I go, "Sure pal, whatever you want." And he kept directing me to darker and darker places, till finally I said, "I think someone from Argentina lives just down the block." When he asked where, I said, "Just open the door and take a look out," and, as he did, I spun around on the seat, put both feet on him and kicked him out the door. Foot down on the gas and took off, listening to him scream. I had had more than enough.'

Vachss breaks off from reminiscence to point out, on our right, the Spofford Juvenile Detention Centre. It holds children from seven or eight years old up to sixteen. It's where several of the boys accused in the Central Park case are held, and it looks indistinguishable from an adult prison. 'Yeah, it's just like Attica, smaller scale that's all,' just in a grimmer neighbourhood than most. Apparently, whether or not sections of the black press think of the boys as victims, their fellow inmates do not, and there have already been several assaults on them inside.

We emerge on to Bruckner Boulevard, joining the traffic

speeding out of the South Bronx. As we pull up at the lights I
notice that the guy in the car next to us is shaking convulsively.
'Yeah, he's a crackhead. You don't want to get in any confron-
tation with him, he's wired like a goddamn Christmas tree.' So
what's his attitude to New York's drug traffic? 'I'm really in
favour of legalizing it. It's made millionaires out of teenage robot
mutants. I've always been astounded by people who say they
have moral qualms against dope, but not liquor stores.'

Over the Triboro Bridge and we're at the eastern end of 125th
St, Harlem's main drag. There's talk lately of Harlem being the
new growth area for gentrification now that lower Manhattan
has been almost entirely reclaimed for the sushi-eating classes.
Vachss says that this is indeed the case: 'Harlem now wouldn't
be in the top ten dangerous areas in this city. It's been incredibly
gentrified. When I was a kid, 96th St was the border; no more,
yuppies are away past 96th. It doesn't necessarily make the area
any better but it does mean a better level of city services.'

We're not heading for Harlem, though; instead we're going
back down the East River Drive towards where I'm staying,
where we'll pick up a bite to eat. As we drive down the
conversation finally shifts from New York as urban hell to
matters of writing. I ask Vachss whether he plans writing the
Burke novels indefinitely. 'I've written a lot of short pieces
recently because that's more my taste, anyway. I don't want to
delude myself, there's some market for the books I'm writing,
enough to ensure the promotion and so on that I want, but I
don't hear anyone beating down my door, asking for a mainstream, so-called, novel. Still I'm not done writing the one book
that I wanted to write, so it's a little premature for me to switch.'

He mentions that his novels are now translated into most of
the languages into which books are translated, and that they
seem to be finding an audience world-wide – apart from South
Africa, where he won't let them be published. Then the conversation turns to other writers. I ask how he likes Nick Tosches's
portrayal of his old neighbourhood. He says that he was unimpressed by Tosches's knowledge of weaponry and leaves it at
that. Then he asks me how I got on with James Ellroy. I tell him
and then Vachss tells me he's been seeing a fair bit of Ellroy:
'Poor James, he's learning about life the hard way. He always

wanted to do something to assist me in what I do so I hooked
him up as a big brother to a proper little sociopath. James is
hanging in tough, but there is nothing in his background that
enables him to deal with someone who just doesn't have certain
cards in their deck. But he's stuck with it. You know, though he
writes about all these horrible folk, he'd never met any. Now he
has, you can see that it's truly shocking to him that there could
be young children who don't have any feelings.'

We pass Bellevue Hospital. 'That's where you go if you get
shot or stabbed,' says Vachss. So has he been so wounded? 'I've
been shot at without anyone ever succeeding in hitting me, and
sliced but never stabbed,' he says (neat distinction, huh). Then
Vachss points out a team of black girls going off to play Double
Dutch, ultra-intricate skipping routines and this leads me to
mention my fondness for doo-wop, the street-corner vocal harmony sound of New York in the 1950s, performed particularly
by blacks and Italians. Turns out that this is Vachss's great
musical love. He reaches down, switches on the tape machine
and suddenly the sound of the Chantels – one of the few all-girl
doo-wop groups, best known for the transcendent 'Maybe',
written by their fourteen-year-old lead singer Arlene Smith –
floods the car. We listen for a while and Vachss sighs and says,
'There's so much more emotional content in a song like this than
in anything the modern groups do.'

On 25th Street we park and find ourselves an anonymous
diner, quiet on a Saturday morning. Once I've ordered bacon
and eggs and stuff I ask Vachss to give me a rundown on how
his career took him here. 'I began professionally as an investigator for the federal government tracking down chains of sexually
transmitted diseases. That naturally led on to children and
naturally made you sick. I'm not a naïve person, I was raised on
these streets and I still didn't believe that people would have sex
with a nine-month-old baby. But a nine-month-old baby with
rectal gonorrhoea answers that question. Ever since, my life has
followed a thematic direction . . . case worker then supervisor for
the City Department of Social Services. I was in charge of a unit,
generic social work.

'After that was Biafra. The deal was billions of dollars had
been raised for starving Biafran kids and the war reached a stage

that no other war had reached, in that a Red Cross plane was actually shot out of the sky and Biafra became landlocked, so there was no way in and no more reports as to what was happening to the aid. So a group of foundations essentially looked for someone crazy or stupid enough to try and penetrate the war zone on their own and report back as to whether the money was actually being translated into food, and if not, make some suggestions as to how it could be. And that's the mission that I undertook. In order to do that I had to go to Lisbon, Geneva, Angola, South Dahomey. I finally got inside, did what I was supposed to do, didn't take long. I spent the rest of the time trying to get out and that was it. No more to it than that.

'After that I had a number of organizing jobs ... Chicago, Indiana. I ended up running a centre for transplanted migrants, Appalachians, in Chicago. After that got how I wanted it to be, I drifted. I was always drifting at this time. I went to Massachusetts and ran a re-entry centre for former prisoners. Out of that came running a maximum-security prison. Out of that came the final total failure of my health, which was residual from Biafra and all the injuries. At which point I entered law school. And I went to law school with the malice aforethought of only representing children. Because many of the teenagers that I had in the prison really came there because of what was done to them before they did it to others. I worked through law school at, for me, some relatively intellectual jobs, as a planner and analyst, finished law school, and drove a cab till I raised enough money to open my own office, and I have been in practice ever since.'

So it wasn't a case of Vachss having been, himself, abused? 'I grew up on the westmost fringe of Little Italy. My mother raised me alone during the war and when my father returned – my father was a horribly abused child and the abuse only stopped when he reached his full size – my father made up his mind he would never use violence against children. Though he was a violent man; if you met him in a bar he'd knock you down. But no, not only was I not abused, compared to my peers I was utterly coddled.'

The cases in Vachss's books tend to involve abused children, child pornographers, snuff-movie makers. Burke is no social worker; he has no belief in rehabilitating the paedophiles and sadists that he simply refers to as 'freaks'. Burke's street justice is swift and brutal, but Vachss is not prepared to accept that Burke's war on the freaks amounts to a *Death Wish*-style vigilante credo. 'Burke is not a vigilante. He never goes after anyone gratuitously. He is no white knight, he never does anything unless he's compensated. I don't call a vigilante someone who goes after people outside of the law, if he is himself outside of the law.'

The question that remains is why, having established himself as a lawyer, he started writing thrillers? 'I wrote a lot of non-fiction (on child abuse) and it struck me that the audience was limited by the genre, it was just reaching a professional audience; the kind of material I'm dealing with needs to be in the public domain, and the best way to do it is to write "fiction".'

As for why Vachss chose to write thrillers rather than 'serious fiction': 'I think what I'm writing is quite serious and has been accepted as such, but it is about crime. I couldn't write a poem about kiddy pornography. Perhaps my vocabulary is closer to the gutter than the ivory tower, but it doesn't mean I'm not serious about what I'm doing.'

There is little doubt about that. Throughout both our meetings it has been quite clear that he is far less concerned with discussing his work as a writer than talking about his writing as one part of a personal crusade against the peculiar problem of child abuse. The objection which can be made to Vachss's furious and graphic fiction is that in dealing with such taboo areas in a popular medium the writer involves himself in voyeurism and a complicity with the exploitation he condemns. Vachss weighs this and replies, 'I think that any time you write about evil and you write about it accurately you risk replicating it. If you write about child pornography you risk depicting it in such a way that it could be titillating to those interested in such a subject. But I think if you are not willing to come close to the line you don't come very close to reality.'

I suggest that his disgusted attack on the Times Square sex trade could be seen as a promo for the pro-censorship lobby. 'My position on pornography is quite simple. You can argue about *Penthouse* or *Playboy* or things of that ilk. Child pornography, a picture of a child engaged in a sexual act, is a photograph of a crime and you cannot argue about that. It is, per se, illegal, illicit and immoral. It is unfortunate that my work is taken up by people with whom I am not allied. For example, if you misread my work, and you'd have to do it deliberately, you could decide that I have an anti-homosexual bias. Which is absolutely untrue and I stand for the proposition that a paedophile and a homosexual are two different creatures entirely, yet there are people who are homophobic who seize on my work and say that this is homosexuality run amok. It's no such thing any more than someone molesting a little girl is heterosexuality run amok.'

And now it's time for him to move. We leave the diner and Andrew Vachss, the undisputed king of the hard-boiled kung-fu novel, gets into his car, reflexively locks the door, and drives off to a fortified home somewhere in the city, shared with his wife and his dogs; in his car the sound of the Chantels singing about the heartbreak of love, with a mixture of teenage longing and childish naïveté. Some part, perhaps, of why Vachss does what he does.

Epilogue

Sometime later in the day I'm doing some shopping, presents and such like. The search for the perfect baseball cap takes me to 42nd Street, a place called Herman's just east of Times Square. It's no better than anywhere else, but rather than settle for a wasted journey I decide to head further west down 42nd St, to see whether it really is as grim as Vachss paints it. West of Times Square the street's camera, music and T-shirt stores start to be leavened with amusement arcades – full of the blank-eyed teenagers who inhabit amusement arcades the world over, mostly black and Hispanic here – and with sex shops. I go into a couple of these and the merchandise looks to be identical to that in LA, except that the 'pile it high, sell it fast' ethos seems more in evidence here, and the stores all seem to have private cine booths at the back where you can go and feed quarters into the slot, watch one of a selection of videos, and masturbate in a kind of very public privacy.

The depravity on offer quickly starts to look tiresomely familiar, but neither it nor the environment seems precisely dangerous. So I am on the point of giving up when I decide to try one more place. This is a smaller narrower establishment, more dimly lit than the other places on the street. It's a single room with racks of videos and magazines to the right, a row of cubicles to the left. Looking at the display of magazines I soon realize that here there is nothing but bondage, domination and fetishism, whips and boots, piss and shit. There are just a few men in here, notably more smartly dressed than in the other places, and quieter, tense and intent. Then I look at the cubicles. Most are occupied and on the outside of each door is a selection of photos and some come-on copy describing the delights of the video visible inside. These delights seem heavily to feature bound women and men in Nazi uniforms and, in truth, most of the stills just look like cheap and tacky costume drama, and I suspect that the iniquities inside are somewhat tamer than suggested, but still I am seized by a sudden sense of clamminess and claustrophobia – a sense that this place is pervaded by desires that I am tempted to call simply evil, sexual fantasies blurred into nightmares. I have to get out, and as I leave I look up at the cash desk, raised six feet high and next to the door. Here sit two guys, completely impassive, looking as if they come from a country where life is not the most valuable of commodities regularly traded.

And at this point I begin to feel, not afraid precisely, but sick maybe. Sick of all the baseball caps that say, 'Shit happens' and of the gun shops and the sex shops and the bad beer and sick really of all the evil that people do, all the viciousness, and sick at last of being fascinated by it and, worst, of seeing bad things not as bad but as research, as material.

And that's when I knew it was time to go home.

Bibliography

A selective list of works by the authors interviewed (most recent British edition unless otherwise noted):

James Lee Burke
   The Lost Get Back Boogie (US only – Henry Holt)
   The Neon Rain (Vintage)
   Heaven's Prisoners (Vintage)
   Black Cherry Blues (Mysterious Press)
James Crumley
   One to Count Cadence (US only – Vintage)
   The Wrong Case (US only – Vintage)
   The Last Good Kiss (US only – Vintage)
   Dancing Bear (US only – Vintage)
   Whores (Denis MacMillan)
James Ellroy
   Brown's Requiem (US only – Avon)
   Clandestine (US only – Avon)
   Blood on the Moon (Mysterious Press)
   Killer on the Road (new title for *Silent Terror*) (US only – Avon)
   The Black Dahlia (Mysterious Press)
   The Big Nowhere (Mysterious Press)
Joe Gores
   Final Notice
   Interface   } (All out of print)
   Hammett
   Come Morning
James Hall
   Under Cover of Daylight (Mandarin)
   Squall Line (Heinemann)
Gar Anthony Haywood
   Fear of the Dark (US only – Penguin)
   Not Long for This World (US only – St Martin's Press)
Carl Hiaasen
   Tourist Season (US only – Warner)
   Double Whammy (Pan)
   Skin Tight (Macmillan)
George V. Higgins
   The Friends of Eddie Coyle (Robinson)
   The Digger's Game (Robinson)

    Cogan's Trade (Robinson)
    The Rat On Fire (Robinson)
    The Patriot Game (Robinson)
    A Choice of Enemies (Robinson)
    Impostors (Abacus)
    Outlaws (Abacus)
    Trust (Abacus)
Tony Hillerman
    Dance Hall of the Dead (Sphere)
    People of Darkness (Sphere)
    The Ghostway (Sphere)
    Skinwalkers (Sphere)
Eugene Izzi
    Bad Guys (Grafton)
    King of the Hustlers (US only – Bantam)
    Prime Roll (US only – Bantam)
Joseph Koenig
    Floater (Penguin)
    Little Odessa (Penguin)
    Smuggler's Notch (Viking)
Elmore Leonard
    The Big Bounce (Penguin)
    Swag (Penguin)
    Unknown Man Number 89 (Penguin)
    The Switch (Penguin)
    City Primeval (Penguin)
    Split Images (Penguin)
    Stick (Penguin)
    Glitz (Penguin)
    Freaky Deaky (Penguin)
Sara Paretsky
    Killing Orders (Penguin)
    Toxic Shock (Penguin)
    Burn Marks (Chatto)
Nick Tosches
    Hellfire (Plexus)
    Cut Numbers (Mandarin)
Andrew Vachss
    Flood (Pan)
    Strega (Pan)
    Blue Belle (Pan)